BREAD

BREAD

the breads of the world and how to bake them at home

CHRISTINE INGRAM and **JENNIE SHAPTER**

HERMES HOUSE

This edition is published by Hermes House

Hermes House is an imprint of Anness Publishing Ltd
Hermes House, 88–89 Blackfriars Road, London SE1 8HA
tel. 020 7401 2077; fax 020 7633 9499
info@anness.com

© Anness Publishing Ltd (1999, 2003)
Published in the USA by Hermes House, Anness Publishing Inc.
27 West 20th Street, New York, NY 10011; fax 212 807 6813

A CIP catalogue record for this book is available from the British Library.

PUBLISHER: Joanna Lorenz
EXECUTIVE EDITOR: Linda Fraser
EDITORS: Janet Charatan, Jo Lethaby and Jenni Fleetwood
DESIGNER: Nigel Partridge
PHOTOGRAPHERS: Nicki Dowey (recipes) and Amanda Heywood
HOME ECONOMISTS: Jennie Shapter (recipes) and Jill Jones
EDITORIAL READER: Catherine Sillence
PRODUCTION CONTROLLER: Julie Hadingham

Previously published as *The World Encyclopedia of Bread and Bread Making*

1 3 5 7 9 10 8 6 4 2

NOTES
For all recipes, quantities are given in both metric and imperial measures and, where appropriate, measures are also given in standard cups and spoons. Follow one set, but not a mixture, because they are not interchangeable.

Standard spoon and cup measures are level.
1 tsp = 5ml, 1 tbsp = 15ml, 1 cup = 250ml/8fl oz

Australian standard tablespoons are 20ml. Australian readers should use 3 tsp in place of 1 tbsp for measuring small quantities of gelatine, cornflour, salt, etc.

Medium eggs are used unless otherwise stated.

CONTENTS

INTRODUCTION

There is something undeniably special about bread. The flavour of a good loaf, the texture of the soft crumb contrasting with the crispness of the crust, is almost a sensual experience. Who can walk home with a fresh baguette without slowly, almost absent-mindedly breaking off pieces to eat en route? Or resist the promise of a slice of a soft white farmhouse loaf, spread simply with butter? Most people have their own favourite: ciabatta, rich with olive oil; dark, malty rye; honeyed *challah* or a Middle Eastern bread, freshly baked and redolent of herbs and spices. Whatever the shape or texture, bread has a special place in our affections.

Even today, at the end of the 20th century, when bread is taken largely for granted, seen as an accompaniment or a "carrier" for other foods, we still have a sense of its supreme significance. In some languages the word "bread" means "food", and in certain of the more rural parts of Spain and Italy, for example, you may find that bread is blessed or kissed before being broken or eaten. There are numerous rituals and traditions attached to bread. Slashing the dough with a cross or making a sign of the Cross over the loaf before baking was believed to let the devil out. Cutting the bread at both ends was also recommended to rid the house of the devil. One extraordinary custom was

BELOW: Cutting a cross in an unbaked loaf was believed to let the devil out.

ABOVE: Just a few of the many shapes and types of bread.

sin-eating, a practice at funerals, whereby someone would eat a loaf of bread and by so doing would take on the sins of the dead person.

The obvious explanation for bread's importance is that until quite recently, it was for many, quite literally the "staff of life" – the single essential food. Today, most people have more varied diets. Potatoes, pasta and rice are all enjoyed in the West and are important staple foods, but in some countries, for example France and Italy, bread is easily the most popular of the carbohydrates, eaten with every meal and in many cases with every course.

Like wine tasters, true aficionados taste bread *au naturel* in order to savour its unique taste and texture, unadulterated by other flavours. Good as this can be, the best thing about bread is that it goes so well with other foods. Throughout Europe bread is most frequently cut or broken into pieces to be eaten with a meal – to mop up soups and sauces or to eat with hams, pâtés and cheese. Dark rye breads, spread with strongly flavoured cheese or topped with smoked fish, are popular in northern Europe, and in the Middle East breads are split and stuffed with meats and salads – a tradition that has been warmly embraced in the West too. In Britain and the USA, the European custom of serving bread with a meal, with or instead of potatoes or rice, is catching on, but sandwiches are probably still the favourite way of enjoying bread. Sandwiches have been going strong for a couple of hundred years – invented, it is said, by John Montagu, 4th Earl of Sandwich, so that he could eat a meal without having to leave the gaming table. Although baguettes and bagels are naturally ideally suited for linking bread with meat, the sandwich, clearly an English concept, is unique and continues to be the perfect vehicle for fillings that become more and more adventurous.

BREADS OF TODAY

Figures show that throughout Europe bread consumption declined after World War II. Until then it was the single most important food in the diet, but due to increased prosperity, which meant a wider choice of other foods, and mass production, which led to bread becoming increasingly insipid and tasteless, people moved away from their "daily bread". The situation was more noticeable in some countries than others. In France, Italy and Spain, where people continued to demand the best, eating of bread did not decline so sharply, although even in those countries, the quality did deteriorate for a time.

BELOW: In northern Europe, dark rye bread is served sliced with colourful, rich-tasting toppings.

In Britain, however, most bread was notoriously bland – the ubiquitous white sliced loaf being little more than a convenient shape for the toaster. In supermarkets, certainly, there was a time, not so long ago, when apart from the standard pre-wrapped white loaf, the only baked goods on sale were croissants and a selection of fruited teabreads, vaguely labelled as "Continental". Yet within the last ten years, things have improved by leaps and bounds. Perhaps supermarkets, finding that the smell of freshly baked bread enticed shoppers into their stores, installed more in-store bakeries. Or perhaps shoppers who travelled abroad and sampled the breads of other countries created a demand for better breads made with better flours, using more imaginative recipes and untreated with additives.

Nowadays there is a huge choice of breads both from independent bakeries and from the large supermarkets. Italian ciabatta and focaccia are now a regular sight, even in the smallest food stores, as are the various Spanish, Indian and Middle Eastern breads. There is an increasingly interesting choice of German, Danish, Scandinavian and eastern European breads and, among the French breads, there is now a truly good range on offer. If the supermarket has an in-store bakery, baguettes are likely to be freshly baked and some are now as good as the real thing. The availability of *pain de campagnes*, *levains* and other rustic breads means that you can choose breads to suit the style of meal you are serving, while sweet breads, such as brioches and croissants from France, *pane al cioccolato* from Italy and numerous offerings from Germany mean that there is much more to choose from than simply toast at breakfast and malt loaf at tea time.

Local bakers, although competing with the supermarkets, have paradoxically benefited from the range on offer from supermarkets. The more breads there are available, the more people feel inclined to try other baked goods. Small bakers who could easily have lost customers to the big stores, have risen to the challenge by producing their own range of country-style and fine breads. Craft bakers are

ABOVE: A huge range of traditionally baked French breads are offered for sale in this specialist bakery.

producing traditional breads, at the same time experimenting with recipes they have devised themselves. Bread making has never been a tradition that stood still. The best craft bakers have ensured that bread making has continued to evolve, resulting in the emergence of all sorts of corn and barley breads, mixed grain loaves and a range of new sourdoughs.

Added to this are the many European-style bakeries. Set up and run by émigrés from all parts of Europe and beyond, these bakeries are the best source of many of the most authentic European breads. In supermarkets you will invari-

BELOW: Traditional country-style breads are enjoying a renaissance.

ably find ciabatta or focaccia, but for *paesano*, *pagnotta* or *pane sciocco* you are likely to need an Italian baker, who will be only too happy to provide you with the loaves and tell you all about them while they are being wrapped.

Once you have found a bakery you like, there are no particular tips for buying bread; the baker will be pleased to explain the different styles of loaves and advise on their keeping qualities. Crusty breads, such as baguettes, round cobs or Italian country loaves are known as "oven bottom" or "oven bottom-baked", which means they have been baked, without tins or containers, on the sole of the oven or on flat sheet trays. They are evenly crusty, although the type of dough, the humidity during proving, the steam in the oven and the heat itself determines whether the crust is fragile or chewy. Loaves, such as the English farmhouse, baked in metal tins, characteristically have a golden top, but with thinner crusts on the sides. Rolls or breads baked up against each other have even softer sides and are described as "batch-baked". Sourdough breads are made without yeast – using a natural leaven instead – and are often labelled as "yeast-free" breads or "naturally leavened". There are many varieties, some made entirely from wheat, some from rye, others from a blend of both of these or other cereals. They are normally heavier than an average loaf, with a dense texture and pleasantly tart flavour.

HISTORY

Bread seems to be a recurring theme in history. Most people could be forgiven for thinking that history was driven by great scientists and ambitious men. But look closer and you will find that the incentive behind many of our greatest inventions was the availability, production and delivery of food – our "daily bread" in the widest terms. The wheel, the plough and the windmill right through to steam and motorization all plot a course that was concerned specifically with agriculture and producing food. Similarly, the aspirations of any king or queen were intimately connected with the feeding of their people. The poorer and hungrier the population, the more insecure was their ruler's position. "Give them bread and circuses!" said Juvenal in the 1st century AD, referring to the Roman mob, in a constant state of unrest because of poverty and starvation; and Queen Marie Antoinette famously said "Let them eat cake", on being told that the peasants were rioting because they had no bread. Almost all revolutions came about because of famine, and bread was the single food that might alone have averted such an event.

BELOW: By the 1st century AD, Roman bakers had perfected their craft, as this mural shows..

THE FIRST BREAD

Archaeology and history show that bread has been eaten since the earliest times. Remains of stone querns indicate that cereal was ground in prehistoric Britain to make a branny-type grain. It is likely that this would have been fashioned into

ABOVE: Distributing bread to the poor in Paris after the famine in 1662.

cakes and cooked over an open fire to make a coarse flat cake. At the same time in Egypt, where civilization was considerably more advanced, bread was a regular part of daily life and indeed the Egyptians are credited with being the first people to make bread. Paintings on the walls of tombs depict bread being offered to the gods and the flat oval-shaped breads look uncannily like *aiysh*, the Egyptian bread still eaten today. Other pictures show round or cone-shaped breads and it is likely that they were all leavened, since the water from the Nile contains the same strain of yeast that is used in baking today. The Greeks initially made unleavened breads, but during the last millennium BC leavens were introduced to raise their breads and the loaves were baked in bread ovens. Once wheat flour replaced barley meal, the Greeks became very partial to bread, their bakers producing a huge range of different breads made with honey or milk or sprinkled with sesame or poppy seed, according to one account written in the 1st century AD.

Elsewhere, the leavening of bread became commonplace, even if at first it might have come about by accident. Natural yeasts exist in the air around us and a warm paste of flour and water will

ABOVE: Throughout Europe, windmills were built to make milling easier.

spontaneously start to ferment if left for a couple of hours, so leavened bread is probably almost as ancient as the unleavened cakes baked over hot stones. Sourdoughs made by this natural method became popular in many parts of Europe, and the traditions continue to this day with sourdough ryes from eastern Europe and Germany, wheaten *levains* such as *pain de campagne* and Italian country loaves from more southerly regions.

In ancient Britain, about the time of the Roman invasion, beer barm – the yeasty froth on fermenting liquor – began to be used as a leaven. Barley was by far the most important crop at that time and ale was widely brewed. Once the use of natural leavens had become widespread, it would have been but a small step to realize that beer barm, with the same sweet/sour smell, could be used as well.

In Biblical times, leavened bread was common. In the Book of Genesis, Lot, the son of Abraham, welcomes two angels to his house and "baked for them unleavened bread", which suggests that leavened bread was the more usual food for non-angels. Today, Jews bake unleavened bread – *matzos* – for Passover, in remembrance of the Hebrews' escape from Egypt, and unleavened bread is frequently the bread for ritual or sacred occasions.

Bread also plays a central role in Christianity. Jesus fed the five thousand

BELOW: Originally, bread ovens were made of fireproof stone or bricks.

with bread, and at the last supper he broke unleavened bread (it being Passover), giving thanks to the Lord and literally identifying with it, with the words "this is my body", the act of which is recalled in every Christian Mass.

BREAD IN BRITAIN AND EUROPE DURING THE MIDDLE AGES

The Romans brought wheat, oats and rye to Britain along with many of their bread-making techniques. However, while for a time bread making became more sophisticated, it suffered a setback once the Romans had left. During the Dark Ages, the growing and harvesting of cereal and then the making and baking of bread would have been a hit-or-miss affair. Families would have gathered cereals from their local fields and threshed the grain either in their own home or by using a quern stone belonging to the village.

By the Middle Ages, however, horses had begun to be used for ploughing and cultivation began to be more organized. The watermill and then the windmill were invented, probably first in England and then elsewhere in Europe. Perhaps this was something of a mixed blessing, for while the mill certainly took the backache out of the task, the lord of the manor retained rights over the mill and would oblige the serfs who worked his land to pay a tithe for the use of the mill. To add insult to injury, the bakehouse, often adjoining the mill, also made a charge to the families who used it and in a period when cottages were flimsy constructions without ovens or even chimneys, families often had little option but to take their bread to the communal oven.

The loaves themselves were normally huge, weighing more than 4.5kg/10lb, and would be expected to feed the family for several days. Made of a mixture of grain – wheat, barley, millet and rye – they would have been coarse mealy loaves. If the winters were not too harsh, the summers warm and the rainfall neither too great nor too little, harvests would be good and people could survive on a diet of bread, ale and pottage – a kind of stew made of pulses and meat. However, after a poor harvest, cereal became scarce and people would have to scratch around for almost anything that could be ground to a meal. Acorns and crushed roots were often the stand-bys in times of famine in Europe, while in England the poor would have to resort to horse bread, a type of mealy cake made of ground beans, so-called as it was normally fed to animals.

BELOW: In 15th century France bread was still cooked over an open fire.

ABOVE: This 16th century bake-house in Scandinavia was built next door to a public bath – perhaps the oven also warmed the water.

In 1266 laws were introduced in England, known as the Assizes of Bread, which regulated that the weight of bread should be fixed to a certain price. For the price of one penny it was set down that three types of bread should be available: white loaves made from bolted (sifted) flour, which were the lightest breads, wheaten loaves made of more coarsely sifted meal and weighing half as much again, and finally the household loaf, the heaviest of all three and made of unrefined meal. The Assize system was deeply unpopular with bakers, but it nevertheless continued for some 450 years, which testifies to the importance the government attached to bread being available and affordable for all the populace.

BRITAIN IN TUDOR TIMES

Bread and pottage continued to be the staple foods for most people of England

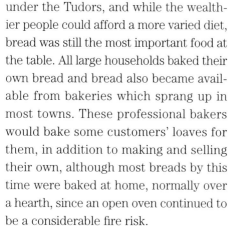

under the Tudors, and while the wealthier people could afford a more varied diet, bread was still the most important food at the table. All large households baked their own bread and bread also became available from bakeries which sprang up in most towns. These professional bakers would bake some customers' loaves for them, in addition to making and selling their own, although most breads by this time were baked at home, normally over a hearth, since an open oven continued to be a considerable fire risk.

For the poor, most bread was made of a mixture of grains, which would vary depending on the part of the country: rye in Norfolk; barley in north-west England and the lowlands of Scotland, Wales and Cornwall; and oats in the uplands of Wales and the Scottish Highlands. For the poorest, a mixed grain called maslin was often used, while peasant bread made from peas and beans continued to be made during severe hardship.

Although the more affluent people did eat plain brown bread, they also began to acquire a liking for white bread. White bread was considered superior for several reasons: it was more expensive, owing to the time and effort required to sift out the bran, and it implied prestige; added to which the Church used a white bread called Pandemain, by definition more refined, as the sacramental bread. People took this to mean better, and white bread acquired a cachet which has only really been dented in the last 20 years.

Known by various names, this white bread eventually came to be known as manchet. Manchets were made from the finest wheat flour and were relatively small, sometimes not much bigger than a large roll; compared with the large plain breads, they were not considered sufficient for one person at a meal.

Another common practice, dating from the Middle Ages and surviving until the end of the 16th century, was the use of trenchers. These were thick slices of bread from large four-day-old wholemeal loaves, which served as plates for both the less affluent and the wealthy, hard-baked for the purpose and cut into squares or oblongs. The custom was also practised in

France, and trencher breads were made in Corbeil and sold in the markets of Paris. Meat and fish would be placed on top of each slice, the bread soaking up any gravy. Those who were still hungry would then eat their trencher – from where we get the expression "trencherman", someone renowned for the amount he eats. In wealthy families it would have been unseemly to eat the trencher, not to say unnecessary, as there would have been sufficient food offered at table. Instead, the servants would take the pieces of bread and give them to the almshouses.

LATER CENTURIES

Within the British Isles and across Europe, the lot of the peasant farmer contrasted sharply with that of the wealthy. During the 18th century the price of wheat rose steeply. In Britain, the Corn Laws, which were largely responsible for the price increases, were finally repealed in 1846. In France, the State's faiiure to respond to the crisis resulted in revolution. Around this time, the potato – introduced to Europe at the beginning of the 17th century – finally gained acceptance. In France and the south of England, wheat continued to be the favoured staple, but potatoes were used increasingly and by the middle of the 19th century, potatoes were as much a staple as bread. For the poor, bread and potatoes together formed the basis of a meagre diet. In Ireland, however, potatoes were often the only food, resulting in the catastrophic famine of the 1840s when potato blight struck.

BELOW: Most affluent homes had a built-in oven, fired by wood or peat.

ABOVE: In Victorian times all large households baked their own bread.

BAKING METHODS

The first means of baking or cooking a bread was simply by placing the dough on a heated stone over the dying embers of a fire. This technique is not dissimilar to that used today by the Australian bushmen when making their damper bread. The first English settlers in Virginia also used the same principle for their maize breads, baking the dough over hot ashes or in hot sand. The advantage is that no hardware or utensils are required; the disadvantage is that the bread, even if leavened, is mainly flat. At some point someone came up with the idea of placing a pot over the bread. The steamy heat caused the bread to rise and variations on this theme continued for hundreds of years among poorer people.

At the same time, most villages had a bakehouse, either attached to the mill or owned by the baker. Farmers and larger households often had their own bread ovens, fired with wood and furze (gorse). Although these fuels were cheap to collect, lighting and heating the oven would have been a time-consuming process and for most households it would be lit only once a week. After the week's bread had been baked, biscuits and cakes, which required lower temperatures, would be placed in the cooling oven.

Originally, ovens were heated using wood that was burnt on the oven floor. Once the oven was hot, the embers were removed using a long-handed tool, called a peel. These ancient ovens were built of fire-proof stone, and later replaced by bricks. The stone or bricks would become white hot and then very gradually the heat would decrease as the bread was baked. Flat breads, such as the Italian *focaccia*, would have been the first breads to go into these immensely hot ovens, where they would be baked quickly and crisply. Larger loaves would then be baked, the slowly decreasing heat ensuring that the bread had a good thick crust, which meant that it kept well for the days ahead.

In the USA, Australia, Britain, France and other parts of Europe, enthusiasts have restored these wood-burning ovens and their bread, which is made to traditional recipes, is quite delicious.

In Ireland, bread was cooked in a type of Dutch oven, which was set in peat with burning embers piled around it. A similar type of oven is still used by the people of Dutch ancestry in South Africa, who make their pot bread by baking it in a cast-iron pot piled high with smouldering embers.

GRAINS AND MILLING

Wheat is by far the most popular cereal for bread making. First grown in Asia Minor, it has been cultivated for some ten thousand years. For most of that time, the sowing and cultivating, threshing and milling were laborious jobs that required toil and effort for both farmer and miller. Today, mechanization makes the task of getting bread to our table far less arduous, and the skills acquired from our ancestors, although refined, are still very much with us today.

Wheat is a member of the grass family, and flour is produced from the grains in the ear. It is a tolerant cereal and grows in a wide range of climates, although it prefers cooler temperatures. There are two basic species of wheat: bread wheat used in baking, and durum used for pasta. Of the bread wheats, the so-called hard ones, which contain a higher proportion of protein, are best for bread flour.

THE WHEAT GRAIN

The wheat grain is one of nature's perfect foods. Crammed with energy and low in fat, it contains fibre, carbohydrates, protein and important vitamins and minerals.

The wheat grain is 5mm/¼in long and golden when ripe. The ripeness of wheat is determined by its colour; a farmer may also chew a few grains to check that the wheat is dry and crunchy.

WHOLEMEAL (WHOLEWHEAT) GRAIN

This is the whole grain from which wholemeal flour is made. Wheat grains are cleaned to remove grit and debris before milling, but nothing else is removed.

BRAN

The bran is the thin, papery skin covering the wheat grain. Some or all of it is removed for brown and white flour respectively. Bran cannot be digested, but it does provide valuable fibre in the diet and can be bought separately for use in bran loaves and for other baking purposes.

WHEAT KERNEL

This is the inner part of the wheat grain, revealed when the bran has been peeled away. It is made up of starch bound together by gluten, the protein needed for bread making to give dough its elasticity. Strong wheats tend to contain a greater proportion of gluten and are therefore the preferred wheats for bread making.

WHEAT GERM

This tiny wheat seed is rich in vitamins B and E, salts, proteins and fatty acids. It is present in wholemeal flour but partly removed in brown flour. Wheat germ can

BELOW: Nowadays, most of the barley grown in Europe is used for brewing.

ABOVE: The ripeness of wheat grain is determined by its golden colour.

be bought separately for adding to loaves or sprinkling over the sides of the baking tins prior to cooking bread. Since its natural oil eventually becomes rancid, wheat germ will keep for only a short period. Store in the fridge and check the "use-by" date on the packet.

OTHER GRAINS
BARLEY

Barley has been grown across Europe for centuries, and was used for bread making when wheat was expensive and rye was unavailable. Today the grain is mostly grown for brewing.

BUCKWHEAT

Buckwheat is a member of the same family as rhubarb and dock and is therefore not strictly a cereal. It is now mostly grown in north-east Europe.

CORN (MAIZE)

The term "corn" has given rise to considerable confusion. In Britain it was historically used to describe the predominant cereal crop of a region (for instance, wheat in England and oats in Scotland). An English field of corn, therefore, meant a field of wheat, not the tall annual grass with yellow edible grains, which was also known by its 16th century Spanish name – maize (*maiz*).

Sailors from Spain and Portugal, who accompanied the early explorers, were

ABOVE:: At Crowdy mill in North Devon, England, flour is still milled in the traditional way.

responsible for introducing corn into Europe. Until then it was unknown in the Old World, although a staple crop in the southern parts of America. It needs higher temperatures and more sunshine than wheat and is therefore grown mainly in the more southerly parts of Europe. It is still widely grown in Mexico and the southern states of America.

MILLET

Mostly grown for animal feeds, millet thrives in both tropical and arid countries.

OATS

Oats have been cultivated in northern Europe for centuries, but although among the most nutritious of all the cereals, they were mostly grown for animal feed. Thanks, however, to the Scots' love of porridge this grain continues to be cultivated for human consumption.

RICE

Widely grown in China and other parts of Asia, as well as the USA and parts of Spain and Italy, rice is an important cereal crop. Rice flour contains no gluten, but can be used in the same way as cornflour.

RYE

Rye prefers colder, dry climates and acid soils and is therefore ideally suited to the cooler parts of Europe, such as Germany, Scandinavia, northern Russia and Poland.

SPELT

This is one of the oldest cultivated species of wheat. It continues to be grown, but only in small areas in Germany and other parts of northern Europe.

MILLING

Flour is milled by passing the grain through a series of grinders. Traditionally, these were huge stones that were placed closer and closer together and turned by water or wind power. Nowadays the stones have been replaced by steel rollers, driven by machine. The ribbed cylinders separate the bran and wheat germ from the white kernel and the flour is sifted through a series of increasingly fine meshes. The advantage of roller mills, apart from the obvious one of not being dependent upon the weather for power, is that the rollers themselves wear far better than grindstones, which needed replacing regularly. The disadvantages are that the rollers automatically expel the bran and wheat germ and the faster process means that the flour loses some of its flavour and character.

GRIST

The grist is the blend of different wheats a miller selects to make flour. Most flours are made from a mixture of wheats.

WINDMILLS

The stone towers of old windmills are still dotted across Europe. Although they are a reminder of a simpler age, windmills were complex machines that required a great deal of skill. The miller was consequently an important and respected member of the community. Farmers who had spent much of a year growing and harvesting their crop relied on the miller to turn their efforts into flour so that they could feed their families.

The principle of the windmill is very simple. Huge grindstones, turned by the action of the wind on the sails, slowly milled the grain into flour. The miller's task was to make sure the stones turned at a steady speed: too slowly and the grain would pile up, too quickly and it would overheat and spoil. It was most important to ensure that the hopper remained topped up with grain, for if there was no grist on the mill, the stones would spark and the whole mill could catch alight.

Nowadays only a small amount of flour is milled using windmills. Compared with modern methods, the process is very slow. Nevertheless a few smaller flour producers use windmills for their stoneground flours and thus keep this tradition alive.

BELOW: This 17th-century windmill is a reminder of a simpler age.

INGREDIENTS FOR BREAD MAKING

—

WHEAT FLOURS

The simplest breads are a mixture of flour and water and some type of leavening agent. Beyond that narrow definition, however, lies an infinite number of possibilities. The flour is most likely to come from wheat, but may be derived from another type of grain or even, in the case of buckwheat, from another source entirely. The liquid may be water, but could just as easily be milk, or a mixture. Yeast is the obvious raising agent, but there are other options. Salt is essential, fats are often added, and other ingredients range from sweeteners like sugar or molasses to dried fruit, spices and savoury flavourings.

WHITE FLOUR

This flour contains about 75 per cent of the wheat grain with most of the bran and the wheat germ extracted. Plain flour is used for pastry, sauces and biscuits; while self-raising flour, which contains a raising agent, is used for cakes, scones and puddings. It can also be used for soda bread. American all-purpose flour is a medium-strength flour, somewhere between the British plain and strong white flour. Soft flour, sometimes known as American cake flour, has been milled very finely for sponge cake and similar bakes.

UNBLEACHED WHITE FLOUR

Unbleached flour is more creamy in colour than other white flours, which have been whitened artificially. Bleaching, which involves treating the flour with chlorine, is becoming increasingly rare and the majority of white flours are unbleached, although check the packet to be sure. In Britain, flour producers are required by law to add, or fortify their white flours with, certain nutrients such as vitamin B1, nictinic acid, iron and calcium. These are often added in the form of white soya flour, which has a natural bleaching effect.

RIGHT: Organic flours are being used increasingly for bread making.

STRONG WHITE/WHITE BREAD FLOUR

For almost all bread making, the best type of flour to use is one which is largely derived from wheat that is high in protein. This type of flour is described as "strong" and is often labelled "bread flour", which underlines its suitability for the task. It is the proteins that combine to form gluten when mixed with water, and it is this that gives dough its elasticity when kneaded, and allows it to trap the bubbles of carbon dioxide given off by the yeast. A soft flour produces flat loaves that stale quickly; conversely, if the flour is too hard, the bread will have a coarse texture. A balance is required and most millers blend hard and soft wheats to make a flour that produces a well-flavoured loaf with good volume. Most strong white flours have a lower protein content than their wholemeal equivalent and a baker would probably use a flour with a protein level of 12 per cent. The protein value of a flour can be found listed on the side of the packet under "Nutritional Value".

FINE FRENCH PLAIN FLOUR

French bakers use a mixture of white bread flour and fine plain flour to make baguettes and other specialities. Fine French plain flour is called *farine fluide* in its country of origin because it is so light and free-flowing. Such is the popularity of French-style baked goods that this type of flour is now available in supermarkets.

WHOLEMEAL FLOUR

This flour is made using the whole of the wheat grain and is sometimes called 100 per cent extraction flour: nothing is added and nothing is taken away. The bran and wheat germ, which are automatically separated from the white inner portion if milled between rollers, are returned to the white flour at the end of the process. *Atta* is a fine wholemeal flour used for Indian breads (see Other Flours).

STONEGROUND WHOLEMEAL FLOUR

This wholemeal flour has been ground in the traditional way between two stones. The bran and wheat germ are milled with the rest of the wheat grain, so there is no separation of the flour at any stage. Stoneground flour is also considered to have a better flavour, owing to the slow grinding of the stones. However, because the oily wheat germ is squashed into the flour, rather than churned in later, stoneground flour has a higher fat content and may become rancid if stored for too long.

ORGANIC WHOLEMEAL FLOUR

This flour has been milled from organic wheat, which is wheat produced without the use of artificial fertilizers or pesticides. There are organic versions of all varieties of wholemeal and white flours available from most large supermarkets and health-food shops.

STRONG WHOLEMEAL/
WHOLEMEAL BREAD FLOUR

A higher proportion of high gluten wheat is necessary in wholemeal flours to counteract the heaviness of the bran. If the flour is not strong enough, the dough may rise unevenly and is likely to collapse in the oven. The miller selects his grist (the blend) of hard and soft wheat grains, according to the type of flour required. Bakers would probably look for a protein content of about 13.5 per cent; the strong flours available in supermarkets are normally between 11.5 and 13 per cent.

ABOVE: A selection of different wheat flours and grains. Clockwise from top right: strong white flour, stoneground wholemeal, wholemeal, wheat germ, organic wholemeal, plain white flour, organic plain flour, semolina, organic stoneground wholemeal and Granary flour. The three flours in the centre are (clockwise from top) brown, spelt and self-raising flour.

GRANARY FLOUR

Granary is the proprietary name of a blend of brown and rye flours and malted wheat grain. The malted grain gives this bread its characteristic sweet and slightly sticky flavour and texture. It is available from healthfood shops and supermarkets.

MALTHOUSE FLOUR

A speciality flour available from some large supermarkets and healthfood shops, this is a combination of stoneground brown flour, rye flour and malted wheat flour with malted wheat flakes. It resembles Granary flour.

GRAHAM FLOUR

This popular American flour is slightly coarser than ordinary wholemeal. It is named after a 19th-century Connecticut cleric, Rev. Sylvestor Graham, who developed the flour and advocated using the whole grain for bread making because of the beneficial effects of the bran.

BROWN FLOUR

This flour contains about 85 per cent of the original grain, with some of the bran and wheat germ extracted. It produces a lighter loaf than 100 per cent wholemeal flour, while still retaining a high percentage of wheat germ, which gives bread so much of its flavour.

WHEAT GERM FLOUR

A wheat germ flour can be brown or white but must contain at least 10 per cent added wheat germ. Wheat germ is highly nutritious and this bread is considered particularly healthy. Wheat germ bread has a pleasant nutty flavour.

SEMOLINA

This is the wheat kernel or endosperm, once the bran and wheat germ have been removed from the grain by milling, but before it is fully milled into flour. Semolina can be ground either coarsely or finely and is used for certain Indian breads, including *bhatura*.

SPELT

Although spelt, a variety of wheat, is no longer widely grown, one or two smaller flour mills still produce a spelt flour, which is available in some healthfood shops.

OTHER FLOURS

Alternative grains, such as barley, cornmeal and oatmeal, are full of flavour but contain little or no gluten. Breads made solely from them would rise poorly and would be extremely dense. The milled grains are therefore often mixed with strong wheat flour. Rye is rich in gluten, but pure rye doughs are difficult to handle; once again the addition of strong wheat flour can provide a solution.

BARLEY MEAL

Barley is low in gluten and is seldom used for bread making in Britain and western Europe. In Russia and other eastern European countries, however, barley loaves continue to be produced, the flour mostly blended with some proportion of wheat or rye flour to give the loaf volume. These loaves are definitely on the robust side. They tend to be rather grey and flat and have an earthy, rather mealy flavour. Similar loaves must have been baked in parts of the British Isles in the past, when times were hard or the wheat harvest had failed. There are several old Welsh recipes for barley bread, which was rolled out flat before being baked on a baking stone. Finnish barley bread is made in much the same way.

Barley meal is the ground whole grain of the barley, while barley flour is ground pearl barley, with the outer skin removed.

BELOW: Finnish barley bread

Either can be added in small quantities to wholemeal or to white flour to produce a bread with a slightly rustic flavour.

BUCKWHEAT FLOUR

This grain is blackish in colour, hence its French name, *blé noir*. It is not strictly a cereal but is the fruit of a plant belonging to the dock family. The three-cornered grains are milled to a flour and used for pancakes, blinis and, in France, for crêpes or galettes. It can also be added to wheat flour and is popular mixed with other grains in multigrained loaves. It has a distinctive, earthy flavour and is best used in small quantities.

CORNMEAL (MAIZEMEAL)

This meal is ground from white or yellow corn and is normally available in coarse, medium or fine grinds. Coarse-ground cornmeal is used for the Italian dish of polenta; for bread making choose one of the finer grinds, available from most healthfood shops. There are numerous corn breads from the southern states of America, including the famous double corn bread. Corn was brought back to Europe by the Spanish and Portuguese and corn breads are still popular in these countries today, particularly in Portugal. Corn contains no gluten so will not make a loaf unless it is blended with wheat flour, in which case the corn adds a pleasant flavour and colour.

MILLET FLOUR

Although high in protein, millet flour is low in gluten and is not commonly used by itself in bread making. It is pale yellow in colour, with a gritty texture. The addition of wheat flour produces an interesting, slightly nutty flavour.

OATMEAL

Oatmeal does not contain gluten and is only very rarely used by itself for bread making. The exception is in Scotland where flat crisply baked oatmeal biscuits have been popular for centuries. These are baked on a griddle and served with butter or marmalade. Oatmeal can also be used in wheat or multigrained loaves. Choose finely ground oatmeal for making oatcakes or for using in loaves. Rolled oats are not a flour but are the steamed and flattened whole oats. They look good scattered over the crust of leaves and rolls, and add a pleasant flavour.

RICE FLOUR

Polished rice, if ground very finely, becomes rice flour. It can be used as a thickening agent and is useful for people with wheat allergies. It is also occasionally used for some Indian breads.

STORAGE

Although most flours keep well, they do not last indefinitely and it is important to pay attention to the "use-by" date on the packet. Old flour will begin to taste stale and will make a disappointing loaf. Always store flour on a cool dry shelf. Ideally, the flour should be kept in its bag and placed in a tin or storage jar with a tight-fitting lid. Wash and dry the jar thoroughly whenever replacing with new flour and avoid adding new flour to old. Wholemeal flour, because it contains the oils in wheatgerm, keeps less well than white flours. Consequently, do not buy large quantities at a time and keep it in a very cool place or in the salad drawer of the fridge.

ABOVE: A selection of non-wheat grains and specialist flours. Clockwise from top centre: rye flour, buckwheat flour, cornmeal, bajra flour, organic rye flour, millet grain, jowar flour, gram flour and atta or chapati flour. In the centre are (clockwise from top) barley meal, fine oatmeal and rice flour.

RYE FLOUR

Rye is the only other cereal, apart from wheat, that is widely used to make bread. It has a good gluten content, although the gluten in rye is different from wheat gluten, and rye doughs are notoriously sticky and difficult to handle. For this reason, rye meal is often blended with other flours to create a dough that is more manageable. There are as many different rye meals as there are wheat flours, ranging in colour and in type of grind. Pumpernickel and other dense and steamed box-shaped rye breads use a coarsely ground wholemeal rye, while finer flour, which contains neither the bran nor the germ, is used for the popular crusty black breads.

INDIAN FLOURS

ATTA/CHAPATI FLOUR

This is a very fine wholemeal flour, which is normally found only in Indian grocers where it is sometimes labelled *ata*. As well as being used to make chapatis, it is also the type of flour used for making rotis and other Indian flat breads.

BAJRA FLOUR

This plant grows along the west coast of India. The grains are a mixture of yellow and grey but when ground, the flour is a more uniform grey. It has a strong nutty aroma and a distinct flavour. *Bajra* bread or *rotla* is cooked, like all unleavened breads, on a griddle.

JOWAR FLOUR

Jowar grows over most of central and southern India. The flour, ground from the pretty pale yellow grains, is a creamy-white colour. The flat breads usually made from this flour, called *bhakris*, are roasted on a griddle and are traditionally served with a rich-flavoured, spicy, coconut, garlic and red chilli chutney.

GRAM FLOUR

This is a flour made from ground chickpeas. It is also known as *besan*. The Indian missi rotis – spicy, unleavened breads from northern India – are made using gram flour or a mixture of wholewheat and gram flours.

YEAST AND OTHER LEAVENS

Almost all breads today are leavened in one way or another, which means that a substance has been added to the dough to initiate fermentation and make the dough rise.

Without yeast or another leavening agent, the mixture of flour and water, once cooked, would be merely a flat, unappetizing cake. At some point in our history, our ancestors discovered how dough, if left to ferment in the warmth, produced a lighter and airier bread when cooked.

The transformation of dough into bread is caused by yeast or another leavening ingredient producing carbon dioxide. The carbon dioxide expands, the dough stretches and tiny pockets of air are introduced into the dough. When the bread is cooked the process is set and the air becomes locked in.

LEAVENING AGENTS

The most popular and most widely known leavening ingredient in bread making is

BELOW: Clockwise from top left: fresh yeast, dried yeast, fast-action dried yeast and easy-blend dried yeast.

yeast. However, raising agents such as bicarbonate of soda and baking powder are also used for making certain breads.

YEAST

Yeast is the most popular leavening agent for bread making. It is simple to use, more reliable than a natural leaven and considerably quicker to activate. Conventional dried yeast, easy-blend and fast-action yeast are all types of dried yeast, produced for the convenience of those making bread at home. Almost all bakers prefer fresh yeast, since it is considered to have a superior flavour and to be more manageable and reliable. However, when fresh yeast is not available or convenient, dried yeast is a handy substitute.

There are several ways of adding yeast to flour. Fresh yeast is usually blended with lukewarm water before being mixed into the flour; conventional dried yeast is first reconstituted in warm water and then left until frothy; easy-blend and fast-action dried yeasts are added directly to the flour.

THE SPONGE METHOD

Some yeasted breads are made by the sponge method, whereby the yeast is dissolved in more lukewarm water than usual, and then mixed with some of the flour to make a batter. This can be done in a bowl, or the batter can be made in a well in the centre of the flour, with only some surrounding flour included at the start, as in the recipe for split tin loaf. The batter is left for at least 20 minutes – often much longer – until bubbles appear on the surface, a process known as sponging. It is then mixed with the remaining flour, and any other ingredients are added. The advantage of this method is that it enables the yeast to start working without being inhibited by ingredients like eggs, fat and sugar, which slow down its action.

Many French breads are also sponged. A slightly different technique is used and the batter is left to ferment for a lot longer – for 2–12 hours. The slow fermentation creates what is described as a *poolish* sponge, and makes for a wonderfully flavoured bread, with very little acidity, yet with a fragile and crunchy crust. *Pain polka* is made by this method, as are the best baguettes. Two factors affect the rise: the temperature of the room and the wetness of the mixture. A wet sponge will rise more quickly than a firmer one. Italian bakers employ a similar process called a *biga*. This uses less liquid and the sponge takes about 12–15 hours to mature. For an example of the use of a *biga* starter, see the recipe for ciabatta.

BAKING POWDER

This is made up of a mixture of acid and alkaline chemicals. When these come into contact with moisture, as in a dough or a batter, the reaction of the chemicals produces tiny bubbles of air so the dough rises and becomes spongy, just as it does with yeast. Unlike when making yeast-leavened breads, however, it is important to work fast as the carbon dioxide will quickly escape and the loaf will collapse.

BICARBONATE OF SODA

Bicarbonate of soda, sometimes just called soda, is the leavening ingredient in Irish soda bread. It is an alkaline chemical which, when mixed with an acid in a moisture-rich environment, reacts to produce carbon dioxide. Cream of tartar, an acid that is made from fermented grapes, is commonly used in conjunction with bicarbonate of soda for soda breads, or else the soda is combined with soured milk, which is naturally acidic. Buttermilk may also be used.

LEFT: Pain de campagne is one of the many French sourdough breads.

BREWER'S YEAST

Old cookery books sometimes call for brewer's yeast or ale or beer barm. Until the last century, this was the common and only leavening ingredient. Since then brewer's yeast has acquired something of a cult status, and during the 1950s in the USA and Britain it was considered a wonder food owing to its nutritional value. It is not however, suitable for bread making, being too bitter, and should only be used for making beer.

NATURAL LEAVENS

Natural leavens, made using a medium of flour, or grown from potatoes, yogurt, treacle or buttermilk were once very popular and are enjoying a renaissance.

SOURDOUGHS

Sourdoughs are breads based on a natural leaven. An authentic sourdough relies entirely on the wild yeasts that exist in the air. Given the right conditions, any dough of flour and water or batter of vegetable origin will start to ferment spontaneously and will continue to do so if starch or sugar is added to feed it. Recipes for some of the traditional American and German breads use a variety of rather surprising starters for their sourdoughs, from potatoes to treacle. With the renewed interest in rustic breads, there are all sorts of sourdough breads in supermarkets and specialist bakers, and numerous books explaining how to make them at home. There are many, many types of sourdough. In France the sourdough method is known as the *chef* or *levain*, and is used for *pain de campagne* as well as for sourdough baguettes.

Despite their many variations, sourdoughs do have some elements in common. Each begins with a "starter", which can take anything up to a week to ferment and become established. This "starter" or leaven is used, daily by bakers or less frequently by home bread makers, for the day's bread. A small amount of the dough is then kept back and used for the next batch of bread. Alternatively, a slightly more liquid starter can be made and kept in the fridge until it is ready for use. Each time part of the starter is used, the remaining starter is refreshed with equal amounts of flour and water. Looked after in this way, some starters have been known to survive for many years. Starters for sourdoughs, as well as the breads themselves, vary hugely – not only from country to country but from village to village. Many recipes, and indeed many bakers, recommend using a little yeast to get started since a true starter is likely to be rather a hit-or-miss affair. Wild yeasts may be all around us, but for some reason they seem to vanish as soon as you decide to make a sourdough. Starters also improve with age, so do not be discouraged if your first sourdoughs are rather bland. After a few attempts, you should find your breads developing their own tangy personality.

YEAST KNOW-HOW

◆ Yeast needs warmth to activate it, but must not be subjected to too hot a temperature or it will die. Whether dissolving yeast in water or adding liquid to the yeast and flour, make sure the liquid is not too warm. The optimum heat is 38°C/100°F. If you do not have a thermometer, experts recommend mixing 300ml/½ pint/1¼ cups boiling water with 600ml/1pint/2½ cups cold water, and measuring the required water from the mixture.

◆ If you are using easy-blend or fast-action dried yeast you can afford to have the water slightly hotter, since the yeast is mixed with the flour, and the heat of the water will rapidly dissipate.

◆ Check "use-by" dates on dried and fast-action yeasts. If a product is past its "use-by" date, replace it. If it is marginal and you cannot immediately replace it, take a measuring jug and pour in 120ml/4fl oz/½ cup warm water (43–46°C/110–115°F). Add 5ml/1 tsp sugar, stir to dissolve and then sprinkle over 10ml/2 tsp dried yeast. Stir and leave for 10 minutes. The yeast should begin to rise to the surface after the first 5 minutes, and by 10 minutes there should have developed a rounded crown of foam that reaches to the 250ml/8fl oz/1 cup level of the measuring jug. If this happens the yeast is active, if not, the yeast has lost its potency and should be discarded.

◆ The amount of yeast you require should not increase proportionally as the amount of flour increases, so take care if you decide to double the quantities in a recipe. You will not need to double the amount of yeast. Similarly, if you halve a recipe, you are likely to need proportionally more yeast or be prepared to wait longer for the bread to rise.

ADDITIONAL INGREDIENTS

ABOVE: Welsh bara brith is packed with dried fruits.

Although flour and yeast are the most obvious ingredients used in bread making, there are a number of other ingredients that are just as important.

WATER OR MILK

As a general rule, savoury loaves are made using water; teabreads and sweeter breads use milk. Whatever the liquid, it is always heated slightly. Breads made with milk are softer in both the crumb and the crust than those using water.

SALT

Almost all bread recipes add salt at the beginning, stirring or sifting it right into the flour.

Salt is one of the few essential ingredients in bread making. It is important for both flavour and the effect it has on the yeast and dough. Essentially, it slows down the yeast's action – which is why it should not be added directly to the yeast. This means that the dough rises in a controlled and even way, giving a well-risen even loaf. Too little salt means the loaf will stale more quickly; too much and the crust will harden, so do take care when measuring salt.

LEFT: The French petit pains au lait, made with milk rather than water, have a lovely soft crumb and crust.

SUGAR

Sugar, once invariably added to all breads (usually with the yeast), is now no longer necessary for savoury breads since modern yeasts can be activated without it. However, some bakers still prefer to add a little sugar, even when making savoury baked goods, contending that results with sugar are better than when it is omitted.

White and brown sugar, honey, treacle and golden syrup can be used to sweeten teabreads and fruit breads. Sugars are normally added with the flour, while liquids, such as treacle and honey, are more often stirred into the lukewarm liquid so that they are gently warmed as well.

BUTTER AND EGGS

Enriched breads are made with the addition of both butter and eggs and normally use milk rather than water. These breads, such as Sally Lunn, barm brack and many of the festive European breads, have a delicious cake-like texture and soft crust. The butter is either melted or diced and the eggs beaten before being worked into other ingredients to make a fairly sticky batter. This is then beaten by hand or in an electric mixer. In some instances, the butter is kneaded into the dough after the initial rising, since large quantities of butter can inhibit the action of the yeast.

BELOW: Sally Lunn, one of the richest breads of all, is traditionally served sandwiched with clotted cream.

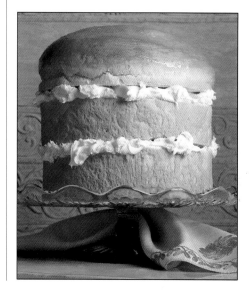

ABOVE: Panettone is enriched with eggs and egg yolks.

BELOW: Red lentil dosas are spiced with turmeric and black pepper.

FRUIT

Almost any dried fruit can be added to bread. Raisins, sultanas, currants and mixed peel have always been popular for fruit loaves. Chopped dates, apricots and prunes can all be kneaded in, as can more exotic fruits, such as dried mango or papaya. Fruit can be added to a dough during mixing or left until the second kneading. If adding at the second kneading, warm the fruit first, so that it does not inhibit the action of the yeast. If you are using an electric mixer or food processor for kneading, note that the blades, particularly on the food processor, will chop the fruit. This spoils both the appearance and the flavour of the loaf, so only knead by machine to begin with, then knead the fruit in by hand after the initial rising.

FATS

Fats, in the form of butter, oil, lard or vegetable fat, are sometimes added to savoury loaves. They add flavour and help to preserve the freshness of the loaf. The Italians particularly love adding olive oil to their breads, which they do in generous quantities. Although oils and melted butter can be poured into the flour with the yeast and liquid, solid butter or fats are normally kneaded into the flour before the liquid is added.

NUTS, HERBS AND OTHER SAVOURY INGREDIENTS

Some of our favourite breads today are flavoured with herbs, nuts and other

BELOW: Ciabatta, like many Italian breads, is made with olive oil.

such savoury ingredients. *Manoucher*, "Mediterranean nights" bread, is a rainbow of colours. Based on the Italian *focaccia*, it contains rosemary, red, green and yellow peppers along with goat's cheese. The Italians add olives or sun-dried tomatoes to their ciabatta, while walnut bread (*pain aux noix* in France, *pane con noci* in Italy) is one of the best-known and best-loved savoury loaves.

Nuts, herbs, pitted olives and sun-dried tomatoes should be roughly chopped before being kneaded into the dough after the first rising.

SPICES

The sweet spices are cinnamon, nutmeg, cloves and ginger, and for savoury breads cumin, fennel, caraway and anise impart a delicious flavour. Mace, pepper and coriander seeds can be used for both sweet and savoury breads. Spices can be added with the flour or kneaded in with fruit or nuts, or other ingredients.

TECHNIQUES

USING YEAST

There are several different forms of yeast, some easier to use than others, but none of them particularly tricky if you follow a few simple rules. Whichever yeast you use, it must be in good condition – neither old nor stale – and must not be subjected to too much heat.

USING FRESH YEAST

Fresh yeast is available from baker's shops, healthfood shops and most supermarkets with an in-store bakery. It is pale beige in colour, has a sweet, fruity smell and should crumble easily. It can be stored in the fridge, wrapped in clear film, for up to 2 weeks or can be frozen for up to 3 months. A quantity of 15g/½oz fresh yeast should be sufficient for 675–900g/ 1½–2lb/6–8 cups flour, although this will depend on the recipe.

1 Put the yeast in a small bowl. Using a spoon, mash or "cream" it with a little of the measured water until smooth.

2 Pour in the remaining measured liquid, which may be water, milk or a mixture of the two. Mix well. Use as directed in the recipe.

USING DRIED YEAST

Dried yeast is simply the dehydrated equivalent of fresh yeast, but it needs to be blended with lukewarm liquid before use. Store dried yeast in a cool dry place and check the "use-by" date on the tin or packet. You will need about 15g/½oz (7.5ml/1½ tsp) dried yeast for 675g/ 1½lb/6 cups flour. Some bakers add sugar or honey to the liquid to which the yeast is added, but this is not necessary, as the granules contain enough nourishment to enable the yeast to work.

1 Pour the measured lukewarm liquid into a small bowl and sprinkle the dried yeast evenly over the surface.

2 Cover with clear film and leave in a warm room for 10–15 minutes until frothy. Stir well and use as directed.

WATER TEMPERATURE
For fresh and regular dried yeast, use lukewarm water; for easy-blend and fast-action yeast the water can be a little hotter, as the yeast is mixed with flour before the liquid is added.

USING EASY-BLEND AND FAST-ACTION DRIED YEASTS

These are the most convenient of the dried yeasts as they can be stirred directly into the flour. Fast-action yeasts and some easy-blends contain a bread improver, which eliminates the need for two kneadings and risings – check the instructions on the packet to make sure. Most of these yeasts come in 7g/¼oz sachets, which are sufficient for 675g/ 1½lb/6 cups flour. Do not store opened sachets as the yeast will deteriorate quickly.

Sift together the flour and salt into a medium bowl and rub in the fat, if using. Stir in the easy-blend or fast-action dried yeast, then add warm water or milk, plus any other ingredients, as directed in the recipe.

BELOW: Small, shaped rolls are very quick to make using easy-blend yeast.

MAKING A YEAST DOUGH BY THE SPONGE METHOD

This method produces bread with an excellent flavour and soft texture. The quantities listed are merely an example and can be increased proportionately. See individual recipes.

1 Mix 7g/¼oz fresh yeast with 250ml/ 8fl oz/1 cup lukewarm water in a large bowl. Stir in 115g/4oz/1 cup unbleached plain flour, using a wooden spoon, then use your fingers to draw the mixture together until you have a smooth liquid with the consistency of a thick batter. (Do not add salt to the sponge as this would inhibit the yeast.)

2 Cover with a damp dish towel and leave in a warm place. The sponge will double or triple in bulk and then fall back, which indicates it is ready to use (after about 5–6 hours).

3 The sponge starter is now ready to be mixed to a dough with the remaining flour and any other ingredients, such as butter as directed in the recipe.

MAKING AN ITALIAN STARTER (*BIGA*)

If you wish to make an Italian *biga* for Pugliese or a similar Italian country bread, use 175g/6oz/1½ cups unbleached plain flour. Cream the yeast with 90ml/6 tbsp lukewarm water, then pour it into a well in the centre of the flour. Gradually mix in the surrounding flour to form a firm dough. The dough should be kneaded for a few minutes and then left, covered with lightly oiled clear film for 12–15 hours.

MAKING A FRENCH SOURDOUGH STARTER (*CHEF*)

It is not difficult to make a sourdough starter. The starter can be kept in the fridge for up to 10 days, but for longer than that it should be frozen. Bring the starter to room temperature before adding to the next batch of bread.

1 Place 115g/4oz/1 cup flour in a large bowl and add 75ml/5 tbsp water. Mix together, then knead for 3–4 minutes to form a dough. Cover the bowl with clear film and set aside at room temperature for 2–3 days. The flour that you choose will depend on the bread you wish to make; it can be wholemeal, white or rye, or a combination of two or three.

2 After 2–3 days, the mixture will rise and aerate slightly and turn a greyish colour. A soft crust may form on top of the starter and it should develop a slightly sweet-sour smell.

3 Remove any crust that has formed on top of the starter and discard. Stir in 120ml/4fl oz/½ cup lukewarm water to make a paste and then add 175g/6oz/ 1½ cups flour. The flour can be wholemeal or a mixture of wholemeal and white. Mix together to make a dough, then transfer to a work surface and knead lightly until firm.

SOURDOUGH

The actual word "sourdough" is thought to have come from America as this style of bread was commonly made by pioneers and the word was sometimes used to describe old "Forty-Niners". However bread made by the sourdough method dates back long before the 19th century. Many traditional European rye breads are based on this method, particularly in Germany and Scandinavia where the sour flavour of the leaven complements the flavour of the rye.

In Britain sourdoughs are sometimes called acids or acid breads. Some restaurants and home bread makers have their own favourite acid breads, but generally there is not much of a tradition of sourdoughs in the British Isles. Except in Ireland, where soda was popular, ale barm (the fermentation liquor from beer) was the most commonly used leaven for bread making until it was replaced by baker's yeast around the middle of the last century.

4 Place the ball of dough in a bowl, cover again with clear film and leave for 1–2 days at room temperature.

5 Remove and discard any crust that forms. What remains – the *chef* – can now be used to make a sourdough bread, such as *pain de campagne rustique*. To keep the *chef* going, save about 225g/8oz of the dough each time.

6 Place the dough starter in a crock or bowl, cover and keep in the fridge for up to 10 days or freeze.

MIXING, KNEADING AND RISING

The sequence and method of adding ingredients to make your dough is surprisingly important. For some breads, fresh or dried yeast is dissolved in lukewarm water and then stirred into the flour; if easy-blend dried yeast or fast-action dried yeast is used, this is added directly to the flour with warm water or milk added afterwards. Read your recipe carefully before starting and warm your bowls if they are in the least bit chilly, so that the yeast gets off to a good start.

MIXING

The easiest way to mix the dough is with your hand but, if you prefer, start mixing with a spoon until the mixture is too stiff to stir, then mix by hand.

1 If using fresh or regular dried yeast, mix it with lukewarm water or milk as described in the recipe. Sift the flour, salt and any other dry ingredients (including easy-blend or fast-action dried yeast, if using) into a large, warm mixing bowl.

2 If using butter or lard, rub it in. Make a well in the centre of the flour mixture and pour in the yeast mixture with the remaining lukewarm water. If oil is being used, add it now.

3 Mix the liquid into the flour using your hand, stirring in a smooth, wide motion so that all the dry ingredients are evenly incorporated and the mixture forms a dough. Knead lightly in the bowl.

KNEADING

Kneading is something you just cannot skip in bread making. If you do not have strong wrists, or simply do not enjoy it, you will have to resort to using the food processor, which takes all the effort – and much of the time – out of kneading. Better still though, learn to love it.

Kneading dough, whether by hand or machine, is the only way of warming and stretching the gluten in the flour. As the strands of gluten warm and become more elastic, so the dough becomes more springy. It is the elasticity of the dough, combined with the action of the yeast, that gives bread its light, springy texture. Insufficient kneading means that the dough cannot hold the little pockets of air, and the bread will collapse in the oven to leave a heavy and dense loaf.

HOW TO KNEAD BY HAND

1 Place the mixed dough on a floured surface and flour your hands generously.

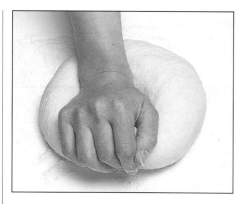

2 Press the heel of your hand firmly into the centre of the dough, then curl your fingers around the edge of the dough.

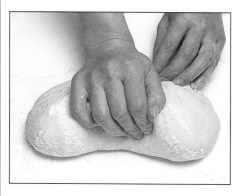

3 Pull and stretch the dough towards you and press down again, giving the dough a quarter turn as you do so.

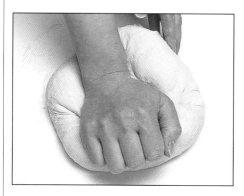

4 Continue pressing and stretching the dough, making quarter turns so that it is evenly kneaded. After about 10 minutes the dough should be supple and elastic; however, some breads need more kneading, so do check the recipe.

ADDING EXTRA INGREDIENTS

Ingredients, such as olives, can be added after kneading, or they can be kneaded in after the first rising.

KNEADING IN A FOOD PROCESSOR

Unless you have an industrial-size machine, it is likely that your food processor will only be able to knead moderate amounts of dough. Don't attempt to knead more dough than recommended by the manufacturer as it may damage the motor. If necessary, knead in small batches and then knead the dough balls together by hand afterwards.

Fit the dough blade into the processor and then blend together all the dry ingredients. Add the yeast mixture, and extra lukewarm liquid and butter or oil, if required; process until the mixture comes together. Knead for 60 seconds, or according to the manufacturer's instructions, then knead by hand on a floured board for 1–2 minutes.

KNEADING IN A FOOD MIXER

Check the manufacturer's instructions to make sure bread dough can be kneaded in your machine.

Mix the dry ingredients together. Add the yeast, liquid and oil or butter, if using, and mix slowly, using the dough hook. The dough will tumble and fall to begin with, and then it will slowly come together. Continue kneading the dough for 3–4 minutes or according to the manufacturer's instructions.

RISING

This is the easy part of bread making – all you need now is to give the dough the right conditions, and nature and chemistry will do the rest. While kneading works and conditions the gluten in the flour, during rising (proving) the yeast does the work. The fermentation process creates carbon dioxide, which is trapped within the dough by the elastic gluten. This process also has the effect of conditioning the flour, improving the flavour and texture of the eventual loaf.

The number of times you leave your bread to rise will depend on the yeast you are using and the recipe. An easy-blend or a fast-action yeast needs no first rising, but dough using fresh yeast and other dried yeasts normally requires two risings, with some recipes calling for even more.

TEMPERATURE AND TIME

For most recipes, dough is left to rise at a temperature of about 24–27°C/75–80°F, the equivalent of an airing cupboard or near a warm oven. At a cooler temperature the bread rises more slowly and some of the best-flavoured breads, including baguettes, use a slower rising, giving the enzymes and starches in the flour more time to mature. The quantity of yeast used will also determine the time required for rising. More yeast means quicker rising.

1 Place the kneaded dough in a bowl that has been lightly greased. This will prevent the dough from sticking. Cover the bowl with a damp dish towel or a piece of oiled clear film, to prevent a skin from forming on top.

2 Leave to rise until the dough has doubled in bulk. At room temperature, this should take 1½–2 hours – less if the temperature is warmer; more if the room is cool. It can even be left to rise in the fridge for about 8 hours.

A FEW SIMPLE RULES

◆ Warm bowls and other equipment.

◆ Use the correct amount of yeast: too much will speed up the rising process but will spoil the flavour and will mean the loaf stales more quickly.

◆ If you have a thermometer, check the temperature of the lukewarm liquid, at least until you can gauge it accurately yourself. It should be between 98°–108°F/37°–43°C. Mixing two parts cold water with one part boiling water gives you water at roughly the right temperature.

◆ The amount of liquid required for a dough depends on several factors – type of flour, other ingredients, even the room temperature. Recipes therefore often give approximate quantities of liquid. You will soon learn to judge the ideal consistency of a dough.

◆ Do not skimp on kneading. Kneading is essential for stretching the gluten to give a well-risen, light-textured loaf.

◆ Avoid leaving dough to rise in a draught and make sure the ambient temperature is not too high, or the dough will begin to cook.

◆ Always cover the bowl during rising as a crust will form on top of the dough if the air gets to it. Clear film can be pressed on to the dough itself or can be stretched over the bowl. Either way, oil the film first or the dough will stick to it as it rises.

◆ Remember: the slower the rising, the better the taste of the bread.

KNOCKING BACK, SHAPING AND FINAL RISING

KNOCKING BACK

After all the effort by the yeast to create a risen dough, it seems a shame to knock it back. However, this process not only redistributes the gases in the dough that were created by fermentation, it also rein-vigorates the yeast, making sure that it is evenly distributed, and ensures the bread has an even texture. It should take only a few minutes and the bread is then ready for shaping. The dough is fully risen when it has doubled in bulk. If you are not sure that it is ready, test by gently inserting a finger into the centre of the dough. The dough should not immediately spring back. If it does, leave for a little longer.

1 Knock back the risen dough using your knuckles. Americans call this "punching down the dough", which is an accurate description of the process. Having knocked back the dough, place it on a floured work surface and knead lightly for 1–2 minutes.

SHAPING

There are several ways of shaping the dough to fit a loaf tin.

1 The easiest way is to shape the dough roughly into an oval and place it in the tin, with the smooth side on top.

2 Alternatively, roll out the dough into a rectangle, a little longer than the tin. Roll it up like a Swiss roll, tuck in the ends and place the roll in the tin, with the seam-side down.

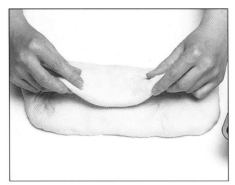

3 Another method for shaping the dough is to roll it out into a rectangle and fold it in half lengthways, pinching the edges together on the sides and flattening the dough out slightly with the heel of your hand. Fold the dough over once more to make a double thickness and pinch the edges together again. Now gently roll the dough backwards and forwards until it has a well-rounded shape.

4 Fold in the two short ends and place the dough in the prepared tin with the seam along the bottom.

1 Shape the dough into a round and then press along the centre with your hand. Turn the dough over, so that the smooth side is uppermost.

2 Shape the dough into a round or oval and place it on a baking sheet.

TIPS

◆ Always knock back the dough after the first rising and knead lightly to redistribute the yeast and the gases formed by fermentation, otherwise you may end up with large holes in the loaf or the crust may lift up and become detached from the crumb.

◆ Rising the dough in a warm place is not always necessary – it is simply a method of speeding up the process. Dough will rise (albeit very slowly) even in the fridge. However, wherever you decide to rise your dough the temperature must be constant. Avoid draughts or hot spots, as both will spoil the bread and may cause it to bake unevenly.

◆ Some breads may need slashing either before final rising or during this period (see next section).

SHAPING A BAGUETTE

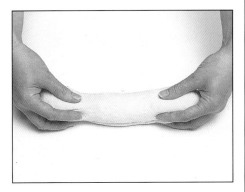

1 Divide the dough into equal pieces. Shape each piece into a ball and then into a rectangle measuring 15 × 7.5cm/ 6 × 3in. Fold the bottom third up and the top third down lengthways. Press the edges together to seal them. Repeat twice, then stretch each piece to a 33–35cm/13–14in loaf.

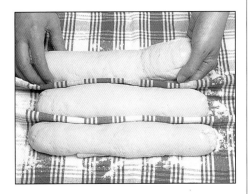

2 Place within the folds of a pleated, floured dish towel or in *bannetons*.

SHAPING A PLAIT

1 Divide the dough into three equal pieces. Roll each piece into a 25cm/10in sausage about 4cm/1½in thick.

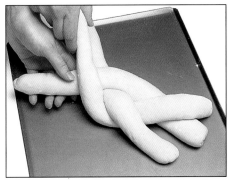

2 Place the three "sausages" on a greased baking sheet. Either start the plait in the centre, plaiting to each end in turn, or pinch the pieces firmly together at one end then plait.

3 When you have finished, pinch the ends together, and turn them under.

FINAL RISING

After shaping the dough and placing it on the baking sheet or in the tin, there is usually a final rising before baking. Depending on the warmth of the room, this can take ¾–1½ hours, although in a very cool room it may take up to 4 hours. Cover the dough so that the surface does not crust over. Oiled clear film placed over the tin or directly on the bread is the best method. The timing is important as over-rising means the loaf may collapse in the oven, while too little proving will mean the loaf will be heavy and flat.

BELOW: A loaf ready for the final rising.

BELOW: After rising the dough should be double in size – no more.

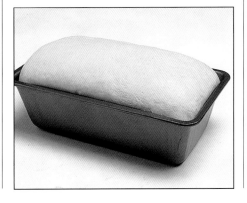

PROVING BASKETS

Professional bakers use proving baskets called *bannetons* for baguettes, and circular *couronnes* for round loaves. Some are lined with linen. Proving baskets are available from good kitchenware shops but, depending on the shape you require, you can improvise with baskets and/or earthenware dishes. Simply dust a linen dish towel liberally with flour and use to line the container.

BELOW: A proving basket will give your loaves a professional finish.

CHOOSING TINS

Choosing the right size of loaf tin can be a tricky business. If it is too small the dough will spill over the top. If it is too large, the final loaf will be badly shaped and uneven. As a general rule the tin should be about twice the size of the dough. Professional bakers use black tins, which are considered to be better than shiny metal ones as they absorb the heat better, giving a crisper crust. Always warm a tin before using and then grease it with melted lard, vegetable oil or unsalted butter. Experiment to see what you find most successful. Baking sheets should also be greased or buttered to prevent sticking.

TOPPING AND BAKING

The actual baking is perhaps the simplest part of the bread-making process, yet even here the yeast still has a part to play and it is important that you play your part too, by making sure conditions are as ideal as possible. When the loaf goes into the oven the heat kills the yeast, but for the first few minutes, there is a final burst of life and the bread will rise even further before the entire process is set and the air is finally locked in.

PREPARING TO BAKE
While the shaped dough is having its final rise, you will need to preheat the oven to the required temperature. It is important that the oven is at the right temperature when the bread goes in – almost always a hot oven, between 220–230°C/425–450°F/Gas 7–8, although check the recipe since sweet loaves or those containing a lot of butter cook at a lower temperature. Many recipes suggest that the oven temperature is reduced either immediately after putting the bread in the oven or some time during cooking. This means the bread gets a good blast of heat to start with, and then cooks more gradually. This mimics the original bread ovens, which would have cooled down slowly once the embers had been removed.

SLASHING
Once the loaf is ready for baking, all that is needed is to slash and glaze the loaf. This is done not only for appearance, but also to improve the baking of the loaf. When the loaf goes into the oven, the yeast will continue to produce carbon dioxide for a short time and the loaf will rise. This is called the "spring". Slashing provides escape routes for the gas and gives direction to the spring, so that the loaf will open out around the slashes and retain an even shape. Loaves that have not been allowed enough time to rise will tend to have more spring, and it is therefore important to slash these fairly deeply. If you think your loaf may have over-risen, only slash it gently.

You will also find that some recipes suggest slashing either before the final rising

or some time during it. This will depend on how much you want your loaf to "open up". The earlier it is slashed the more the split will develop. However, unless the recipe specifies otherwise, the general rule is to slash the loaf just before you put it in the oven.

ABOVE: *Cob or coburg – just before baking, slash a deep cross across the top of the loaf.*

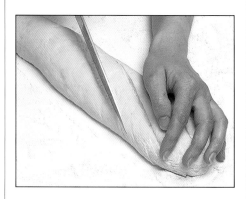

ABOVE: *Baguette – slash four or five times on the diagonal just before the baking process.*

ABOVE: *Porcupine – slashing not only looks attractive, but gives a wonderful crunchy crust to this bread. Make five or six cuts across the bread in one direction, then cut again at right angles, chequerboard fashion.*

ABOVE: *Tin loaf – part-way through rising, make one deep slash along the length of the loaf.*

GLAZING
Glazing has two important functions. It gives an attractive finish to the loaf and it introduces moisture during cooking. This moisture produces steam which also helps to expand the gases in the loaf and ensures it cooks through completely. Glazes also change the consistency and taste of the crust. Bread can be glazed before, during or just after baking: sometimes recipes will suggest all three. If you glaze before and during baking, take care not to brush sticky glazes up to the sides of a tin or let the glaze drip on to the baking sheet, thereby gluing the bread to its container. This will cause the loaf to crack and rise unevenly.

All sorts of glazes can be used – egg yolk, egg white, milk, butter, sugar solutions, salt solutions and olive oil are regularly used. They also help the toppings to stick to the surface of the loaf.

ABOVE: *Brushing a plait with beaten egg yolk and milk before baking gives it a golden glaze and a professional-looking finish.*

TOPPINGS

There are as many toppings as there are glazes, if not more, all of which add to the appearance, taste and texture of your finished bread. The dough can be rolled in a topping before the second rising, or it can be glazed and sprinkled with the topping just before baking. Try poppy seeds, grated cheese, caraway seeds, oats, cracked wheat, sea salt, sunflower seeds, sesame seeds, herbs, cornmeal or wheat flakes as alternative toppings.

For basic breads and rolls, toppings are simply a matter of preference – for dinner parties it's always nice to offer people a selection of white and wholemeal rolls, each sprinkled with a different topping. Some breads classically have their own particular topping. *Challah*, for instance, is traditionally sprinkled with poppy seeds, pretzels are covered with sea salt or caraway seeds, while the long thin grissini can either be rolled in sesame or poppy seeds. Rolled oats add a soft texture to loaves, and many traditional British and American loaves, such as

ABOVE: Roll the dough for a Granary loaf in sunflower seeds.

ABOVE: A split tin loaf can be dusted with flour before baking.

ABOVE: Grated cheese

ABOVE: Cornmeal

ABOVE: Cracked wheat

ABOVE: Chopped fresh herbs

ABOVE: Rolled oats

ABOVE: Chopped black olives

ABOVE: Poppy seeds

ABOVE: Sea salt

ABOVE: Sesame seeds

ABOVE: Wheat flakes

ABOVE: Sunflower seeds

English cottage loaf and San Francisco sourdough bread have no toppings as such, but a dusting of flour gives an attractive matt sheen to the finished loaf.

Grated cheese and fried onion rings also make more substantial as well as tasty and attractive toppings and many of the Italian breads excel themselves in their rich variety of toppings – whole green or black olives, chunks of sun-dried tomatoes and roasted peppers are frequently added to ciabattas and focaccias. As with glazes, toppings can also be added during and sometimes after cooking. Small breads, such as Vienna rolls, are baked until just golden, brushed with milk or cream and then strewn with sea salt, cumin or caraway seeds. They are then returned to the oven for a few more moments until cooked.

ABOVE: Caraway seeds

BELOW: For a dinner party or a buffet meal, bake a batch of rolls with assorted toppings.

BAKING TIMES

This will depend on the recipe, the size of the loaf and the heat of the oven. As a general rule, rolls take about 20 minutes, round country breads 40–50 minutes and tin loaves a little longer, 45–60 minutes. To check if bread is ready, remove it from the oven and tap firmly on the base of the loaf with your knuckles. It should have a hollow sound. If it seems soft or does not sound hollow, bake for a little longer.

ABOVE: Check rolls are ready by gently turning one over in a clean dish towel. The underside should be firm and golden, with no trace of moisture.

ABOVE: To check that a loaf is cooked, tap the base with your knuckles. It should be firm and sound hollow.

ADDING MOISTURE TO THE OVEN

A baker's oven is completely sealed and therefore produces the necessary steam for an evenly risen loaf. At home, glazing helps to produce steam, as does a tin of boiling water placed in the bottom of the oven, or you can spray water into the oven two or three times during cooking.

WHAT WENT WRONG

DOUGH WON'T RISE

You may have forgotten the yeast or the yeast may be past its "use-by" date and is dead. To save the dough, make up another batch, making certain the yeast is active. This dough can then be kneaded into the original dough. Alternatively, dissolve the new yeast in warm water and work it into the dough. Another time, always check that yeast is active before adding to flour.

SIDES AND BOTTOM OF BREAD ARE TOO PALE

The oven temperature was too low, or the tin did not allow heat to penetrate the crust. To remedy this, turn the loaf out of its tin and return it to the oven, placing it upside-down on a shelf, for 5–10 minutes.

CRUST TOO SOFT

There was insufficient steam in the oven. You could glaze the crusts before baking next time and spray the inside of the oven with water. Alternatively, place a little hot water in an ovenproof dish in the bottom of the oven during baking. This problem particularly besets French breads and other crusty loaves, which require a certain amount of steam in the oven.

CRUST TOO HARD

Using too much glaze or having too much steam in the oven can harden the crust, so use less glaze next time. To soften a crusty loaf, leave it overnight in a plastic bag.

CRUST SEPARATES FROM THE BREAD

This is caused either by the dough drying out during rising, or by the oven temperature being too low and the dough expanding unevenly. Next time, cover the dough with clear film or waxed paper to prevent any moisture loss while rising, and ensure that the oven is preheated to the correct temperature, so that heat penetrates uniformly throughout the loaf.

SOFT PALE CRUST

This could be because the bread was not baked for long enough or perhaps the oven temperature was too low. When you think bread is ready, tap it firmly underneath; it should sound hollow. If it does not, return the bread to the oven, only this time placing it directly on the oven shelf.

LOAF IS CRUMBLY AND DRY

Either the bread was baked for too long or you used too much flour. Next time check the quantities in the recipe. It is also possible that the oven was too hot. Next time reduce the temperature and check the loaf when the crust looks golden brown.

LARGE HOLES IN LOAF

Either the dough was not knocked back properly before shaping or it was not kneaded enough originally.

BREAD HAS A YEASTY FLAVOUR

Too much yeast was used. If doubling recipe quantities, do not double the amount of yeast but use one and a half times the amount. In addition, do not overcompensate for a cool room by adding extra yeast unless you don't mind a yeasty flavour. Wait a little longer instead – the bread will rise in the end.

LOAF COLLAPSES IN THE OVEN

Either the wrong flour was used for a particular recipe or the dough was left too long for the second rising and has over-risen. As a rule, the dough should only double in bulk.

LOAF IS DENSE AND FLAT

Too much liquid was used and the dough has become too soft, or was not kneaded enough. Check the recipe for quantities of liquid needed until you are confident about judging the consistency of the dough. The dough should be kneaded firmly for at least 10 minutes.

BREAD-MAKING MACHINES

Bread makers may take the fun out of bread making, but if you enjoy home-made bread on a daily basis, they make it an incredibly easy process. All you need to do is add the correct ingredients, press the right buttons and – hey presto – a few hours later, you have a freshly cooked loaf of bread!

Many bread makers have a timer switch, so that you can programme your bread to be ready for when you get up in the morning. Almost all bread makers will make a variety of different types and sizes of loaves, and many have a feature where the bread maker does the kneading and rising, with the baking up to you – useful for French loaves, pizzas or any other breads that are not a standard loaf shape.

THINGS TO LOOK OUT FOR WHEN BUYING A BREAD-MAKING MACHINE

◆ Unless you are likely to need only one small loaf a day, choose a machine with the option of making small, medium and large loaves.
◆ "Rapid-bake": this cuts down on resting time, and by recommending extra yeast, also cuts down on rising. You will get a loaf in under 2 hours.
◆ Dough (or manual) cycle: allows you to remove the dough prior to shaping when making loaves that are not the standard "loaf" shape.
◆ Crust colour: some bread makers have the option of a dark, medium or pale crust.
◆ Sweet bread cycle: breads that are high in sugar or fat need to bake at slightly lower temperatures, other-wise these ingredients tend to burn. A sweet bread cycle means that the bread-making machine will automat-ically adjust the heat to allow for this, if programmed to do so first.
◆ Timer feature: this useful feature allows you to set the bread maker so that the bread is ready for when you get up in the morning or when the children come home from school.

USING A BREAD MAKER

1 Add the easy-blend or fast-action yeast to the bread tin. If you are making a quick or rapid-bake loaf, you may need to add up to one and a half times the usual quantity of yeast, but check the manufacturer's recommendation.

2 Add the remaining ingredients to the bread tin and place in the machine. Select the type of loaf you wish to bake, the size and colour of the crust.

3 Dried fruit, olives or other ingredients used to flavour breads are added after the initial kneading. This is to ensure that they are not broken up too much. Depending on the type of loaf you chose to make, your bread will be ready to eat in 2–5 hours.

TIPS FOR CONVERTING RECIPES

Once you're familiar with your bread machine and confident using suggested recipes, you will probably want to adapt some of your own favourite recipes. A loaf baked in a bread-making machine will, of course, always be "loaf-shaped", but since most bread makers have a dough cycle (where the dough is kneaded but not baked), it is possible to prepare rolls, ciabatta and baguettes – indeed most breads featured in this book. It is impor-tant that you reduce the recipe according to the maximum capacity of your machine (and even further if you wish to make a small loaf).

Make sure that the proportions of all the essential ingredients for the recipe are approximately as follows:

FOR A 450G/1LB LOAF
Flour: 225–300g/8–11oz/2–2¾ cups
Liquid (water or milk):
180–250ml/6–8fl oz/¾–1 cup
Salt: 1.5–5ml/¼–1 tsp
Fat: 10–45ml/2 tsp–3 tbsp
Salt: 10–45ml/2 tsp–3 tbsp
Dried yeast: 7–15ml/1½ tsp–1 tbsp
FOR A 675G/1½LB LOAF
Flour: 350–450g/12–16oz/3–4 cups
Liquid (water or milk):
250–300ml/8–10fl oz/1–1¼ cups
Salt: 2.5–7.5ml/½–1½ tsp
Fat: 15–60ml/1–4 tbsp
Salt: 15–60ml/1–4 tbsp
Dried yeast: 7–15ml/1½ tsp–1 tbsp

◆ If adding fruit or other ingredients, reduce the quantities proportionately.
◆ Always use a fast-action yeast.
◆ If adding eggs, remember that one large egg is roughly equal to 60ml/4 tbsp liquid, so reduce the liquid accordingly.
◆ When adapting a recipe, monitor the machine carefully and make a note of any adjustments you may need to make. For instance, pay attention to whether the mixture is too moist or whether the machine struggles to knead the dough. If the loaf is too tall, this may be because you've added too much liquid, yeast or sugar, or added insufficient salt.

Bread-making Equipment

Bread making is not an exact science and you do not need a fully equipped kitchen with state-of-the-art utensils if you decide to have a go. In the long run, though, you may decide that some things are essential and others could be useful.

Scales/Weights
Balance scales are more accurate but spring balance scales are easier to use and more convenient (especially if you have a tendency to lose the weights). Bear in mind, if buying scales for bread making, that you will probably be using large quantities of flours and will therefore need large-size scales with a deep basin.

Measuring Jugs
Heatproof glass jugs are most convenient as liquids can safely be heated in them in

Below: Be sure to get scales with a large measuring bowl.

the microwave and they are dish-washer safe. Measurements should be clearly marked on the outside; be sure to buy jugs with both imperial and metric measurements so that you can follow any recipe with ease.

Measuring Spoons
These are always useful in the kitchen for adding small quantities of spices etc. A set of spoons measures from 1.5ml/ ¼ tsp to 15ml/1 tbsp.

Food Processor
Most food processors can mix and knead dough extremely efficiently and in

Left: Sieves for flour or spices

a fraction of the time it would take by hand. Always check the instruction book about bread making since only the larger machines can handle large amounts of dough, and you may find that it is necessary to knead the dough in batches.

Food Mixer
An electric mixer fitted with a dough hook will knead dough in a time similar to that taken to knead by hand but with much less effort. Small machines can cope with only small amounts of dough and if you are considering buying a machine for bread-making purposes, make sure that the equipment is suitable for the quantities of bread you are likely to want to make.

Sieves
Some finer breads may require the flour to be sifted so it is worth having at least one large sieve for flours and a smaller sieve should you wish to add ground spices or dust the loaves with flour or icing sugar after baking them.

COOK'S KNIFE

You will need a sharp knife for slashing the dough – either during rising or just before baking. Some recipe books suggest using a razor for this job but the blade does need to be very sharp indeed. Since a good cook's knife can be kept in razor-sharp condition, this is the preferable option and adds a professional touch to your loaves.

ABOVE: A selection of glass bowls

BOWLS

If you have not got a selection already, it is worth buying some now since it is not possible to make bread (at least in the kitchen) without at least two good-sized bowls. Choose a bowl with a wide mouth, which is still deep enough to contain the batter or dough. A smaller china or glass bowl is also useful (although you can use the measuring jug) for making up dried yeast.

ABOVE: Bread knife and cook's knife

LEFT: Dough knife/scraper

ROLLING PIN

Some doughs need to be rolled out and you will need a large rolling pin for this job. A wooden rolling pin that is long and smooth and has no separate handles is ideal for bread making.

ABOVE: Rolling pin

DOUGH KNIFE OR SCRAPER

This is extremely handy when kneading dough by hand. The rectangular piece of steel on a wooden handle is particularly useful in the early part of kneading, for lifting and working sticky or difficult doughs. The blades normally measure about 10 × 13cm/4 × 5in and should ideally be slightly flexible rather than rigid.

ABOVE: Pastry brushes

BREAD KNIFE

A dull knife can wreak havoc on a fresh loaf of bread, so make sure you use a good bread knife. Bread should be cut in a sawing motion, which is why bread knives have long serrated blades. A plain cook's knife, although it will cut through the bread, will spoil the texture of the crumb.

PASTRY BRUSH

This is essential for glazing loaves and rolls. Choose a good, wide brush. It is worth spending extra for a brush that will not lose its bristles. Use a brush made from natural fibres; nylon will melt if used for brushing hot loaves during cooking.

BREAD TINS

Bread tins come in all sizes and it is worth having a selection. Include a 450g/1lb and preferably two 1kg/2¼ lb tins so that you can make loaves in a variety of shapes and sizes. If the tins are labelled with their dimensions, rather than their capacity,

BELOW: Shallow loaf and cake tins

look out for 18 × 7.5cm/7 × 3in (equivalent to 450g/1lb) and 23 × 13cm/9 × 5in (equivalent to 1kg/2¼ lb). Other useful sizes are 30 × 10cm/12 × 4in and 25 × 10cm/10 × 4in. Professional bakers prefer matt black tins, which absorb the heat better than the shiny ones and therefore make the crust crisper. The wider

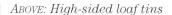

ABOVE: High-sided loaf tins

shallow tins are mostly used for fruit breads. Tin loaves are baked in plain, high-sided tins; farmhouse loaves are slightly shallower and tins may be stamped with the word "Farmhouse". Cake tins are sometimes used for bread making. Monkey bread, for instance, is baked in a 23cm/9in springform ring cake tin, while buchty – breakfast rolls that are batch-baked – require a square, loose-bottomed cake tin with straight sides that will support the rolls as they rise.

Several speciality breads are baked in a deep 15cm/6in cake tin. These breads include *panettone* and Sally Lunn.

If you are fond of baking focaccia, you will find a 25cm/10in pizza pan or shallow round cake tin invaluable.

MOULDS

There are various sizes of brioche mould for the traditional fluted brioche, including individual bun size. A *kugelhopf* mould is a fluted ring mould essential for making the Alsace or German *kugelhopf* or the Viennese *gugelhupf*. A savarin mould is a straight-sided ring mould for

savarins and other ring-shaped breads. If you don't have the correct mould, it is sometimes possible to improvise. Boston brown bread, for instance, can be baked in a special mould, but the heatproof glass jar from a cafetière coffee jug can be used instead, or even two 450g/1lb coffee tins, without the lids, work perfectly well once they have been washed and dried.

BAKING SHEETS
When buying baking sheets, look for ones that are either completely flat, or have a lip only on one long edge. This makes it easier to slide bread or rolls on to a wire rack. Strong, heavy baking sheets distribute the heat evenly.

MUFFIN SHEETS AND PATTY TINS
Muffin sheets with 7.5cm/3in cups are very useful for making elaborately shaped rolls like the aptly named New England Fantans, while the larger patty tins and Yorkshire pudding tins come into their own for specialities like Georgian Khachapuri. The tins support the dough while it is filled with cheese and then tied into a topknot.

FLOWER POTS
Earthenware flower pots can also be used for baking. These need to be tempered before being used for bread. Brush the new, perfectly clean pots liberally inside and out with oil and place in a hot oven (about 400°F/200°C/Gas 6) for about 30 minutes. (This can conveniently be done while you are cooking something else.) Do this several times until the pots are impregnated with oil. They can then be used for baking bread and will need very little greasing.

BELOW: Baking sheets and patty tins

BELOW: Earthenware flower pots make unusual moulds for loaves.

LEFT: A French fluted brioche mould and a savarin or ring mould

LONGUETS

Longuets are moulded pieces of steel, like corrugated iron, used for baking baguettes. They are designed with the professional baker in mind and are unlikely to be suitable for an average size oven.

BAKING STONE

Baking stones are now widely available, sold principally for pizzas but also useful for making thick crusted loaves. They are the nearest thing to replicating an authentic brick-floored oven. The stones are heated in the oven and then the bread is placed on top.

BANNETONS AND COURONNES

These are the canvas-lined proving baskets used by French bakers for their bread: *bannetons* are used for baguettes, *couronnes* for round loaves. In Germany, sourdough bread is sometimes proved in a floured basket, which has the effect of creating a crust that looks like wicker.

GRIDDLE

This is a heavy cast-iron pan used on top of the stove for griddle cakes, soda farls, bannocks and even Indian breads like missi rotis and chapatis. Weight is the important feature with griddles, so that heat can be evenly dispersed.

Griddles can have handles or have the more old-fashioned design of a hooped handle over the entire pan, often with a small hoop in the centre which would have been used to hang the griddle over a peat fire. In Scotland, where they are still widely used, griddles are also known as girdles.

Square-shaped griddles that come with metal hoops for muffins and crumpets are also available in good kitchen shops. The hoops have a diameter of about 10cm/4in and are about 2.5cm/1in deep.

BELOW: This short, deep banneton is ideal for shorter French loaves.

ABOVE: Very long bannetons are designed for supporting baguettes during the final rising.

BELOW: A griddle for pikelets and other free form breads, such as griddle-baked soda bread and oatcakes.

BREADS OF THE WORLD

Bread is a particularly fundamental aspect of a country's cuisine – it reflects the climate and geography, as well as the customs, culture and religious beliefs of the people. This comprehensive guide includes the world's best-loved breads and many less well-known loaves, too. It will help you recognize the different breads that are sold in supermarkets and bakeries, act as a guide if you are travelling abroad, and encourage you to sample local breads, whether you've travelled halfway across the world, or simply moved to a new area.

BRITISH BREADS

British bread is now considered as good as any bread from Europe, something that could not have been said 20, or even 10 years ago. In the 1970s and 80s British holiday-makers discovered the delights of French baguettes, Italian ciabatta and all the other wonderful breads of Europe, and began asking why their own bread was so uninteresting. Many small bakers, of course, had been producing excellent bread for years, a delight for their customers but unknown to all those who shopped mostly in supermarkets. Things changed when supermarkets introduced their own in-store bakeries. Suddenly fresh bread was easily and readily available. The equation was simple. Fresh bread tasted great; people started eating more of it, and thus more bread, and in greater diversity, was made and sold. It's an equation where everyone gains. Bread is relatively cheap; it's an excellent food; it can be eaten with almost any meal and there is now a huge choice for the consumer. Small bakers have risen to the challenge of the supermarkets by producing their own speciality breads. All sorts of sourdoughs, ryes and corn breads are now available, along with a vast range of the more traditional British breads. The following breads are among the better known shapes, and are the breads you are

RIGHT: A bloomer can be distinguished by the diagonal slashes across the top.

likely to find in almost any good bakery and in most supermarkets, too. White breads are defined by their shape rather than the dough, and the majority of loaves are made using the same dough. However, once you start tasting and comparing breads, you will discover that the shape, the method of cooking and even the amount of slashing on the loaf will alter the flavour.

BATCHED BREAD

These loaves are baked together without tins so that there are no crusts along the sides, the individual loaves being broken apart when baked. The top crust is normally soft. Brick or sister brick loaves are two loaves baked together in large square or rectangular tins and then broken apart to give a half-batched effect.

BLOOMER

This is a popular oven bottom-baked loaf, i.e. one that is baked without a tin, either on a tray or on the sole of the oven. It has a plump, oval shape and is distinguished by five or six diagonal slashes across the upper crust. A bloomer from a good baker's has a soft crumb and a fragile and sharp crust. However, shop-bought bloomers that have been pre-wrapped in plastic often have a disappointingly flabby crust. Bloomers can be made

ABOVE: Batched loaves are not necessarily uniform in shape, but always have soft sides. White and brown loaves are available.

ABOVE: Cornmeal loaf (top) and brown and white cobs. The even texture of the crumb on the cob loaves means that they make excellent toast.

using brown wheat flour, rye or multigrain; however, the most popular type is white.

COB

The cob is perhaps the oldest and most basic of British loaves. The loaf is round and completely plain without slashes or decoration, and is oven-baked and crusty. The word "cob" is an old English word for a head, and plain round loaves made with coarse, brown meal would have been the basic loaf for many families for genera-tions. Cobs today can be white, but are usually brown, wholemeal or Granary.

COBURG

This white, round, oven bottom-baked loaf has a cross slash on the upper crust, dis-tinguishing it from the cob. Some bakers slash the loaf before the final rising to produce a wide-spread loaf with four clover-leaf corners. Others slash more conservatively for a loaf that retains its basic round shape.

PAN COBURG

This loaf is baked in a shallow round tin, the diagonally slashed crust rising up and over the sides of the tin to look a bit like a cauliflower, a name by which it is also known. Specialist craft bakers sometimes make this loaf, either on order or because they have an appreciative clientele, but it is a popular bread to make at home.

CHEQUERBOARD

Also known as a porcupine or rumpy loaf, this bread is cross-hatched to give a "che-querboard" crust. The loaf is usually floured before being cut, and the deeper the cuts, the more the crust will spread.

CORNMEAL

This is not a traditional British loaf, but is becoming increasingly popular, especially among some of the small craft bakers who have developed their own recipes, blending cornmeal with a strong white or wholemeal flour. Sometimes whole corn kernels are also added to give a delicious loaf with good texture.

DANISH

A traditional – or proper – Danish loaf is a round loaf with one central lengthways cut. Originally oven bottom-baked to give a good crust, it was always made using white flour – unlike the cobs and coburgs

RIGHT: A good Danish loaf should have a soft floury crust and a fairly dense crumb.

BELOW: Hovis loaves come in various sizes but all have the familiar tin shape with "Hovis" on the sides.

which would have used the cheaper and more widely available brown meal. Danish loaves today, however, are as likely to be more oval in shape. A good Danish from a bakery still has the firm crust and is cut with frequent and deep diagonal slashes on the top. A common supermarket version of a Danish is a pre-wrapped, cylindrical sliced loaf that is distinguished mainly by the lightness of the crumb. Although this is advertised as virtue, there is very little that can be said in its favour, since it is bland to the extent of being quite tasteless. So, whenever possible, buy from your baker instead.

FARMHOUSE LOAF

Farmhouse tins are shallow and somewhat squat, producing the characteristic plump tin loaves. At

RIGHT: Plaits can be elaborate. Most are enriched with eggs and butter.

one time special bread tins were used, which impressed the word "Farmhouse" along the side of the loaf. This was a fashion introduced towards the end of the last century when there was a move away from the "whiter-than-white" breads that had become immensely popular, to a more healthy bread. The original farmhouse loaves were made using a brown flour to satisfy the instincts of the more health conscious, although ironically today most farmhouse loaves are white. Today some craft bakers make their own special farmhouse breads using a dough that has been fermented for longer than usual, but the majority of farmhouse loaves are made using exactly the same dough as other white breads. The difference, as is often the case, is in the shape.

HOVIS

No sooner had the poor in Britain been converted to the values and merits of white bread, than a movement began to persuade people that breads containing wheat germ, the bits discarded by the roller mills, were highly valuable nutritionally. A flour was developed that put the wheat germ back into the flour, after first stabilizing it to prevent rancidity. The flour was called Hovis (from the Latin *hominis vis*, meaning "the life of man") and one of the most enduring proprietary breads was born. All Hovis loaves, whether baked at home or bought from a bakery, are made using Hovis flour, although there are a variety of different mixes, some containing more of the wholemeal along with other

grains. Hovis loaves have their name impressed along the side and some are quite delicious. Pre-packed and sliced loaves have less character.

INNES

Innes Original is one of the few sourdough loaves widely available in Britain today, although individual bakers may well make their own favourite sourdough.

PLAIT

Specialist bakers often produce their own plaited loaves, which can be made from anything between three and eight strands of dough. They mimic the popular European and

Jewish breads but are no less British for all that, having been made by craft bakers for generations. They are normally white and can be crusty, made using plain dough, or they can be enriched with butter, eggs and milk and are therefore soft.

SPIRAL

Several of the European breads are shaped by rolling the dough into a sausage shape and then twisting it around to make a spiral or snail shape. Specialist bakers may produce their own particular favourite, which may be white and crusty or enriched and sprinkled with poppy seeds or glazed with egg.

ABOVE: A spiral loaf

RIGHT: Ground nuts give this walnut bread a slightly beige colour.

WALNUT BREAD

There are two styles of British walnut loaf, though the French *pain aux noix* is more commonly available. The white bloomer-shaped walnut loaf contains coarsely ground walnuts while the walnut Granary is made using larger chunks of walnut. Both are fairly soft loaves with an airy texture.

OPPOSITE: The white farmhouse loaf produced today (top) is somewhat squat in shape with a characteristic central slash. Wholemeal and Granary loaves (left and right) can be tin-baked or oven bottom-baked.

BELOW: The obvious choice for making sandwiches is the eponymous sandwich loaf, but any tin or split tin loaf works well, despite the more irregular shape.

TIN/SPLIT TIN LOAVES

These loaves are baked in tins, the crust either forming a domed shape (tin), or being slashed along the centre before baking (split tin), so that there is a larger crust area. The crust is normally fairly soft, particularly on loaves that have been pre-packed. A sandwich loaf, which is baked in a completely enclosed tin, is – as the name suggests – popular for making sandwiches since all the slices are conveniently square.

VITBE

Like Hovis, this is another loaf made from a proprietary brand of flour, which also returns the stabilized wheat germ to the white flour. There are several VitBe loaves: the original wheat germ bread and a Hi-Bran loaf.

VIENNA BATONS

A Vienna baton is a slashed long loaf which was, until very recently, the British approximation of the French baguette. The crumb is light and airy, the crust crisp and flaky.

The French baguette was developed partly from a process that originated in Vienna where steam was injected into the oven. Known as the "Vienna" technique, the process was adopted by British bakers in the forlorn hope of reproducing the increasingly popular baguette. The experiment wasn't entirely successful. Vienna batons resemble baguettes only in shape. Their light airy crumb and crisp flaky crust nevertheless has a character of its own and they are surprisingly good, sliced, topped with grated cheese, then toasted and added to French onion soup.

ENGLISH BREADS

ENGLISH OATMEAL BREAD

Oats have always been an important crop in England and other parts of the British Isles, although mainly for animal feed. Oatmeal contains no gluten, so breads made entirely using oats were inevitably flat, baked on stones or on a griddle. Many parts of England, as well as Wales and Scotland, have their own traditional oatmeal cakes, but the meal can be used for baking loaves if it is mixed with wheat flour.

CORNISH SAFFRON CAKE

This Cornish sweet bread is yeast-leavened, enriched with fruit and spiced with nutmeg, cinnamon and saffron. Saffron was an important crop in England in the 16th century and although it gradually declined, it continued to survive in the West Country, where numerous traditional breads and cakes include the tiny strands of saffron, adding a delicate flavour and pretty colouring.

LEFT: An English favourite – cottage loaf

RIGHT: Cornish saffron cake is one of the best known of the English currant breads.

COTTAGE LOAF

The cottage loaf must be among the oldest shapes of English breads. The distinctive arrangement of a smallish round loaf baked on top of a larger round loaf seems to be a peculiarity to England and Elizabeth David in her *English Bread and Yeast Cookery* suggests that it might have originated as an improvised way of economizing on baking space in a small oven. The two loaves are wedded together by pushing a wooden spoon handle or fingers down the centre of the two rounds and sometimes the sides are snipped to give an extra crusty finish. Traditionally, cottage loaves would have been baked on the floor of the oven and the best cottage loaves today have a thick, dark bottom crust. Sadly, few high-street bakers have the time or oven space for these celebrated loaves and they are not widely available. For special occasions or on request, some of the smaller specialist bakers will bake a cottage loaf and, no doubt, take great pleasure in doing so.

ABOVE: A harvest loaf gives bakers an opportunity to practise their skill and can be quite spectacular.

GUERNSEY GÂCHE

From this small British island off the coast of Normandy come two breads that are both known as "gâche". The French, brioche-style gâche is highly spiced with cloves and made in proper Normandy style with apples. The British version is heavier, enriched with candied peel and sultanas, and made with eggs and rich Guernsey butter and milk.

HARVEST LOAF

Harvest loaves are not really intended for eating but are made by bakers in the autumn to coincide with harvest festivals in churches and schools. It is a tradition that has happily endured in many of the smaller villages of England and bakers clearly enjoy the opportunity to demonstrate their skill and expertise.

HOT CROSS BUNS

Small yeasted buns have been popular in England since medieval times. Small breads, enriched with eggs, currants and raisins and spiced with nutmeg and cinnamon, were served to accompany wine at the end of a feast. They became a particular Lent favourite among the Elizabethans, who enjoyed displaying their wealth and sophistication by using

CRUMPETS

Crumpets are another traditional bread, and are similar to pikelets and muffins. Recipes for crumpets date from the 18th century and then, just as now, they were always toasted and eaten with lashings of butter. Today, crumpets are made using yeast and baking powder (or bicarbonate of soda and cream of tartar), which accounts for their characteristic holey surface. Crumpets are widely available pre-packed from supermarkets but the superior crumpets from specialist bakers are harder to find and it might be simpler in the long run to make your own.

LEFT: Crumpets are traditionally served warm with butter.

the expensive and much sought-after spices from the Far East. During the Middle Ages it was common practice to mark loaves with a deep cross before baking to ward off evil spirits and, although the custom was abandoned after the Reformation as being popish, the buns made for Good Friday continued the custom for this most significant of religious days. Hot cross buns are now available almost all year round. They normally make an appearance shortly after Christmas so the significance of Easter and the pleasure of enjoying food according to the season, like so many things, is but a distant memory. Small bakers, however, continue to bake their own hot cross buns only during Lent and most have the attraction of not being so horribly over-spiced.

LEFT: Hot cross buns are the traditional Easter treat.

LARDY CAKE

There are many different versions of this unequivocally English bread, but all go by the same name and all are very rich. Originally, lardy cakes were made for celebrations, notably harvest festivals, but as sugar and fruit became more affordable they became popular all year round. Various English counties lay claim to lardy cake. You can certainly eat delicious lardy cake in Lancashire and Yorkshire, and Northumberland, too, has its own speciality. The Midlands and Derbyshire are partial to a very sweet variety, while further south, in Surrey and Hampshire, there are versions of fruitless lardy cakes. The round, flattish breads are made using a basic white dough, which is layered with fat, sugar and fruit. Lardy cake, almost by definition, is very calorific (so be warned) and it contains pork lard and is therefore a prohibited food for vegetarians. The cake is still often sold by weight or by the piece.

ABOVE: A sticky, rich and tasty lardy cake

RIGHT: Lincolnshire plum bread makes a pleasant tea-time treat, spread with butter or damson jelly.

LINCOLNSHIRE PLUM BREAD

Just as with plum pudding or plum cake, plum means dried fruit in this context, namely currants, raisins and sultanas. There are several of these plum breads – fruited breads – sold in supermarkets, distributed by a variety of producers. However, the Lincolnshire plum bread seems to be the best known. This, too, is widely available but visitors to Lincolnshire should try if possible to sample the non commercial version, as baked by smaller specialist bakers.

MUFFINS

English muffins – to give them their correct name and to differentiate them from American muffins, which resemble English fairy cakes – belong to the same tradition as crumpets, although there are several differences, as enthusiasts would be only too keen to point out. Like crumpets, they are a part of an English folk memory that includes the muffin man, winter afternoons in front of the fire, toasting forks and tea time. Although muffins and crumpets are made from the same, or similar, basic recipes, muffins use a stiffer mixture and are consequently thicker with a thin skin or crust on each side and without the characteristic holes of crumpets. Like crumpets, muffins are delicious toasted, either split and then toasted or toasted and then split (it makes a difference!) and served with butter. Pre-packed muffins are available in any supermarket. Bakers also occasionally make their own. (Look out for those made by small craft bakeries, which are likely to have a better flavour and a crisper crust.)

BELOW: Once mostly white, brown muffins are now almost as popular.

to the townspeople. The story goes that Sally Lunn, a Huguenot, brought her recipe from France and adapted it to the English oven. Alternatively, although less romantically, the word is thought to be a corruption of the French *soleil lune* or "sun and moon" cake. Either way, Sally Lunn is a distinctive-

LEFT: Pikelets are a speciality of northern England

looking bread with tall sides and a billowing top like the *kugelhopf* of Alsace. Although there is no one authorized version, Sally Lunn is always made using white flour and yeast, enriched with butter and cream. It can be lightly spiced and slightly citrusy, but should not be over-flavoured. It is often sold in cake shops, split and spread with butter or clotted cream.

SOURDOUGH

There is no tradition of making sourdoughs in England but many of the more adventurous bakers are now producing loaves using a sourdough leaven. There are all sorts of breads using various blends of wheat and rye flours, are made and some using a potato starter. Most loaves of this type are, however, flattish and fairly dense with a definite sour/ acid flavour.

PIKELETS

Some people say pikelet is just another name for crumpet and in some parts of the country the words are synonymous. However, while both pikelets and crumpets have the distinctive holey tops, pikelets are not cooked in rings but are free form in shape, being cooked straight on the griddle like Scotch pancakes or the Welsh crumpets *bara pyglyd* (pronounced piglet, and from which pikelets may well get their name). The mixture for pikelets is very much the same as crumpets, but perhaps a bit thinner for pikelets. Bakers in the counties of Leicestershire, Derbyshire, Yorkshire and Lancashire may produce them on a regular basis, and they are sometimes available from larger supermarkets. Otherwise you will need to find a baker who specializes in regional breads and cakes.

SALLY LUNN

This brioche-style cake is a speciality of the West Country, or more particularly Bath, where supposedly a lass called Sally Lunn once sold her cakes

ABOVE: Sally Lunn, with its delicate citrus flavour, is often sliced into three layers and filled with clotted cream

BELOW: Sourdough

STOTTIE

This flattish bread is native to the northeast of England, where it is widely available, although almost unheard of anywhere else. Almost always white, it is flat with a soft, floury crust, often (but not always) scored with a single slash or cross. Local bakers explain that stotties were traditionally the last things to be baked in the oven at the end of the day, the name itself coming from the local word "stott", meaning to throw to the ground. The bread apparently was ready for eating if it rebounded from the floor! Stottie bread (perhaps as a result of such bad treatment) is rather dry with an open crumb and fairly chewy texture. It is, however, delicious with another regional dish, ham and pease pudding (based on split peas).

STAFFORDSHIRE OATCAKES

Unlike the small, crumbly Scottish oatcake, Staffordshire oatcakes are soft and floppy and are the size of small pancakes. They are known locally as "turnstall tortillas" and they are indeed similar to a tortilla, although unlike the Mexican bread, these are eaten in true English fashion with eggs and bacon for breakfast or butter and honey for tea.

The oatcakes are made from a mixture of oatmeal and flour, yeast and milk or water. It is likely that they have been made in Staffordshire for centuries, as all sorts of oatcakes and griddle cakes were common in the North of England from Tudor times. With the Industrial Revolution though, they became associated with the Staffordshire potteries and while available from many supermarkets, the best are those that are baked on the premises of local bakers in places such as Stoke-on-Trent.

YORKSHIRE FARL

This is a round soda bread, similar to the Irish soda breads, that is cross-slashed into quarters (farls) before being baked.

BELOW: Stotties are a favourite in the north of England.

WELSH BREADS

BARA BRITH

Bara brith is one of the best-known fruit breads of the British Isles. "Bara" is the Welsh word for bread, while "brith", meaning spotted, describes the currants that are an essential ingredient. Although there are brown or "wholemeal" versions, bara brith is normally made using white flour. A good bara brith is yeast-leavened, lightly spiced and fairly dense in texture. Today, raisins and mixed peel are often added, but currants are the essential ingredient and bakers in Wales will commonly plump these first in cold tea, perhaps to emulate the juicy blackcurrants thought to have been the original fruit in bara brith. The bread is sold in most large supermarkets and some delicatessens, but for a really traditional barabrith you may need to travel to Wales, where there are many different versions from which you can choose your own particular favourite.

RIGHT: Bara brith was considered a luxury loaf when dried fruit was expensive. It is still one of the most delicious teabreads.

WELSH COB

Unlike the round English cob, a Welsh cob is something like a cross between an English farmhouse and a stottie. It is baked oven crusty and is normally made from white flour. Usually dusted with flour before baking, these loaves may also have a cut along the centre.

ABOVE: Welsh cob

WELSH COTTAGE

The Welsh cottage loaf, like its English equivalent, is not often made by bakers as it is time-consuming and takes up a lot of oven space. However specialist bakers and some restaurants may produce these loaves for their customers. The bottom half of the loaf is sometimes slashed vertically before the final rising.

WELSH POT BREAD

In the days before families had ovens for baking, people improvised in the most ingenious ways. Dough, which would normally have been a fairly coarse, brown meal, would be moulded in an iron pot and then turned upside-down on to a flat stone lying over a wood-burning fire. Alternatively, the dough was baked in a three-legged pot, which also would be placed over an open fire, and smouldering peat would then have been piled on top. Pot breads like these are not made these days, but occasionally some restaurants will make their own version, using earthenware pots to create interesting and crusty loaves.

LEFT: Welsh cottage

WELSH TINS

Welsh tins have a crusty appearance with a pleasant soft crumb. The white loaves are sometimes cross-hatched but are often, like the wholemeal and Granary versions, left plain. Like most tin loaves, this bread makes great toast and is often served buttered with the delicious, slightly salty Welsh butter.

LEFT: Swansea loaf, now made only rarely, was a popular bread in the 18th century.

BELOW: Left to right: white, wholemeal and Granary Welsh tin loaves

SWANSEA LOAF

Although nowadays fairly rare, this was once the basic loaf for all who lived in Swansea and its environs. It was normally a batch-baked bread, made with a white wheat flour, and would have been sold in the markets. Some local restaurants that specialize in Welsh food may bake this bread for guests, or there are museums around Swansea that give regular exhibitions of bread making: the bread is made and baked as you watch, so that you have the opportunity of tasting it as it once really was – made by traditional methods, baked in old-fashioned ovens and served still warm.

SCOTTISH BREADS

ABERDEEN BUTTERY ROWIES

Scottish bakers, especially when explaining their wares to the uninitiated, may well describe these delicious little rolls as Scottish croissants. There are certainly similarities. Although the shape differs, rowies being round or oval, they are both made in a similar way: layered with butter so they have a delicious texture that resembles pastry. Rowies, however, are lighter and more savoury than croissants, using less butter but more salt. They are widely available in Scotland, less so as you move further south.

LEFT: Despite the name, soft rolls are slightly crusty.

SELKIRK BANNOCK

This fruited loaf is popular throughout Britain and is available from most large supermarkets, although there was once a time when these breads were only made in the town of Selkirk. It is a round loaf (normally white) and, unlike barm brack and bara brith to which it is often compared, should be completely unspiced. It, too, contains fruit, some versions using only sultanas, others containing currants and candied peel as well. Traditionally it would have been made with lard, making it similar to lardy cake, but most shop-bought versions today use butter or vegetable fat instead, although some older recipes may still suggest a mixture of butter and lard.

BARLEY BANNOCK

"Bannock" is an Old English word of Celtic origin and was probably the first word used to describe bread, as long ago as the 5th century AD. The word still has a rather antiquated ring to it. It generally describes a type of flat, scone-like bread and in Scotland the two words "bannock" and "scone" are used interchangeably. Bannocks were originally unleavened breads, made with barley or oatmeal and cooked on a griddle. Such flat, dense breads are unheard of these days. Most of today's bannocks are made using baking powder or bicarbonate of soda as a raising agent, which gives them a light, airy texture. Some craft bakeries produce bannocks using a natural leaven. The sour flavour is something of an acquired taste, especially when coupled with that of the barley. The breads are still cooked on a griddle and have the characteristic earthy flavour of barley.

MELROSE LOAF

This is Scotland's best-known soda bread. It is a proprietary bread, made by a bakery in south of Scotland. It is a wholemeal, malted loaf with a dense texture and is a popular bread for breakfast, often being spread with butter and marmalade.

LEFT: Aberdeen buttery rowies

SCOTCH BREAD

Scottish bakers are renowned for their bread and these fine loaves are the most popular bread in Scotland, used for sandwiches and toast. Often simply called a "plain" loaf, the bread has the characteristic soft sides of a batch-baked loaf and the top is baked to a dark brown. It has a particularly good flavour, thanks to the longer than usual fermentation period.

MORNING ROLLS

These soft and flattish, floury rolls are to be found in every bakery and supermarket in Scotland. They are called "baps" in some parts of Scotland; in other parts such a word is completely unheard of and the rolls are called "morning rolls" or just "rolls". The product, however, is clearly the same: made with plain, rather than strong flour, the rolls can be wholemeal or brown, but are more commonly white. They are made with lard, which is rubbed into the flour. This is mixed to a dough with milk and water and, of course, yeast, creating the characteristic soft texture. The rolls are normally batched together on large baking trays and are pulled apart after cooking so, like batched bread, they have little or no side crust and are often almost square in shape. A little dimple in the centre of the roll, pressed into the dough just before baking to stop the tops blistering, is a sign of a true traditional morning

ABOVE: Scotch bread is mostly used for sandwiches.

RIGHT: Morning rolls may be known by different names in Scotland but are all similar, being white, flattish and soft.

roll but these marks frequently disappear in the oven and their absence should not deter you from buying the rolls if they look and smell fresh. They are best eaten very fresh, and are noticeably salty, like most Scottish bread. They are popular almost any time of the day, but are a favourite at breakfast, for bacon "butties" and with various fillings. A variation of Scottish "baps" or morning rolls are soft rolls. Confusingly, these rolls are often not as soft as morning rolls. They have a golden glaze, which is produced by brushing the rolls with cream both before and after they are baked.

IRISH BREADS

WHITE SODA BREAD

Soda bread is the traditional bread of Ireland, which has quite different bread-baking traditions from mainland Britain. The old Irish hearth had no built-in oven, and bread was cooked either on a griddle set over the fire, or in a *bastable*, a type of Dutch oven or oven-pot that would have been set in the smouldering peat. These methods continued to be popular even when iron cooking ranges were introduced to Ireland, and even today specialist Irish bakers will make their traditional breads in cast-iron casseroles with the lid on. Another significant difference in bread making in Ireland was the popularity of bicarbonate of soda, as opposed to yeast, as a raising agent. Buttermilk provides the necessary acid to the alkaline bicarbonate of soda and the best soda breads are made using this, although cream of tartar is often used as an alternative to the buttrmilk.

There is a vast range of different soda breads, and almost every bakery in Ireland, as well as most restaurants, has its own favourite recipe. Outside Ireland there is still a reasonable selection of white, brown and wholemeal soda breads available in most supermarkets. Better still are those breads made on the premises by craft bakers. If the baker is Irish, so much the better.

RIGHT: Soda bread can be baked whole and then broken into farls.

Irish round soda bread is normally marked with a cross. Cut the bread into quarters before cooking, and you have soda farls. These are either baked in the oven or cooked on a covered griddle and have a pale, crusty, floury appearance.

RIGHT: Barm brack is one of Ireland's most delicious teabreads. Toast and eat with butter or just cut into chunks or serve with jam

OATMEAL SODA BREAD

In a country with a history of more than its fair share of poverty, almost any edible material that could be ground to a meal would have been used for making bread. Oatmeal is high in protein and would have made a nourishing if flattish bread.

BARM BRACK

This is the Irish version of the Welsh bara brith, the words also translating as "speckled bread". It is linked with several Irish festivals, notably St Brighid's Day – 1 February and the first day of spring – and the festival of Luanasa, which celebrated the start of harvest on 1 August. Barm brack is associated with Hallowe'en and there is also a tradition of baking a wedding ring into the bread, the finder being thus assured of becoming engaged before the year is out. The traditional barm brack, normally made with white flour, is one of the few yeasted Irish breads. Made with sugar, sultanas, mixed peel and currants, it is enriched with butter and eggs. Barm brack is quite delicious by itself, spread with jam or toasted and buttered. It is widely available in Britain and is well worth looking out for.

POTATO BREAD

Potatoes, since their introduction in the 17th century, have been an essential food in Ireland. At various times, up to and including the early parts of the 20th century, wheat was scarce and expensive. Potatoes were regularly used to help "stretch" the flour, producing a nourishing and, if lard was available, a well-flavoured griddle bread. Today, potato breads made by blending mashed potatoes with some proportion of white flour are baked by Irish bakers and some restaurants. The dough is then normally marked or cut into farls and either cooked over a griddle or baked in the oven.

RIGHT: Soda farls are wedges of soda bread, cut from a loaf either before baking or after.

RIGHT: This potato bread was formed into a star shape before being baked.

SODA FARLS

As already mentioned in the entry on white soda bread, the term "farl" describes a wedge-shaped soda bread (usually a quarter of a loaf). The word derives from "fardel", which meant "fourth part", and in Ireland, soda bread is often marked into quarters, or "farls", before baking, as indeed is the Yorkshire farl. In addition, some are actually cut into farls (either into quarters or thirds) before baking, to give a thick wedge-shaped bread with a good crust. Most of these soda farls are made using a white flour, although some are wholemeal breads, made with Irish-milled flour and creamy buttermilk. Properly made, soda farls, like soda bread, are delicious. Their main problem is that they stale quickly, so if possible, consume on the day of purchase.

WHEATEN LOAF

This wheaten loaf is a soda bread that is baked in a tin, so that it is "loaf" shaped, rather than the usual rough round. In Ireland, round soda breads are often called "cakes" or "cakes of bread"; whereas a tin-baked soda bread is called a loaf. Wheaten loaves are normally made with soft Irish wholemeal flour.

BELOW: An Irish wheaten loaf, which is a type of soda bread.

FRENCH BREADS

The French are passionate about their bread. A baguette is one of France's most potent symbols and, whether carried in a basket, strapped to a bicycle or simply tucked under a schoolboy's arm on the way to school, it is as much a sign that you are in France as are the streets of Paris or the vineyards of Provence.

Bread is eaten with every meal and with every course apart from dessert. Although, as in most countries, pre-packaged bread is available, the French seem to attach much importance to their bread, and consequently most families eat fresh bread bought daily – if not from their local *boulangerie*, then at least from the fresh bread counter of the supermarket.

By far the majority of loaves consumed in France are baguettes but there are nevertheless many other types of French bread. The *pain de campagne* and the *levains* are popular throughout the country but there are also countless regional breads of all shapes and sizes. Home-made bread is relatively unusual in France, which surely must be because excellent fresh bread is so easily and readily available. Every village has at least one *boulangerie* where bread is made three or four times a day. French people shop daily – sometimes twice daily – for their bread. Baguettes have to be eaten as fresh as possible, and walking or cycling to the bakery is a small price to pay for the treat.

BAGUETTE

The baguette was developed in Paris in the 1930s and came about due to a combination of factors. White bread was becoming increasingly popular, being synonymous, so it was believed at the time, with quality and excellence. The new baker's yeasts that had been developed meant bakers could experiment with other ways of adding yeast to flour, and mechanized kneading and steam ovens led to substantial improvements in techniques and baking. There are many explanations today for why the best baguettes (and they are not all excellent, even in France) are such a delight, yet so difficult to recreate. The soft French flours certainly play a significant part, producing a soft, light crumb with a wonderful wheaty flavour. The small amounts of yeast used, together with a long kneading and rising period and finally, but not least, the skill of the baker, all contribute to the flavour and texture of a baguette, with its sharp, thin crust and delicious, soft crumb.

The baguette was first known as *pain de fantaisie* ("fancy bread") but the word baguette, meaning "stick", was soon adopted, being obviously the more descriptive nomenclature. *Flutes*, *bâtards*, *ficelles*, *pains* and *petits pains* all belong to the same family, made using the same dough and method. *Pain* is a rounder French bread, normally found only in rural areas. The *bâtard* ("bastard") is a cross between the baguette and the *pain*. It is shorter and slightly fatter than a baguette but weighs about the same. The *flute* is a slim 200g/7oz baguette, while the little *ficelle* ("string") is slimmer still, weighing half as much as a baguette. The baguette itself measures some 68cm/27in in length and weighs 250g/9oz. *Petits pains* are individual sized breads and are often eaten for breakfast.

The baguette has been available outside France for some 20 years and thankfully continues to get better and better.

ABOVE: French baguettes: there are many different varieties, but they should all have a crisp crust and a soft crumb.

Other baguette-style breads are *baguette à l'ancienne* or *baguette de tradition*, *baguette rustique* and *baguette campagne*, often dark, slightly floury and with small paper labels. These breads are an effort by some traditional bakers to recreate the original baguette, as opposed to the modern version, which has, particularly since the 1970s, been subject to ever-faster production methods. These "traditional" baguettes may be made by a sourdough method, can contain rye or other grains or may be a wholemeal or bran version. You will need to ask to find out.

Although breads sold as French sticks are worth avoiding, more and more baguettes, sold either by French-style bakeries or by discerning supermarkets, can be very good. They are likely to contain the essential soft wheat and may have been imported from France part-baked.

VIENNA ROLLS

These little milk breads and their cousins, *petits pains au lait*, are enriched with milk and egg and are normally served for breakfast. Do not confuse French Vienna rolls with British rolls of the same name, which are a crusty torpedo-shape and made with a plain dough. French

LEFT: Vienna rolls are soft and slightly sweet, making a good choice for breakfast.

Vienna rolls are similar to bridge rolls and are fairly small and soft. They may be slashed three or four times across the top, while *petits pains au lait* are rounded, often with a cross cut on top, or long and tapered at either end. They sometimes have a sprinkling of sugar on top.

BRIOCHE

Brioche is one of France's favourite breakfast breads, made with white flour and yeast, enriched with butter, milk and eggs and sweetened with just a little sugar. It is similar to many of the British enriched breads, such as Sally Lunns, although generally richer, using a half to three-quarters butter to flour ratio, which is as rich or richer than most pastries. Although not as popular as croissants outside France, brioche makes a perfect bread for breakfast, with its soft texture and rich flavour. It tastes wonderful served with marmalade or a fruit conserve.

Brioche is made in a variety of shapes and sizes. The most

ABOVE: A loaf-shaped brioche and small individual brioche buns.

RIGHT: The unmistakable crescent-shaped croissant is popular at breakfast almost everywhere.

famous is undoubtedly the *brioche à tête*, with its fluted sides and little brioche cap perched on top, and which in turn comes in various sizes – from individual buns to large loaves. The *brioche Nanterre* is made by arranging six or eight balls of brioche dough in a zigzag pattern along the bottom of a loaf pan, while the *brioche Parisienne* is made in a similar way, but with nine or ten balls of dough placed in a circle. Both rise to fill out the pan but the divisions still exist so that small chunks can be broken off.

Savoury brioche, made using cheese in place of some of the butter, is becoming more widely available outside France. This is likely to be loaf-shaped, rather than the traditional round, and can be used for savoury dishes (as indeed can the sweeter versions). One of the most delicious ways of using savoury brioche is to hollow out the centre and stuff with wild mushrooms or grilled peppers.

CROISSANTS

Another essentially French creation, these popular pastries are available almost everywhere, served not only for breakfast but stuffed with savoury fillings and sold wherever there is a demand for food that can be eaten on the hoof. In France, a distinction is drawn between the *croissant au beurre*, which is small and straight and is made using butter, and the *croissant ordinaire*, which is the more familiar crescent shape made with vegetable fat. The distinction is by no means clear cut, however, as some producers who use only butter in their croissants favour the crescent shape. If the croissants are pre-packed, you can check the packet; otherwise you will need to ask your baker. Ideally, buy croissants fresh in the morning from a local baker, when they will be soft inside, with a slightly crackly crust.

EPI

This translates as "wheat ear" and is the traditional bread at harvest festivals, the French equivalent of a harvest loaf. The little ears of bread are made separately and fashioned into sticks or into a large round called a *couronne* ("crown"). The breads can then be broken off, piece by piece, for eating. *Epis* are normally made using a baguette-style dough and are light and crusty.

FOUGASSE

These large, flat breads are quite unmistakable with their deep cuts representing branches of a tree, cogwheels or even the grate of a fire. They are a speciality of Languedoc and Provence although they originally came from Italy and are closely akin to the Italian focaccia. Sometimes known as *fouacés*, or "hearth bread", they were traditionally baked on the floor of the oven after the embers had been

ABOVE: Epi is an unusual bread.

scraped out, but while it was still too hot to bake a normal loaf. There are several varieties of *fougasse* – most use a sourdough-style leaven and all are flat, deeply cut and baked in a very hot oven.

PAIN DE CAMPAGNE

Next to baguettes, this is the best-known of French breads. In spite of its name, the loaf was the invention of a Parisian baker and is as much enjoyed in towns and cities as it is in the country. Made using a *chef* starter, it has a thick, slightly grey and floury crust and a discernibly sour smell and taste. No rules exist for its shape, although, like almost all French bread, it is oven bottom-baked (i.e. without using tins) and is therefore a convenient round (or a rather misshapen) baton. Outside France and in French cities, the breads are normally of manageable size, weighing about 450g/1lb, but visit a rural *boulangerie* in France and you will find huge cartwheel-size breads or sturdy, long loaves, which will keep a large family going for several days. These are sometimes called *pain ménage* ("household bread") and may be sold by weight. Since it is very

LEFT: Fougasse is the equivalent of Italy's focaccia but has characteristic slashes.

much a local product, you will find the bread changes from region to region, even from village to village. Although most use white wheat flour, rye meal and wholemeal grain is occasionally added, especially for *pain de campagne rustique*, and the flavour and shape will vary enormously. Being a sourdough bread, it keeps well for 4–5 days and indeed is better the day after baking – quite the opposite of the refined baguette.

Pain de campagne is widely available in supermarkets. Shop around for the variety you prefer.

RIGHT: Pain de Campagne comes in many shapes and sizes.

PAIN AUX NOIX

This favourite French bread, although it translates as "nut bread", is understood to be walnut bread. The walnuts give it a teabread feel, but it is very much a savoury bread, best served with soft cheese, such as Brie or Camembert or, if you prefer, strong-flavoured Cheddar or Stilton. It is made using a wholemeal bread flour, which contrasts and complements the nutty and savoury walnuts.

PAIN DE MIE

This is the French version of a British sandwich loaf. It is cooked in an enclosed tin, so that the bread has square sides and a soft crust, making it the ideal shape for sandwiches. Unlike the British loaf, however, it is normally enriched with milk and butter so that, in flavour, it is more like brioche than a plain white loaf.

PAIN DE SEIGLE/PAIN AU SEIGLE

Pain de seigle is French rye and the choice bread for eating with oysters. Regulations insist that it must contain at least two-thirds rye, the remaining proportion made up with wheat flour, which gives it a lighter flavour and colour than German and Scandinavian rye breads. *Pain au seigle* ("bread with rye") needs contain only some 10 per cent rye and is a lighter bread again.

PAIN POILÂNE

This proprietary loaf is produced and distributed by the famous Poilâne bakers in Paris, not just throughout France, but all

ABOVE: Pain au seigle (left) contains a small amount of rye and has a mild flavour. A brown pain de mie (centre) stands alongside pain aux noix (right), a savoury walnut loaf which is excellent with a strong cheese.

over the world. Based on the traditional and long-forgotten country loaves of France's past, the bakery prides itself on the methods used for making and baking the bread – a natural sourdough leaven is kneaded briefly but long fermented, then hand-moulded and finally baked in wood-fired ovens. Because the sourdough method, by definition, produces a different loaf each time, breads in the shop can vary to a surprising degree, some being wonderful, others disappointing.

PAIN POLKA

A speciality bread of the Loire region, this is an oval or round loaf, somewhat flat and criss-crossed with deep slashes. It is baked using the *levain* method of keeping back part of the previous day's dough and using this as the starter for the bread.

PAIN BATTU AU FROMAGE

This is a cheese batter bread, which uses Parmesan cheese, a fact that suggests that the bread originally came from Italy or the Alpes-Maritimes region of France. The cheese is stirred into the batter and also sprinkled over the top before baking, to give a golden crust. The bread can be loaf-shaped or baked in brioche-style individual tins.

PAIN ALLEMAND AUX FRUITS

This translates as German fruit bread, but is nevertheless a French bread from Strasbourg, a city on the border with Germany. Strasbourg is in the heart of Alsace, a region famous for its rich breads, notably *kugelhopf*. *Pain Allemand* is a rich fruit bread

ABOVE: Pain polka can be plain or may contain chopped olives.

LEFT: Pain poilâne is easily recognized by the four slashes making a rough square on its top.

ABOVE: There are many variations on pain au levain (back) but all will be made using the sourdough method. The boule de meule is a very substantial loaf best eaten with hearty soups and stews.

that is spiced with cinnamon, cloves and aniseed and rich with raisins, prunes, apricots and figs. It is, needless to say, a festive bread.

PAIN AU LEVAIN

A white or sometimes wholemeal bread that has become almost as popular in the United Kingdom as it is in France. A *levain* is a bread made by the natural sour-dough method, *levain* being the French expression for a sourdough. The breads come in a variety of shapes, often resembling a rather short and flat baguette, or can be moulded into rough squares. *Pain rustique* is made using the same sour-dough method, but using a proportion of wholemeal flour or a blend of grains.

BOULE DE MEULE

The word *boulangerie* comes from the French word for a round of dough, *une boule*, which also accounts for the name of this bread. *Boule de meule* translates literally as a round of stoneground dough, which pretty well sums up this bread, except that it is baked, ideally on the sole of the oven, until it is crusty. *Boules de meule* are normally quite large, with an excellent flavour.

GÂTEAU DE GANNAT

This rich festive bread is popular in the Gannatois region of France. Its principal distinguishing feature is the fromage blanc which is stirred into the batter-like dough with eggs and butter to make a soft crumbly loaf with a sweet/sour flavour. This taste is particularly noticeable if brandy has been added.

PAIN DE PROVENCE

Provence is so rich in all sorts of wonderful foods that it would be nonsense to

RIGHT: Cereale is normally a torpedo-shaped loaf.

ascribe a single bread to this region. If you visit Provence you are likely to find a range of pains de Provence, either fashioned roughly into small loaves or made into slender baguettes. Along with the herbs of Provence – savory, thyme and basil – the dough is made with lavender flowers and fennel. It has a heady flavour and is superb served with cheese or to accompany a soup.

CEREALE

This is a well-flavoured light brown loaf with a good crust and a tender crumb. It is made from eight cereals and seeds and typically includes wheat, corn, rye, millet, malted wheat and oats, with sunflower and sesame seeds. The shape is quite distinctive. *Cereale* is usually formed into a broad torpedo shape and is lightly dusted with flour.

BELGIAN BREADS

PISTOLET

Pistolets are the Belgian equivalent to the croissants of France. They are small, butter-enriched round rolls, easily distinguished by their central indentation, which is made using a stick dipped in oil before baking. They have a soft texture under a thin, glossy crust and can be found in many parts of northern France, too, where they are just as popular as they are in their native Belgium. *Pistolets* are normally enjoyed for breakfast or for tea, split and spread with preserve or, alternatively, are broken into chunks and eaten French-style dipped in café au lait.

CRAMIQUE

A popular Belgian teabread, this is stuffed with raisins and enriched with butter and milk. It is rather squat in shape and can be made using a wholemeal or a white flour, or a blend of the two. Whiter versions have a soft crumb with the texture and flavour of brioche, while the wholemeal *cramique* has a more malted flavour. Bought fresh, *cramique* is wonderful simply buttered or spread with a preserve. Breads that are two or three days old taste good toasted, buttered and spread with jam, or served with a soft cheese, such as brie or camembert.

ABOVE: Fruity cramique

ITALIAN BREADS

Italian bread has had something of a renaissance in the past few years and rightly so. Italian breads are a delight, delicious served with pasta, fish, meats and poultry, as well as cheese. Any Italian baker will tell you that there are thousands of different Italian breads. This could actually be true should anyone ever try to count! Italy was once made up of a number of independent states, and each developed its own favourite cuisine, including, of course, breads. Geography and climate played a part, as did prosperity. Some of the best-known loaves, such as ciabatta and *pagnotta* are "national" breads, available everywhere. Other breads – the more peasant-style loaves – from rural areas would have been coarse, mealy loaves, made with whatever grain could be gathered together. Olive oil was frequently added, not only for flavour, but to add extra nourishment and to help the keeping qualities of the loaf. Nowadays these rustic loaves are still made using olive oil. They are normally white, although wholemeal and mixed grain loaves are not unheard of. They can be yeast-leavened but originally would have been made using a natural leaven. Small bakeries, especially those in the south of Italy, a region only mildly influenced by tourism and fashion, still produce these loaves for their loyal customers, made in the traditional way from time-honoured recipes. If you visit these parts, be sure to buy and sample some of these regional breads; you cannot fail to be delighted. Outside Italy, various country-style breads, such as *pagnotta* and *pugliese*, are available from Italian-style bakers, although these loaves are likely to be standardized. Nevertheless, many first-generation Italian bakers in Britain and North America, who learnt their baking skills from their parents and grandparents, bake their own favourite regional bread and these are likely to be as good and authentic as the breads of their homeland.

The distinguishing feature of most Italian breads, especially those bought from an Italian-style baker, is the shape rather than the dough. By and large, bakers do not make up different doughs for different breads – they would not have the time, the space or the labour. The difference lies in the shaping, the slashing and the baking – a small distinction you may think, but wait until you try the bread and you will be surprised.

BIOVA

This regional bread comes from the north of Italy, around Piedmont. It is cylindrical in shape with little pointed horns. Made with lard, it has a thick crust and soft crumb and has an excellent flavour.

CARTA DA MUSICA

This extraordinary harvest sheaf loaf from Sardinia, also sometimes called *carasaù* is made with paper thin leaves of dough, piled up to make a tower that looks like a stack of uneven shaped pancakes. The leaves of bread are brittle but can be eaten as a snack with an aperitif or with salads. Alternatively, the leaves of bread can be softened in a light dressing or even just water and olive oil, then wrapped around a filling.

CIABATTA

This ubiquitous loaf has surprisingly not suffered for all that it is produced on a massive scale so as to be available from almost every supermarket in the country.

LEFT: Carta da musica means sheets of music and does look not unlike sheets of parchment piled on top of each other.

LEFT: Plain ciabatta served with olive and sun-dried tomato versions.

It is an oval, slightly flattish loaf, and looks rather like a squashed slipper, which is what the word, rather unromantically, means. It is made with generous quantities of olive oil and has a thin, friable crust. The crumb is light, holey and slightly chewy. Ciabatta is delicious served as an accompaniment to soups or tomato salads, as it will mop up the juices beautifully.

Like the French baguette, ciabatta is a relatively new shape of bread. It is normally a white loaf, made using a sponge dough method – flour, yeast and water are fermented for up to 24 hours before being incorporated into the rest of the dough. Another particular feature of ciabatta, making it a tricky bread to bake at home, is the soft consistency of the dough. It has a minimum of 75 per cent water and oil and is thus quite unlike any other kind of bread. A long kneading process also contributes to ciabatta's unique flavour, which should be sweet/sour, as well as its texture: a crisp crust and an open crumb. Numerous flavourings can be added to ciabatta – from olives and sun-dried tomatoes to cheese and walnuts. Many supermarket loaves are sold part-baked and should be finished off in a hot oven before being served. The final baking enhances both the flavour and texture of what is undeniably one of the world's favourite breads.

FOCACCIA AND FOCACCETTE

Focaccia is another Italian bread that has captured the imagination of the rest of the world. Known variously as "Italian country flat bread", *pizza rustica* or *pizza genovese,* it is a large, flat bread, slightly puffy when fresh and dimpled all over the surface with little indentations. It can be round, square or a rather misshapen rectangle; shape is not particularly important. This is the original Italian hearth bread, made from surplus pieces of dough and baked at a very high heat before the oven cooled slightly for the massive family loaves. It is easy to imagine the children waiting impatiently for their share of the warm bread as it came out of the oven. Today, most shop-bought focaccia, particularly those from supermarkets, are round and can be rather bland in flavour. However, Italian bakers who know and love this bread, will produce far more tasty loaves, baking them in a very hot oven so that, like pizzas, they are floury and flecked with black.

Focaccia is a wonderfully versatile bread. Apart from the olive oil that is kneaded into the basic dough, the flattish bread can be sprinkled with sea salt, herbs,

BELOW: Focaccia is often sprinkled with crushed rosemary.

onions, prosciutto or cheese. Smaller versions of focaccia, *focaccette,* are small rolls sprinkled with salt and onions.

GRISSINI

These long, thin breadsticks, mainly popular as an aperitif, are made from wheat flour and have been cooked until completely dry, so that they are basically all crust and no crumb. The better grissini are made using olive oil; best of all are those that are hand-made by craft bakers, having considerably more character than the bland, smooth breadsticks available in most supermarkets.

Grissini come from the north-west of Italy, around Turin and Piedmont. Here they also make a more substantial type of breadstick, called *francescine.* These are thicker breadsticks with a softer centre and they not only have a better flavour, but have a decidedly good crunch, too. Grissini are mostly made using white flour, although wholemeal ones are sometimes available, especially if made on the

ABOVE: The best grissini are bought from Italian bakers or delicatessens.

premises by smaller bakers. Grissini are commonly rolled in poppy seeds or sesame seeds or coarsely ground sea salt before baking to add extra flavour.

MICHETTA

This is a round white roll with a well-flavoured crust, which is called *rosetta* in Rome.

MEZZA LUNA

This simple crusty loaf is shaped like a half moon. It is made with the standard white dough used for *pagnotta* and other country breads.

PAESANA

This round, simple white loaf that is cross-cut to divide into farls, tastes rather like focaccia or ciabatta. *Paesana* is generally less rich in olive oil

BELOW: Paesana

and, without the addition of herbs, sun-dried tomatoes or olives, tends be a far plainer loaf than its cousins. It is never-theless very good with soups and stews.

PAGNOTTA

This large, round farmhouse loaf is prob-ably the most common and popular bread in Italy, sold all over the country. Loaves can be small and round, but in Italy some may be huge, cut in portions, each still big enough to feed a large family. The bread is traditionally made using the sourdough method. Outside the country, some Italian delicatessens sell this bread, either imported from Italy or made to an origi-nal recipe. Italian-style bakers, however, do not always use the classic but lengthy process for their breads. They argue that for most, *pagnotta* means a standard wheat loaf, so they use the same dough as for other Italian breads. In Italy *pagnotta* can be white, wholemeal or a mixture, depending on the region, and all types are available outside Italy, with white being the most common.

PANE AL CIOCCOLATO

A yeasted bread made with olive oil and studded with dark chocolate which is kneaded into the dough, it can be whole-meal, but is more commonly coloured a rich brown with cocoa powder. In Italy, chocolate bread is served with mas-carpone or Gorgonzola cheese as a snack.

PANE CON NOCI

There are several different Italian breads

ABOVE: Pagnotta is Italian country bread; loaves can be huge.

LEFT: Pane al cioccolato, made as rolls.

RIGHT: Pane con noci is a savoury nut bread.

that go under the title of "bread with nuts". The oval-shaped bread is similar to the British and French walnut breads, while a slim, flat loaf with sultanas and walnuts is a sweet version of ciabatta.

PANETTONE

Panettone is a Milanese speciality, sold around Christmas as a traditional festive cake. In Italy and in delicatessens outside the country, it is sold wrapped in cellophane and tied with coloured ribbons. For all its richness – made with liberal amounts of butter, eggs and milk, together with sultanas, candied peel and sometimes chocolate – *panettone* is surprisingly light in texture. This may have something to do with the traditional *panettone* shape, which is like a squat cylinder or dome, slightly wider at the top where the bread has billowed out into a deep golden crust.

RIGHT: Pugliese is one of the best-known and loved Italian breads.

PANE DI MAIS

Made using polenta, a coarse ground cornmeal, *pane di*

RIGHT: Panettone is the classic Christmas bread.

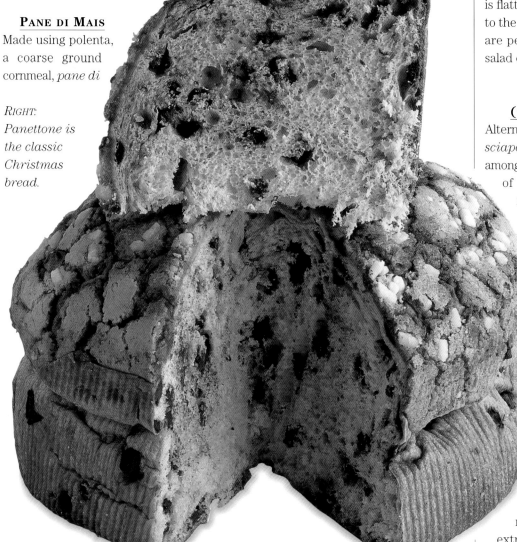

mais is one of the few Italian corn breads. It normally also contains some olive oil. It is flatter than most Italian breads, owing to the high proportion of corn, but pieces are perfect for mopping up sauces and salad dressings.

PANE TOSCANO (TUSCAN SALTLESS BREAD)

Alternatively called *pane sciocco* or *pane sciapo Toscano*, this bread is a favourite among Tuscans, who love it for the flavour of the wheat, which is more pronounced in the absence of salt. The bread was made at a time when salt was heavily taxed. Unlike many Italian breads, *pane sciocco* does not contain olive oil either. If you try eating it by itself, a common reaction is "something's wrong", or "something's missing from this bread". However, eaten with goat's cheese, anchovies, olives or salami, the bread comes into its own.

PUGLIESE

This much-loved Italian bread was once the regional bread from Puglia, in the southern region of Apulia. Perhaps it is the extra virgin olive oil from this region or the excellence of the wheat, but *pugliese*

RIGHT: Sfilatino look like small baguettes.

is considered to be among the jewels of Italian breads, popular all over the country and beyond as well. The bread is normally white, with a pale, floury crust and a soft crumb, quite dense by Italian standards, compared with the holey ciabatta and the open-textured *pagnotta*.

SFILATINO

Looking something like a French baguette that has perhaps been crossed with a baby ciabatta, these little Italian breads are a wonderful addition to the bread counter at the supermarket and are excellent served with an Italian meal. Although similar in shape to the baguette, any comparison ends there. *Sfilatino* loaves are noticeably smaller than the baguette, without the slashes on top and with a darker, more floury crust. Made using lots of virgin olive oil,

the crust is crisper and less flaky than the baguette, while the crumb is softer.

ITALIAN OLIVE BREAD

Olives are grown throughout Italy and it's not surprising to find all sorts of olive bread. The more commercially produced loaves are enriched with eggs and butter and normally contain pitted green olives and sometimes whole olives stuffed, Spanish-style, with red pimiento. Smaller bakers often also produce their own olive breads. These are plainer doughs, which usually contain black olives, sometimes pitted, but sometimes not – so take care when biting into a slice.

TORTINO

Tortino is similar to an olive bread, but is much larger and more rustic, with a dense crumb. It can be stuffed with olives, spinach or tomatoes or a mixture of all these.

SICILIAN SCROLL

Sicily has a strong tradition of bread making. Over the centuries, monks and nuns of the island's many monasteries perfected their baking skills as a sign of devotion to God. Sicilian scroll is unusual in that it contains a high proportion of semolina. Shaped into a broad "S", it has a soft, pale yellow crumb and a crisp crust that is traditionally topped with sesame seeds.

ABOVE: Pane Toscano goes by several names, including "sciocco" and "Tuscan saltless bread". It has a dense crumb, which to palates unused to its salt-free nature is very bland. However, it has its devotees and is good with cheese.

SPANISH BREADS

Bread is the symbol of all food in Spain. In villages, where bread is still often made at home, the housewife will kiss and make the sign of the Cross over the loaf before baking, and children are taught never to snatch bread as this is seen as a sign of disrespect, not only to their parents but also to God.

If you visit Spain, you are likely to find that the first breads of the day are the morning rolls, such as *bollo* or *chica* (meaning "little girl"). Later in the morning the *panadería* (bakery) will start producing larger breads. These are of almost every conceivable shape and size, but will mostly be yeast-fermented, white, wheat breads. Spain is famous for its simple white breads, with their smooth crust and soft white crumb. Bread is eaten with every meal and with every course. More simple still, and a tradition much loved by the Spanish, is the custom of pouring virgin olive oil over fresh bread to eat as a snack at any time of the day.

While wheat is the principal crop, oats, barley and other cereals are sometimes blended with wheat flour for more rustic loaves. In the north-west corner of the country, in Santiago and La Coruña, wholemeal and rye breads can be found. Here, near the north of Portugal, cornmeal is blended with wheat flour to make rich yellow loaves. Corn was brought back to Spain from the New World by sailors returning home, but is not as popular today in Spain as it is in Portugal.

PAN CATETO

This is the traditional Spanish country bread, made from a starter called the *levadura de masa*.

BELOW: The pan gallego often looks like a squashy cottage loaf with a top knot.

HORNAZO

This is a Castilian flat bread customarily made at Easter. The dough is filled with chunks of *chorizo* (spicy sausage), cheese and hard-boiled eggs so that when it is baked and cut, everybody receives a different piece of bread. *Horno* is the Spanish word for an oven, from which the bread probably gets its name. At one time in Spain, people would take loaves of bread, as well as large joints of meat, turkeys or even whole lambs, to the local baker's for cooking in the stone *horno*.

PAN GALLEGO

This country-style bread is made using olive oil and has a pleasant, unassuming flavour. It can be a rather misshapen round, and a whole loaf can be huge. Much of the *pan gallego* sold outside Spain are quarters of a large loaf. The crust is soft and floury, the crumb light with an open texture. Seed *gallego* is a similar loaf but is studded with pumpkin and sesame seeds, which give it a delicious flavour and texture.

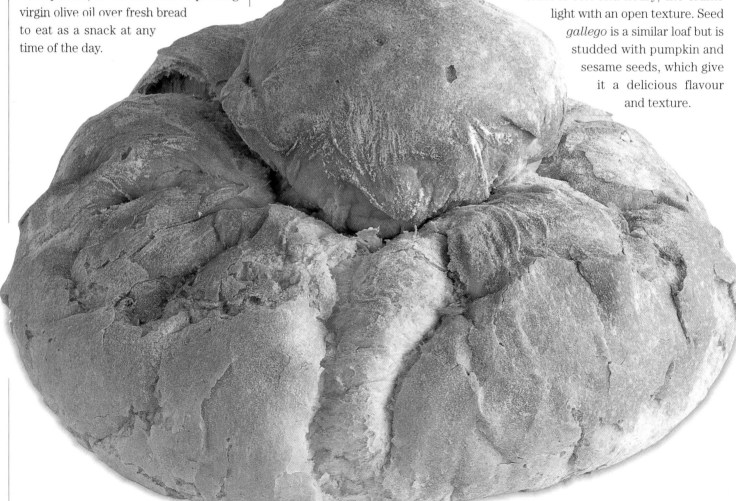

BELOW: Pan aceite

PAN QUEMADO

This is one of the best-known of Spanish sweet breads. It has a rather squashed, sunken look, a bit like an enlarged English lardy cake with its glossy brown top, but in spite of appearances, this is a delicious sweet loaf, a little like a French brioche in texture, although it is made with olive oil rather than butter.

GOFIO

This unusual bread is classified as Spanish, coming as it does from the Canary Islands, but has a fascinating and ancient history that suggests it might more rightly belong with the Arabian or Moroccan breads. Although the Canaries have belonged to Spain for hundreds of years, they were once the home of a group of Berbers called the Guanches. Now extinct, little knowledge of these original people remains apart from a few artefacts. *Gofio*, however, is thought to be a survival of these North African people. The bread is the shape of a large ball and is made from a variety of flours – wheat, barley, corn and gram (dried chick-peas), which are sometimes blended and always toasted before milling. The dough is mixed with water or milk and, although yeast is used today, originally the dough would have been fermented using a natural leaven. Once risen, the bread is baked, either conventionally in an oven or, even today in some parts of the Canaries, in a Dutch oven, a pot-like construction where the embers of the fire are piled around the outside of the pot. The result is a crusty round loaf with a fairly dense crumb, quite unlike the light and airy Spanish breads, and indeed unlike most traditional Moroccan breads as well, which are mostly flat and baked very quickly in unusually hot ovens. Perhaps the scarcity of wheat meant these ancient people needed to be more inventive, or perhaps their settled life on the islands, as opposed to the nomadic life of the Berbers, meant they had more time for the task of baking.

ENSAIMADAS

A speciality of Majorca (Mallorca), these small yeasted pastry buns are the Spanish answer to the croissant, except that instead of being crescent-shaped they look more like little Moorish turbans. Normally a little sweeter than croissants, they have the same soft texture and are served at breakfast with jam or honey in the island's many hotels. Consignments of these little rolls are regularly sent to Barcelona, where they are much appreciated by both tourists and local city dwellers.

A much larger version of the *ensaimada* can also be found in Majorca. This is often topped with cream or a sweet custard-like topping made with pumpkin pulp, sugar, lemon juice and spices. This dessert is particularly popular at fiestas, when the *ensaimada* is decorated with small pieces of marrow and thin slices of *sobrasada*, a type of Majorcan sausage.

MAJORCAN POTATO BUNS

Although a relatively small group of islands, the Balearic Islands have a surprisingly rich and varied cuisine. Along with their own local fish and meat dishes, they have a variety of delicious breads, including these Majorcan potato buns. These small buns are made using either sweet or ordinary potatoes. They have a very sweet taste and are normally eaten at breakfast, during mid-morning or for tea, and are usually served with jam or honey.

PAN ACEITE (OLIVE OIL BREAD)

This is similar to the French *fougasse* and the Italian *foccacia* breads. *Pan Aceite* is commonly a rather misshapen-looking bread. It is baked on the sole of the oven, after being brushed liberally with olive oil (hence the name olive oil bread).

TWELFTH NIGHT BREAD

In Spain and Portugal children receive their presents not on Christmas Day but on Twelfth Night (5 January). Appropriately for the Epiphany, the gifts are delivered by a figure representing the Magi, the three wise men who made their journey from the East to bring gifts to the infant Jesus. It is customary for a special bread called *roscon de reyes* in Spain and *bolo-rei* in Portugal to be baked for this day. The rich teabread is stuffed with fruits and candied peel and traditionally contains a coin or figurine, bringing luck to the person who is given the piece of bread in which it is discovered.

PORTUGUESE BREADS

Portuguese bakers, like their counterparts in other countries, frequently use the same basic dough for making loaves and rolls. It is the shape and manner of baking that gives each bread its own idiosyncratic flavour and texture. Many Portuguese breads are made using a yeasted white flour dough.

ALENTEJANO

This is a white bread with a fairly thick crust and a well-flavoured crumb, which has a distinctive, salty/sour flavour. Like almost all Portuguese and Spanish breads, the bread is oven bottom-baked and has an even, golden crust.

BROA DE MILO

This simple loaf from Minho in northern Portugal, the name of which translates as "corn bread", is normally referred to simply as *broa* and is eaten by everyone. Corn is a popular grain for making bread in Portugal and Spain. The conquistadors and sailors brought home not only potatoes, tomatoes and peppers, but corn as

RIGHT: Alentejano has a good flavour.

BELOW: Papo secos are soft yet crusty.

ABOVE: Rosquilha is an attractive round bread.

well, together with the skills needed to grind it into meal. Corn proved to be a successful crop in the north of Portugal where wheat does not flourish, and it would have been quickly selected as the preferred crop. It is likely that even from the beginning, bakers would have blended cornmeal with wheat in order to provide some gluten, but when this was scarce barley and alfalfa flour was used and, even today, loaves are made from a mixed grain. *Broa de milo* is a robust, well-flavoured loaf, which goes well with Portuguese soups and *cozidos* – stewed meat, vegetables and pulses.

ROSQUILHA

This is a ring-shaped white bread with a pleasant crust and a slightly chewy texture and salty flavour. It will normally be made using the same dough as *alentejano* but the shape means *rosquilha* is crustier, although it does not stay fresh as long. *Rosquilha* can be bought and eaten at any time of day but is very popular for breakfast or during the mid-morning, and is served with coffee.

CANTELO

This wedding bread is a traditional bread from the northern region of Portugal. The loaf is baked in a ring, and custom dictates that the bride and groom break the bread into pieces to give to their wedding guests with a glass of wine.

PAPO SECOS

These small white rolls are a popular breakfast bread all over Portugal. They have a soft white crumb and a delicious crust that is crisp without being hard. Like

RIGHT: Bolo do caco is a hearth bread like focaccia and fougasse.

many breads from Portugal, they are baked with lots of steam which accounts for their good crust yet ensures that the crumb is light and airy.

CARACAS

Caracas are similar in size and shape to *papo secos* but are more akin to an English or Scottish bap, batch-baked and cooked with less steam so they are softer and less crusty.

BOLO DO CACO

This flattish loaf is similar to the Spanish olive oil bread. It is another type of hearth bread, cooked on

ABOVE: If you live near a Portuguese baker, try caracas as an alternative to regular hamburger buns.

the sole of a very hot oven. It is best eaten very fresh with dressed salads or with other foods that have plenty of liquids that need mopping up.

MAIA BREAD

This is a long white loaf, normally made using a plain white dough. It is popular all over Portugal and is one of the better-known everyday breads, eaten with fish soups and salads, and Portuguese cheese.

BELOW: Maia bread is almost always a white loaf and has a good, slightly chewy crust.

GERMAN BREADS

There is an enormous range of German breads. Outside Germany – in Britain for instance – you could be forgiven for thinking that all German breads come in neat packages wrapped in cellophane. These are in fact the *kastenbrots* (box breads) and include the well known pumpernickel. In Germany, however, and increasingly available throughout Europe and North America, there are also the German *krustenbrots* (crusty breads). These are the freshly baked breads, bought from a bakery or from the fresh bread counters at supermarkets, and they are as varied and delicious as the loaves to be found in the rest of continental Europe. The German word *brot* means either wheat or rye bread, with other breads named for the type of grain used in their making: oats, corn or barley.

KASTENBROTS

In the customary way that German words very often describe exactly what they mean, *kastenbrots* translates as "box bread". The bread is steam-baked for some 20 hours in an enclosed tin, which

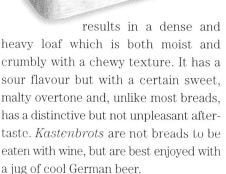

BELOW: Pumpernickel is the best-known of the German kastenbrots.

results in a dense and heavy loaf which is both moist and crumbly with a chewy texture. It has a sour flavour but with a certain sweet, malty overtone and, unlike most breads, has a distinctive but not unpleasant after-taste. *Kastenbrots* are not breads to be eaten with wine, but are best enjoyed with a jug of cool German beer.

These breads almost invariably use rye flour (normally a wholemeal grain that can be coarsely or more finely ground according to the type of bread). The dough uses a natural, sourdough leaven, which adds to the sour taste of the bread and complements the flavour of the rye, with its own earthy taste. The darkest *kastenbrots* contain only rye but wheat flour is added in varying proportions to give a loaf that is lighter in appearance, texture and flavour. Other grains, such as oats or barley, as well as sunflower and sesame seeds, are added to certain loaves, and there are therefore numerous variations on the basic theme. The bread always comes thinly sliced, wrapped in cellophane and clearly labelled. While moist in texture, the bread, with its sweet/sour yet dry flavour tastes best buttered or spread with a soft cheese. Savoury foods, such as smoked salmon, soused herring or German sausage, are most commonly served with the darker breads, but the lighter breads are excellent with marmalade or other sharply flavoured conserves.

PUMPERNICKEL

The best known of all the *kastenbrots*, pumpernickel is also the darkest of these breads. It is usually made with 100 per cent coarsely ground rye grain, and has an unmistakable sour, earthy flavour, but

LEFT: Vollkornbrot (left) is a 100 per cent rye bread, while roggenbrot (back) is slightly lighter, containing some wheat flour. Sonnenblumenbrot (right) is made with sunflower seeds, which give a lighter flavour and a good texture.

some are made with slightly less rye flour and a small amount of wheat flour. Like many German breads, pumpernickel is sometimes flavoured with caraway seeds.

VOLLKORNBROT OR SCHWARZBROT

This is another strongly flavoured bread, the names of which translate as "whole corn" or "black" bread. The whole "corn" in this instance is rye, which again is coarsely ground. The bread also contains molasses, adding to the dark colour and the malty flavour of the bread – which is probably one for devotees only.

ROGGENBROT

Roggen is German for rye, but this bread in fact often contains a small proportion of wheat flour, too. *Roggenbrot* is a dark oblong tin loaf with a hard crust that is sometimes encrusted with whole grains. In spite of the added wheat flour, this is still an intensely flavoured bread, best eaten with strong-tasting foods.

SONNENBLUMENBROT

Sunflower seeds give this bread a pleasant crunchy texture. *Sonnenblumenbrut* is made mainly using rye flour, but a small proportion of wheat flour together with the sunflower seeds makes this a more palatable loaf for those sampling *kastenbrot* for the first time.

WEISENKEIMBROT

This means "wheat germ bread" and it is made using the wheat germ, along with rye grain

and flour. *Grahamsbrot* uses a higher proportion of wholemeal flour, specifically the American-style Graham wholewheat flour.

MUESLIBROT

This is a multigrain *kastenbrot*, made using a muesli-style mix of cereals, chopped nuts and whole grains. It is a popular choice in Germany for those who want a healthy teabread that has plenty of texture and is not overly sweet.

ABOVE: Three krustenbrots: Black Forest (left), Bavarian rye (right) and roggenbrot.

KRUSTENBROTS

These crusty breads are the day-to-day breads of Germany, and are also popular in parts of Canada and in the American states around the Great Lakes, where German emigrés settled in the 1840s. In other European countries, German-style bakers import the flours from Germany or bake them using locally bought flours and meals, but sometimes import the sourdough culture from their native home. Many, although not all, German breads contain rye flour.

LEFT: Weisenkeimbrot (back) is made with both rye and wheat flours, while mueslibrot contains a mixture of cereals, nuts and whole grains.

ABOVE: Landbrot

BELOW: German square rye

and also partly to the long fermentation process. Like most German ryes, it too uses the sourdough principle and consequently has a noticeable yet mild, sour flavour. It is good with German meats and sausages or with creamy cheeses.

LANDBROT

This is a traditional country bread, made using a large proportion of wheat flour but with enough rye to give a pale, beige-coloured crumb. It has an excellent sweet/sour flavour, partly from the rye and partly from the buttermilk, which is used instead of milk or water. It comes in all sorts of shapes and sizes, sometimes with a floury crust and sometimes without. Inside, the bread is always open-textured and slightly chewy, and is good with soups and stews.

ROGGENBROT

Unlike the *kastenbrot* of the same name, this crusty bread contains only rye grain and rye flour. It is a robust, sourdough loaf with a thick, chewy crust.

GERMAN RYE BREAD

There are many varieties of this sturdy loaf, including the well-known Bavarian rye. Rye breads come in various shapes and sizes, but are most often tin or bloomer-shaped. The loaf typically has more rye than usual, but wheat flour is

Rye was once the main cereal in northern Europe. It tolerates the cooler dryer climatic conditions, and for centuries, while the more affluent enjoyed white bread made with imported wheat, the poor continued to eat bread made with the grain that was cheap and readily available. When wheat became relatively inexpensive in Germany white wheat flour was used by all but the very poorest, either by itself or with rye flour. There is consequently a great variety of German breads. Some are baked in tins, but the majority are baked on the floor of the oven and are evenly crusty.

RIGHT: German rye

GERMAN SQUARE RYE

This is an easily recognized bread: it is a large square loaf that is cross-hatched on top. It is often just known as German rye, but unlike other ryes of that name it has a pleasant, gentle flavour, due partly to the blend of rye and wheat flours,

there too, for a lighter texture. Like many German breads, it is made by the sourdough method. The culture is made by mixing rye flour with water to produce just the right balance of acids to work the dough. Although these cultures can last for many years if fed and reinvigorated correctly, most bakers will start a new culture every week, mainly so that they – and you – know what you are getting.

A 100 per cent rye bread contains, as you might expect, only rye flour and is therefore suitable for anyone with an allergy to wheat. This, too, uses the sourdough method and has a dense texture and strong, sour flavour.

GEBILDBROTE (PICTURE BREAD)
Now something of a rarity, these breads can still be found in villages on festive occasions. The bread is moulded into complex shapes and patterns, normally with symbolic meanings. Loaves may be embossed with horses, deer, serpents, flowers and sheaves of wheat or they may be fashioned into shapes of men and women. The origin of this custom most likely dates from pagan times when bread would have been offered to appease the gods. Christianity also used breads in many rituals and many of the *gebildbrote* bear Christian symbols, such as crucifixes, loaves and fishes.

PRETZELS
Although extremely popular as snacks in America, and well known among the Jewish breads, pretzels are nevertheless German in origin. Like *gebildbrote*, pretzels have a symbolic meaning, which may have had its origins in pagan times. The distinctive knot shape is believed by some to have been a symbol for the solar cycle; others believe the crossed arms symbolize the Cross and that pretzels were originally made as a Lenten bread. Whatever the explanation, pretzels clearly have important significance in Germany and beyond – the same symbol of interlocking rings is the sign of a baker's shop throughout northern Europe.

Pretzels are almost always made using white flour and, according to a decree of 1256 in Landshut, it was a punishable

ABOVE: Stollen is a popular Christmas treat in many European countries. It is rich with fruit and often has a sweet marzipan centre.

offence for a baker to bake pretzels from anything but the finest white flour. Unlike the more familiar salted biscuits, German pretzels in many ways resemble a bagel. Along with the white flour, they contain yeast and milk and are poached, sprinkled liberally with sea salt and then baked until the crust is hard and golden. This salty, crunchy crust contrasts with the soft, sweet-flavoured crumb.

ROLLS
There is an enormous variety of German-style rolls. Most are made from white flour and may be sprinkled with caraway or poppy seeds. *Semmel,* with their star-shaped design on top, and *Eiweckerl* are mainly served at breakfast.

STOLLEN
There are many German sweet breads but perhaps the best-known and -loved is stollen, sold almost everywhere as a treat around Christmas. It is an oval-shaped loaf, which tapers at each end. The shape is said to represent the infant Jesus wrapped in swaddling clothes. The bread is packed with sultanas, currants and mixed peel, and is usually spiced and enriched with eggs, butter and milk. Almonds may be finely chopped and added to the dough with the fruit, or they may be ground and made into a paste that is then rolled into the bread, giving it a sweet, moist centre. Stollen is unfailingly delicious, although it is predictably on the calorific side.

FOUR CEREAL BREAD
This dark, solid loaf is made using a blend of cereals but always including both rye and wheat.

BELOW: Four cereal bread.

GOLDGRAIN

Sometimes called a *multigrained* loaf, this baguette-shaped loaf is made using wheat, rye, barley, oats, soya, linseed, sunflower seeds, wheat bran, semolina and millet. For all this vast array of ingredients it is not unduly heavy and it has a texture not dissimilar to a Granary bread, with a wholesome, nutty flavour. Goldgrain sometimes is made with the addition of chopped walnuts. Both varieties are popular in health-conscious Germany and are becoming more easily available elsewhere. They are distributed by several producers.

BELOW: Mehrkorn is available as both a crusty bread and as a thinly sliced box bread.

GERMAN BREAD WITH CARAWAY SEEDS

Caraway is a favourite ingredient in German rye breads, adding its unmistakable aniseed flavour. Although often called "German rye with caraway" or "light rye with caraway", the bread does contain a large proportion of wheat flour, giving it a light texture and flavour.

KUGELHOPF

This bread belongs equally to the Alsace region of France and to Vienna in Austria. There are various ways of spelling *kugelhopf* and even more ways for making and baking it. In Alsace it is a savoury bread made with bacon, lard and/or fromage blanc and cream cheese. The German and Austrian *kugelhopf,* by contrast, is a yeasted brioche-style bread, made using sultanas and raisins and enriched with butter and eggs. A good *kugelhopf* has a delicious citrus flavour, provided by lemon rind and juice.

The *kugelhopf* is baked in a fluted mould with a central funnel, and the top billows out like a "kugel", or ball.

MEHRKORN

Mehrkorn means "more grain" and this bread is a multigrain loaf. The mixture of grains means that the bread is noticeably lighter than many of the principally rye breads.

AUSTRIAN BREADS

As you would expect, a large number of the most popular Austrian breads are similar, if not identical, to those of neighbouring Switzerland, Italy, and Germany. However, Austria may well have been responsible for many of the more elaborate continental breads. It was the Austrians who developed the *poolisch* or sponge method of leavening dough, also used in France. This was particularly popular for white breads or those using finer flours, and breads made by this method were noted for their excellent flavour. Not surprisingly, Vienna became the home of fine baking. Croissants are just one among many delicacies that may originally have come from the master bakers of Austria, although any French person will certainly disagree!

BAURNBROT

While Austria is paradise for all those who love rich breads and pastries, there are still country-style loaves to be found. Not least of these is *baurnbrot,* made using buckwheat and wheat flour and molasses, flavoured with caraway seeds and leavened using a rye sourdough starter. This makes for a robust and strongly flavoured loaf, which tastes best with simple foods, such as country cheeses, sausages and meats, or simply dunked in soup.

DUTCH BREADS

KORNKRACKER

Kornkracker can refer to either loaves or rolls. The bread is popular throughout Germany and Holland. The word means "cracked corn" and the bread is made with cracked whole grain wheat, together with malted wheat and seeds.

DUTCH FRUIT LOAF

This lightly malted Granary loaf rich with fruit and sprinkled with sugar is popular with coffee at any time of the day. It is also a favourite treat for children and is sometimes served with a mild cheese, such as Edam or Gouda.

RIGHT: Kornkracker

DUTCH CRISPBREADS

The Dutch enjoy crispbreads almost as much as the Scandinavians. They are usually served at breakfast, eaten with cheese or smoked hams, or spread with jam or marmalade. The round breads that are commonly available outside The Netherlands are baked until completely crisp. They have a unique, vaguely sweet flavour, which is surprisingly good with savoury foods. Dutch crispbreads come in cylindrical packets and are generally available everywhere.

FRISIAN SUGAR LOAF

This unusual sweet bread is made using whole sugar lumps that melt as the bread is baked to give delicious pockets of sweetness, which contrast with the cinnamon in the soft white crumb.

DUTCH ROGGEBROOD

Holland also has its own varieties of *kastenbrots* and *krustenbrots*. This box-style bread is similar to the German *roggenbrot*, made with rye flour and leavened using the sourdough method. It often contains molasses and is consequently very dark with a strong malty taste.

Holland even has its own pumpernickel, which like the German variety, contains 100 per cent rye flour. The Dutch pumpernickel is a little sweeter than the German version, but with the same strong flavour. It is not for the faint-hearted!

ABOVE: Dutch fruit bread

RIGHT: Dutch crispbreads – popular everywhere.

SWISS BREADS

One of the least accessible and smallest countries of Western Europe, Switzerland has an extraordinary wealth of unusual and tasty breads. There are probably two explanations for this. First, the mountains that cover 70 per cent of Switzerland mean that, until quite recently, villages have existed in relative isolation, and rural traditions, such as baking and bread making, have endured, undiluted by commercialization and mass markets. The other significant factor is that four of Switzerland's five neighbours (the fifth is tiny Liechtenstein) – France, Germany, Italy and Austria – are home to most of the best breads in the world.

As well as producing many loaves that will be familiar to its neighbours, Switzerland has borrowed some of the best breads to develop its own specialities. These, too, reflect the influence of near neighbours and, in common with the pattern elsewhere, rye breads are baked in the north; soft white loaves in the south and east.

BELOW: Crusty bauerruch

APFELNUSSBROT

The name denotes the Germanic origins of this unusual bread, but it seems to be a distillation of a variety of traditions from France as well as Germany. The round, crusty loaf is made from a blend of grains including wheat, rye, barley and spelt, which points to a German influence, yet the apples and walnuts seem typically French and the bread is not unlike the *pain aux pommes* from France The best loaves are said to be found in Valais, in the south of the country.

BANGELI

This crusty loaf is a cross between the French baguette and the long white loaves of Germany. It comes from Basel, a Swiss town on the border of France and Germany, which perhaps explains its hybrid appearance. It is a long loaf that looks rather rustic, with seven or eight horizontal slashes and a thick, floury crust. The bread is often cut into chunks to serve with fondue.

BAUERRUCH

Swiss bakers take an enormous pride in their work and some of the Swiss breads are beautifully crafted, for example the *bauerruch,* which is a rounded crusty loaf shaped in a swirl like a turban or a seashell. It is a fairly dense white or brown bread with a thick, golden crust.

PANIS LUNATIS

This means moon bread. In Switzerland, some believe it was the precursor to the croissant. Indeed moon bread was baked as long ago as the 8th century. Today Swiss bakers sell croissants only, but they always claim to have invented them.

SAKO

Although some wheat is grown in Switzerland, neither the soil nor the climate favour agriculture and the little wheat that was coaxed from the land was frequently blended with other grains to make tasty and healthy loaves. The *sako* is a round multigrain loaf made with eight different cereals. It is usually risen in a floured basket, then turned out for baking. *Sako* is often slashed off-centre across the top and is generally sprinkled with cracked wheat

or rolled oats. It is a somewhat dense loaf, excellent for mopping up soups.

ABOVE: The attractive and simple Swiss peasant loaf

RIGHT: Healthy Vogel loaf

SWISS PEASANT LOAF

There are many variations on the theme of a Swiss rustic loaf, but most are round, free-form loaves, made with a blend of wheat and rye flours but with cracked rye and chopped walnuts giving the loaves a pleasant texture.

VOGEL LOAF

This is a proprietary Swiss loaf that is renowned for its healthy properties. It was developed over 30 years ago by a Swiss nutritionist, Dr Alfred Vogel. A multi-grain bread, it contains kibbled wheat, rye grain and bran, giving it a high-fibre

RIGHT: Zupfe is also known as Swiss braid.

tradition of plaiting bread came from is not known, only that it is extremely old. It may have symbolized the braid of hair offered by the wife or widow of a warrior to ensure his safe return from battle. Shaped into a round, it could have represented the course of the sun, while the crescent may have signified the moon. The Swiss plaited breads are almost always yeast-leavened, made using white wheat flour, and may be plaited with three or more strands of dough. There is really no limit to the baker's art and the Swiss have a reputation for their skill with shaping bread.

GIPFELTEIG

These are essentially tiny croissants and are quite the best thing to eat for breakfast if you are visiting Switzerland. They are so small – three or four will fit comfortably in your hand – and so delicious, that it is easy to consume far too many before you decide you have probably had enough! They resemble, and may be identical, to the tiny croissants you will be served in the Alsace area and other parts of western France and, like them, the bakers use lard as well as butter in the dough to give a texture that is very soft. *Gipfelteig* are best eaten fresh and warm as they are, or spread with a little apricot jam, or some tangy orange marmalade.

WEGGLITAG

These little rolls are often served for breakfast along with *gipfelteig*. The small, oval white rolls are always glazed with beaten egg and notched across the top with scissors to give a crenellated effect and a crunchy crust.

content, which is one of its main selling points. The whole and cracked grain gives the loaf plenty of texture, yet the flavour is not too strong, making it a popular choice for those who like their fibre to be subtle rather than overpowering.

ZUPFE (ZOPF)

Known variously as *zupfe*, *zopf* or Swiss braid, this is a plaited loaf made from a rich dough, which typically contains soured cream or milk, egg and butter. It has a glossy crust and beautifully light crumb. Like its neighbours, Austria and Germany, Switzerland has a great affection for these rich doughs, which are shaped, plaited or twisted into spectacular loaves. This is where the tradition of the Jewish *challah* – another plaited loaf – is believed to have evolved. Exactly from where the

ABOVE AND BELOW: Wegglitag and gipfelteig are a great way to start the day.

NORDIC BREADS

Rye, oats and barley were once the only crops that would grow in the cooler climate and acidic soils of northern Europe. While wheat was imported for the prosperous, for the majority of people, bread was inevitably made using one type or a blend of these cereals. Rye, which contains gluten, was favoured for leavened bread since it would rise and produce a lighter loaf. In Norway, however, where there was a fondness for unleavened bread, oats and barley and sometimes pea-flour were for many centuries the favoured ingredients for making their popular *flatbrød*.

Nowadays, wheat can be grown in the more temperate parts of Denmark and Sweden, and of course, being widely imported, white breads are commonly available. Traditionally, the festive breads have always been made from the finest white flours. Scandinavians set great store by their festivals and each year buy or make their Christmas and Easter breads, along with a host of other breads made for celebrations in between.

White breads are particularly popular in the cities, but the Scandinavians continue to love their dark rye breads and visitors will find that there is a wide choice of breads – from the weird and

wonderful breads of Lapland to the *flatbrøds* of Norway, and the rich pumpernickel breads baked in Denmark.

RIGHT: Danish rye bread is lighter in texture and colour than German ryes.

DANISH BREADS

RYE BREAD

There are numerous types of Danish rye breads and you will need to sample a few to discover the ones you like best. Danish ryes tend to be lighter and sweeter than most German ryes. Molasses and malt extract are popular ingredients, adding to the dark colour, but this is tempered by the greater proportion of white wheat flour. Danish ryes also tend to contain a proportion of fat, either buttermilk or butter or both. This helps to

RIGHT: Rye breads are popular throughout Scandinavia.

RIGHT: The plaited tresse

preserve the loaf and gives a richer and more open-textured bread. Danish ryes are the popular breads for *smørrebrød* (the equivalent to the Swedish *smörgåsbord*), the buffet-style open sandwiches topped with meats and cheese.

KERNEBROD

A seeded loaf, normally made with a Granary meal, sprinkled liberally with sunflower seeds and linseeds.

TRESSE

This is a plaited white loaf, enriched with milk, eggs and butter. It may be scattered freely with poppy or sesame seeds and is popular throughout the year, although at one time this loaf was probably made for special occasions.

DANISH FESTIVE FRUIT LOAF (JULEKAGE)

This is one of the most famous of all the Danish Christmas loaves. Christmas is a hugely important festival in all parts of Scandinavia, not only for its Christian significance, but also because it heralds the halfway point of the long Nordic winter. Similar breads, filled with fruit, nuts and spices, and enriched with butter and eggs, are made all over Scandinavia. *Julekage* is traditionally spiced with vanilla and cardamom. Crushed sugar is then sprinkled over the top before baking and, finally, icing sugar is drizzled over the bread when it is cooked.

CARNIVAL BUNS (FASTERLAVNSBOILLER)

Any Dane will be able to tell you about these treats, which they will remember from their childhood and probably now make for their own children. They are traditionally made on the Monday before Shrove Tuesday, which is celebrated not only with breads and cakes but also with some games, including "beating a cat off the barrel", which involves children chasing each other and which thankfully has nothing to do with cats, in spite of its name. The little square or round buns are something like a cross between a bread and an English Yorkshire pudding, made with white flour and yeast and enriched with egg, butter and milk. Carnival buns are flavoured with cardamom and filled with almond paste and sometimes with chopped peel, and are normally liberally dusted with icing sugar.

SMØRREBRØD

The word simply means "buttered bread" but the famous Danish open sandwiches are so much more than that. Delicious toppings – their ingredients limited only by the imagination of the cook – are laid on thin slices of bread. The aim of the exercise is to produce a snack that is as appealing to the eye as it is to the stomach, and the results are as colourful as they are good to eat. Danish sour rye bread is the preferred base, although for some more delicate toppings, such as smoked salmon, baby shrimps, prawns or lobster, a crusty white bread is sometimes used. Fish and shellfish are favourite toppings, one of the most popular choices being pickled herring with marinated onion rings. Liver paste, salami, cheeses (including the famous blue cheese of Denmark), roast pork, hard-boiled eggs – the list of potential toppings is apparently limitless, as is the Danes' capacity for enjoying their favourite lunchtime snack.

NORWEGIAN AND SWEDISH BREADS

NORWEGIAN FLAT BREAD

Flatbrød is the oldest of all the Norwegian breads and was, until fairly recently, the bread most commonly eaten by the people of Norway. A long time ago these wafer-thin crispbreads would have been made with any cereal that was to hand – mostly oats, rye, barley or pea-flour, or a mixture of all these. The unleavened dough would have been rolled into very thin, large circles and baked on a griddle or on a stone over an open fire. The breads were known to last for months, even up to a year, and would be stored on the beams over the kitchen. These days the breads are factory-baked and sold ready-cut into convenient rectangles. Some bakers, however, continue to make their own, and in parts of Norway the large breads are served at harvest meals, dampened with a little water so they become pliable and can be wrapped around Norwegian sweet cheese or other suitable pieces of food.

NORWEGIAN WHOLEMEAL BREAD

This fine bread is made with whole wheat kernels, skimmed milk, yeast, cottage cheese and wholemeal flour, and is topped with crushed wheat.

LEFT: Flatbrød

RIGHT: Lomper is a soft flat bread cooked on a griddle.

LIMPA

Limpa is a Swedish favourite – a leavened rye loaf, sweetened with molasses or honey, flavoured with orange and lightly spiced with cardamom, cumin, fennel and anise. Since wheat flour makes up the greater proportion of flour, the loaf is not as heavy as some rye loaves, although it has the typical dense yet crumbly texture of rye breads. *Vortlimpa* is a far darker loaf than *limpa*, containing a greater proportion of rye flour together with the dark molasses. It, too, contains orange rind, either grated or finely chopped, and can also be made with ground or whole fennel seeds. In spite of the sweet molasses, this dark, savoury loaf is intended to be eaten with soft cheese or salted herring.

ROGBROD

Røgbröd is the traditional rye bread of Sweden, made in large flat loaves and often containing molasses, which has been valued by Sweden and the other Baltic states since it was first imported. Unlike the flat Norwegian ryes, *røgbröd* is a leavened bread, traditionally made using a sourdough method, but also using normal yeast. Buttermilk is often used instead of ordinary milk, adding to the acidic flavour of the bread, which is also flavoured with fennel or caraway seeds.

Ragbröd is much the same as *røgbröd* – made of rye and often containing molasses – but is shaped into a ring by being rolled out into a flat round and then having a hole cut in the middle. Traditionally, *ragbröd* would have been looped across the kitchen with string, and even today you may see them displayed in such a way in some bakeries.

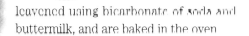

LEFT: Swedish krisprolls

SWEDISH CARDAMOM BRAID

This is a delicious sweet fruit bread, made with white flour, enriched with milk, eggs and butter and spiced with the distinctive flavour of cardamom.

SWEDISH CARAWAY BREAD

This is a half-sweet, half-savoury white bread, made with a little sugar and butter, yet given a subtle savoury flavour by the caraway-seeds.

ST LUCIA ROLLS

Throughout Scandinavia, the days leading up to Christmas are as much a time of festivity as Christmas Day itself. St Lucia Day (13 December) is celebrated widely in Sweden. Children dress up in white and visit each other's homes. They wear crowns of glowing candles, symbolizing the light that will come once winter is over. The favourite food for the children are the little St Lucia rolls, traditionally made with saffron and enriched with eggs, butter and milk. Each bread is shaped in the letter "S" and topped with a raisin.

KNACKERBROD

Sweeter than the Finnish *knackebrod*, these Swedish flat breads are made with rolled oats and taste a little like sweet Scottish oatcakes. Unlike Scottish oatcakes, however, they are leavened using bicarbonate of soda and buttermilk, and are baked in the oven.

SCANDINAVIAN STAR

This unusual and pretty bread is a modern adaptation of some of the best Scandinavian baking traditions. It is made using a blend of white and Granary flours but its fine flavour is due mainly to the sponge method of making the dough, which allows the flavours to develop, and the longer-than-usual rising. Sunflower seeds and linseeds are added for flavour and the bread is liberally sprinkled with sesame seeds before being stamped into its distinctive star shape. The bread has a good crisp crust, while the crumb is soft with a rich nutty flavour. It makes an excellent breaking bread, which is appropriate since pulling off pieces of bread is preferred in Scandinavia to slicing bread conventionally.

SCANDINAVIAN CRISPBREADS

There are many Scandinavian crispbreads, ranging from crisp rusks to wafer-thin biscuits. Norwegian crispbreads are made mainly with whole rye, although there are also many made with a blend of wheat flours. *Krisprolls* are popular in Sweden, eaten at almost any time of the day, but particularly at breakfast. They are baked until entirely crisp and have a noticeably sweet flavour.

LEFT: The Scandinavian star bread, with its liberal sprinkling of sesame seeds looks attractive and has an excellent flavour.

FINNISH AND ARCTIC BREADS

FINNISH KNACKEBROD

This thin, biscuit-like bread with its characteristic central hole is made using a blend of rye and corn. Freshly made *knackebrod* are crisp and are delicious with a fresh goat's cheese or smoked salmon. *Wiborgs kringla* are also from Finland and are similar in many ways to Germany's pretzels: the entwined strands, like a lover's knot, appear in bakers' shop signs in Finland. The enriched yeast bread was traditionally baked on straw, and even today the bread is cooked in a similar way, and it is a feature of the bread that bits of straw need to be pulled off the bottom before it is eaten.

FINNISH EASTER BREAD

For most of Scandinavia, and certainly for those who were better off, most of the original festive breads were made from what was considered the best flour, namely white wheat flour. In the poorer villages and towns, however, most people had to make do with what they could find – usually rye, barley and oatmeal. For festivals special

LEFT: Icelandic bread

breads were made to celebrate using only these three cereals. Easter bread was a particular favourite, moulded in a traditional round, and made with yogurt and honey or molasses and packed with raisins, sultanas and nuts. Easter bread is unlikely to be widely available in the cities, but should you travel through villages at the right time of year, you may find these dark specialities with their shiny tops.

HALKAKA

This heavy black rye bread was once the only food for a number of Finnish peasants during the winter. Extremely large loaves were baked and then gradually eaten over the next few months until the bread was finished and it was time to bake once more.

RIESKA

Further north in Finland, the leavened breads give way to hard flat loaves. *Rieska* is a Finnish word and comes from Lapland, a region that extends across the northern parts of Norway, Sweden and Finland, and most of which is within the Arctic Circle. *Rieska* are round breads, mostly fairly small and rather flattish. They are normally made with oats or barley, but can also be made with potatoes or any starchy food. Although there is no wheat or rye to raise the dough, they do use a little yeast or baking powder, which makes them slightly less dense.

ICELANDIC BREAD

Most Icelandic breads are based on rye. Various loaves are made, from the crusty loaf with open crumb pictured above to the pancake like *flatbrauð*, which are enjoyed with *skyr*, a fresh curd cheese that resembles yogurt.

POLAR FLAT BREAD

Called "polar rounds" or "polar thins", these small breads are easily available, sold in many large supermarkets or in delicatessens as a style of crispbread. They contain a mixture of rye and wheat flours and have a pleasant, slightly nutty flavour. They go well with strong-flavoured cheese, such as goat's cheese.

ABOVE: Polar flat breads are now made commercially.

EASTERN EUROPEAN AND RUSSIAN BREADS

In the cool latitudes of northern Europe, rye, buckwheat and barley were the principal cereals for centuries. Large dark breads made from these flours were not only the staple food, but during severe famine were often the only food for all but the most wealthy. "If we have bread and *kvas* (beer) what more do we need?" goes a Russian saying. Links with southern Europe meant that wheat flour gradually became popular, at first only among the aristocracy but later filtering through to the general population, where the flour was especially used for festive bread and cakes. Today, thanks to genetic manipulation, wheat is widely grown in Russia, Poland and other parts of eastern Europe, but the fondness for breads made from rye and buckwheat continues to this day and these traditional breads are still the mainstay for rural communities.

BLINIS

Although not strictly breads, these little buckwheat pancakes were the equivalent of festive sweet breads in a country where buckwheat rather than wheat was the principal crop. Buckwheat was widely cultivated in Russia in the past. At *Maslenitsa*, the week before

RIGHT: Polish rye bread

LEFT: Polish wholemeal rye uses wholemeal flour with a proportion of rye

Lent, large numbers of blinis were consumed. They are just as popular now, eaten at any time of the year, most famously with *smetana* (a soured cream) and caviare, although also delicious with crème fraîche and smoked salmon. Blinis resemble in shape and size a Scotch pancake, but are normally far darker in colour with a savoury, slightly bitter flavour from the buckwheat flour. The most authentic blinis are made entirely of buckwheat but many are now a compromise with a blend of buckwheat and plain flour. The best blinis are yeast-risen, made using buttermilk or yogurt. Shop-bought blinis may have used baking powder instead and some contain so little buckwheat flour that they hardly merit the name "blini".

Pre-wrapped bought pancakes are best heated slightly in the microwave or wrapped in a cloth in the oven, so that they warm up without drying out.

BARLEY BREAD

Barley bread has long been baked in regions stretching from Finland to the shores of the Black Sea in the Ukraine. Barley made a change from the dark rye breads although, since it contains no gluten, loaves were consequently dense and heavy. Even today, many of the barley breads from the countries around the Baltic Sea are sturdy loaves, made with a blend of barley and wholemeal flour. The bread is generally moist and chewy. Cabbage leaves are sometimes used to line the baking tins, a time-honoured trick which keeps the crust moist.

POLISH RYE

As the name implies, this is made from rye, although some wheat flour is generally added. This bread, however, is made from refined rye meal, unlike Polish black rye which uses a coarser rye and wheat meal. Although they might sound not particularly appetizing, both breads are pleasantly flavoured.

ABOVE: Once the basic loaf for all poor families, Polish sourdough is now baked by craft bakers and is enjoyed by all bread enthusiasts.

RIGHT: Caraway seeds give Polish caraway a noticeable aniseed flavour.

POLISH BLACK BREAD

This is a large flattish and round bread, eaten in Poland, Lithuania and Latvia. Wheat flour is added to give some volume to the loaf, but it is principally made with buckwheat and has a distinctive, rather bitter flavour.

POLISH SOURDOUGH

This is a classic northern peasant-style rye bread. Originally, oats and barley may well have been added to the rye to make a loaf that would feed the family for as long as possible. Each household would take its grain to be milled and the bread would then be set to rise in proving troughs. The blend of grain plus the use of troughs gave a noticeably different flavour and texture to each loaf, from family to family and even from loaf to loaf.

POLISH CARAWAY BREAD

A traditional Polish medium rye bread, this is made with rye and wheat flour flavoured with caraway seeds.

ESTONIAN RYE

This is a sourdough bread made entirely with rye. It is a tin-shaped bread with a distinctive flavour arising from both the rye and the natural leaven.

SWEET PUMPERNICKEL

There are many styles of pumpernickel breads, all made entirely or principally from rye.

RUSSIAN BRAIDED BREAD

Braided yeasted loaves made using white flour are among the most familiar breads of eastern Europe. They are similar, and sometimes identical, to the Jewish *challah* since this part of Europe was home to many Jewish people. Many of these spectacular breads are enriched with milk, eggs and butter and are made as festive breads for special occasions. Others are plainer, sometimes using milk to obtain a softer crust, and are frequently sprinkled with poppy seeds.

RUSSIAN BLACK BREAD

Bread was by far the most important food in Russia until this century. In the 19th century, the Russian peasant ate on average 1.5kg/3–3½ lb of bread a day and even more at harvest time. White breads are now popular in Moscow and other large cities but it is the ryes that are the best-known and -loved of Russian breads. There are numerous types of black breads, varying in colour, density and sour/sweet flavour. Molasses, favoured throughout the Baltic States, is frequently added and originally the breads would have been made on the sourdough principle, although some today are yeast-leavened. Many are similar to German rye breads, since techniques and styles cross borders as easily as weather. A classic Russian black bread, however, is usually made with an equal blend of rye and wheat flour, using a sourdough starter. It

ABOVE: Estonian rye is one of the few tin breads baked in this region.

RIGHT: Russian black bread owes its dark colour to molasses and rye.

is spiced and oven bottom-baked. A round loaf, it has an attractive, coarse top. It is normally roughly broken rather than cut and is often eaten with soups and stews. In the Ukraine a version of a black rye bread is known as *chenyi khilb*, which is another large round loaf.

ROSSISKY

This is among the better-known Russian rye breads and is now made and sold outside Russia in some supermarkets, delicatessens and healthfood shops. It is 100 per cent rye bread, made using a sourdough starter and has a distinctive yet pleasant flavour.

BORODINSKY

This small but compact loaf, traditionally flavoured with crushed coriander seeds, is becoming increasingly available outside Russia. Consequently, it represents, for many, the essence of Russian bread.

The story goes that the wife of a Russian general, Marshal Mikhail Kutuzov, made this sweet, aromatic bread for the army, which was defending Borodino, outside Moscow, from the onslaught of Napoleon's army. Although Napoleon then entered Moscow, the French were shortly forced to withdraw, which led to Napoleon's downfall. The Battle of Borodino thus became enshrined in Russian history and the bread was named

to remember both the eventual victory and the 42,000 men who lost their lives.

The Borodinsky loaf is baked, like the German box breads, in a sealed container; but unlike them it is cooked for only some 2½ hours, and uncovered for the final 15–30 minutes so that the bread is slightly risen with a firm crust. It is made either entirely with dark rye or with a blend of rye and wheatmeal. Barleymeal is also often used, giving an earthy flavour, while buttermilk or yogurt is also occasionally added and enhances the natural sourdough flavour. Molasses, however, is traditionally used and malt is frequently added so that the bread acquires a sweet flavour, albeit with distinct sour/savoury overtones. Borodinsky is the most expensive and most popular of the Russian rye breads, and is served thinly sliced with strongly flavoured fish, such as pickled herring or smoked salmon.

RUSSIAN POTATO BREAD WITH CARAWAY SEEDS

Potatoes were another mainstay for the Russian peasant; breads were often made by using a mixture of a grain and potatoes that had been cooked and mashed. If the mixture included wheat, a flattish but loaf-shaped bread could be made. Caraway seeds were a popular flavouring.

HUNGARIAN CHRISTMAS BREAD

Called *makos es dios kalacs* in Hungarian, this is a popular festive enriched white bread, with the dough rolled around poppy seeds and raisins.

BALABUSKY

These little rolls speckled with caraway seeds are a speciality of the Ukraine, a region known for the variety of its breads. The rolls combine rye and wheat flours in varying proportions, but are made with soured cream, which gives a pleasant acidic flavour. Soured cream and curd cheese are an inheritance from the Tartars who invaded Russia and the Ukraine from Asia in the 13th century. The liking for soured cream, used in bread making and served with bread, is a feature of much eastern European cooking.

KOLACH (KALACH)

Kolach (kalach) is a sweet yeasted white bread, popular at Christmas in Bulgaria and Russia and especially in St Petersburg where it was said it should only be made from the water transported to the city from the Moskva river. It is normally plaited, although in the Ukraine and Moldova it is often formed into a round, like the sun – a reminder of warmer days to come.

KULICH

Kulich is the traditional Russian Easter cake. Apparently, in Tsarist Russia

RIGHT: Rossisky (back) and Borodinsky (front) are the cream of Russian breads.

labourers were not permitted to walk through the kitchen in case their heavy steps caused the dough to fall or the bread to collapse in the oven. The bread is similar to a brioche, made with white flour, eggs, butter and milk and rich with raisins, candied peel, angelica and chopped almonds. The tall, round bread is either glazed or iced and then decorated with glacé cherries, angelica or crystallized fruit. It is served, unusually, by slicing off the top and then slicing horizontally again for eating. The top is then replaced to keep the cake fresh for as long as possible.

The cake was also baked for Remembrance Monday, which is the Russian equivalent to All Souls' Day (2 November), when traditionally it would have been taken to the church in order to be blessed by the priest.

KRENDEL

Krendel or *kolindet* is a popular Russian sweet bread. With its intertwining loops, its shape is reminiscent of a pretzel and, similarly, has a significance that has been lost over the years. These breads were popular for birthdays and to celebrate name-days. They were also given to children on Christmas Eve so they may have been connected with the winter solstice. They are yeast-leavened, made with white flour and enriched with eggs, butter and cream. The breads have a deliciously soft, cake-like consistency and are sometimes served for tea in restaurants or at a *chaikhana* (tea house).

CZECHOSLOVAKIAN HOSKA

Another festive bread, this braided loaf is often decorated with whole almonds and then glazed with egg before and during cooking, so that it bakes to a beautiful golden hue. The bread is quite spectacular and no mean feat for the baker. The three tiers of braids are made successively smaller so that the braids balance on top of each other.

UKRAINIAN RYE

The Ukraine in renowned for its huge variety of breads. It is the second largest country in Europe, after Russia, and almost the entire country is one vast plain of extremely fertile black soils. Once known as the bread basket of the USSR, the Ukraine has a rich tradition of bread making. Emigré bakers in Britain and America, as well as European bread specialists, produce some excellent breads. A popular Ukrainian loaf is a sourdough bread made with a half rye, half wheat flour blend. It is baked on the sole of the oven and has a good chewy crust and a noticeably sour flavour.

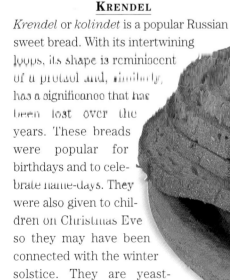

RIGHT: Ukrainian rye is hugely popular wherever these Slav people have settled.

THE BREADS OF GREECE, CYPRUS AND TURKEY

Greece has a wonderful array of breads, arising from historical and geographical influences. Here, not only are there the Arabian-style breads of the Ottoman Empire, but also indigenous breads with a long history, which are still baked, particularly on the islands, by people who keep these traditions alive. On some of the Aegean Islands, up until very recently, the wheat and barley harvested by smallholders would be carried to the windmill for milling into flour. The dough would then be made and shaped, before being taken to the village oven for baking. Such traditions have now almost entirely died out, and in the cities the bakeries are as sophisticated as those anywhere else in Europe. But in many small villages, on the islands or in the mountains, people still buy the simple but large white crusty bread, which is frequently still baked in an old brick oven, the brushwood being collected by the baker or his family each evening ready for the next day's baking.

Throughout Greece, local bakers produce their own particular bread, which necessarily becomes a favourite with their customers. In the cities, the more enterprising bakeries produce a wide range of breads flavoured with raisins, olives and herbs, but among the islands and in the mountains, most loaves continue to be of the plain, farmhouse variety – large and crusty and sometimes scattered with sesame seeds. The bread has a slightly coarse texture, which makes it excellent for mopping up sauces and dressings.

Travelling eastwards from Greece, the leavened breads of Europe give way to the characteristic flat breads of the Middle East. However, inevitably there are breads that are common to Greece and Turkey, partly because of the crossover of ideas and partly because some breads, such as pitta, are so versatile that their popularity endures.

BREADSTICKS

Although similar to Italian *grissini*, Greek and Turkish breadsticks are somewhat chunkier, although just as crunchy. They are mostly sprinkled with sesame or poppy seeds, or may be made using fennel, which gives them a noticeable aniseed flavour. *Koulouria* are similar but the bread has been formed into rings, like pretzels. Sold by itinerant street vendors from their large wicker baskets, these too are often liberally sprinkled with sesame seeds, in which case they are referred to as *thessalonikis*.

PAN BREAD

You are only likely to come across this bread, called *tiganópsomo* in Greek, if you visit the delightful Greek island of Santorini, believed by some to be the site of the lost world of Atlantis. It is a simple unleavened bread, mixed to a thick batter and combined with onions and tomatoes before being fried.

GREEK CELEBRATION BREADS

Bread has religious significance all over the world, but nowhere more so than in Greece. Almost all of the important days in the religious calendar have their own speciality bread – some rich with fruit, eggs and butter, others completely plain, depending on the holy day that is being celebrated.

Prosforo (holy bread) is the bread of the Greek Mass, prepared by bakers every Saturday and taken to the church on Sunday by a member of the congregation. The large, round white loaf is stamped with the church seal and is the Host of the Communion, shared out by the priest to the faithful during the Mass.

LEFT: Breadsticks

RIGHT: Daktyla is a popular Greek bread.

On Clean Monday, which is the first day of Lent in the Greek Orthodox Church, the *lagana* is the centre-piece of a traditional meal of seafood and salads. Clean Monday is so-called since on this day Greek housewives are expected to scrub the kitchens and all utensils, to make sure nothing remains of Celebration – the three-week long festival that precedes the fasting of Lent. Appropriately, the *lagana* is a completely plain unleavened bread, made by local bakers solely for this one day of the year. The dough is formed into a large oval and then sprinkled with sesame seeds before baking.

Tsoureki is the famous Greek Easter bread. The yeasted bread is made from an enriched dough flavoured with orange and spices. It can be coiled into a round, but is more frequently made into a long plait and then scattered with almonds and sesame or caraway seeds and decorated with the characteristic red hard-boiled eggs. If you visit Greece just before Easter, you will find packets of red-dyed eggs sold everywhere. They symbolize the Resurrection and are knocked together after the Midnight Mass

on Easter Saturday evening with the words, "Christ is Risen". On many of the Greek islands, where old customs still continue, *tsoureki* is the traditional Easter gift from children to their godparents.

Another festive and enriched bread is the *christopsomo*, the Greek Christmas bread. The top is decorated with a large cross, fashioned from the dough, the ends of which encircle cherries or walnuts.

OLIVE BREAD (ELIOTI)

Originally this bread was a Lenten food for the priests of the Eastern Orthodox Church, although now *elioti* is produced all over the country and can be enjoyed at any time of the year. It is generally a white bread, enriched with a little olive oil, flavoured with marjoram or oregano and studded with black olives.

DAKTYLA

This unmistakable loaf is a style of bread that belongs equally to Greece, Cyprus and Turkey. Its defining characteristic is the liberal addition of nigella seeds in the bread itself, and the white sesame and black nigella seeds sprinkled

LEFT: There is a rich variety of white breads in Greece, often sprinkled with sesame seeds.

BELOW:
Ekmek

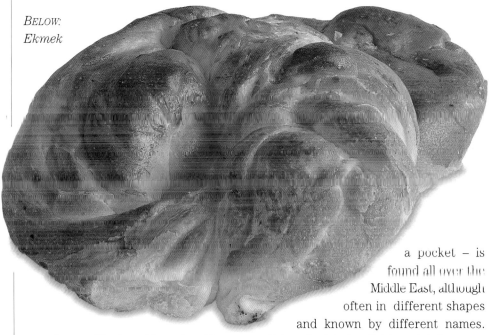

over the top. The bread is oval and is normally large. It has deep slashes along the crust and looks like a large bloomer. It has a slightly peppery flavour thanks to the nigella seeds, and an open, coarse texture.

CILICIAN BREAD

Available now in many countries, these small flat breads sprinkled with cheese and spices are like miniature pizzas.

PITTA (PIDE)

Pitta breads, or *pide* to give them their Turkish name, are probably the best-known Greek and Turkish breads. This style of bread – flat and baked so that it contains

a pocket – is found all over the Middle East, although often in different shapes and known by different names. Although pitta is a flat bread, it is not an unleavened bread. There is little crumb but the crust is soft and it is leavened with yeast; the flatness and characteristic pocket, called the *mutbag*, are due to the method of baking – ideally in an extremely hot clay oven. Pitta breads are widely eaten outside of Greece and Turkey, used as they are intended for stuffing with meats and vegetables. In restaurants in Istanbul, *pide* are served straight from the oven, stuffed with chunks of lamb that has been cooked over hot embers on a nearby spit, and with yogurt and mint. There is a

huge range of different pitta breads available, for example wholemeal pittas, round mini pittas, pittas flavoured with herbs or sprinkled with sesame seeds. They are best eaten warm and, when shop-bought, should be sprinkled with a little water and then placed in a hot oven or under the grill until they begin to puff up.

EKMEK

This is a large round or oval leavened bread, often dimpled like an Italian focaccia, but made simply with a plain white dough. Like pitta bread, the crust is soft and is used either for stuffing for sandwiches, or using as a scoop for picking up food. *Ekmek* can also refer to other breads – the word *ekmek* simply means "bread". In Turkey you will find numerous longish loaves, sometimes made using wholemeal, but normally white flour. More elaborate *ekmeks*, baked in rounds or sprinkled with sesame seeds, can be found in bakeries in the large cities.

BELOW: Sutlu ekmek

RIGHT: Pitta bread is served almost everywhere in Greece and Turkey.

TURKESTAN BREAD

This is a proprietary loaf sold in Britain but said to be based on the bread made by Turkoman tribes who lived in the Turkestan region around the Caspian Sea.

SIMITS

These little crusty golden bread rings are sold in almost every town in Turkey, and generally first thing

ABOVE: Many Turkish bakers still use wood-burning ovens. Breads, such as pide (right) and tuzsuz (left), cook quickly with a beautifully flavoured crust and soft crumb. Hashas (centre) is a large loaf that is cooked as the oven begins to cool.

in the morning when the *simit* seller takes his wares down to the harbour and into the market to entice workers and tourists alike. *Simits* are closely related to bagels, indeed they clearly look like them, and in fact an authentic *simit* is made in the same way as a bagel, being first poached in boiling water before being sprinkled with

LEFT: Simits coated with sesame seeds.

ABOVE: Turkestan bread

sesame seeds and baked. Until quite recently, the *simit* seller would carry the rings piled high on a tray on his head or looped on to long sticks, but nowadays, food regulations mean that *simits* are more likely to be found wheeled around under glass.

THE BREADS OF THE MIDDLE EAST AND NORTH AFRICA

Apart from in Morocco, which bestrides Arabia and western Europe, almost all the breads of this enormous region are versions of flat breads. Tradition and culture play a part here. In many of these regions people have always led a nomadic existence, living in tents and moving frequently from place to place. There was never any time nor inclination for plates or cutlery and when it came to eating, bread was used both as a food in its own right and as a means of conveying other food to the mouth. In addition, fuel was scarce and bread had to be cooked quickly while the fire was hot. Flat breads that cooked in minutes were a far better option than large, sturdy loaves. Even today, clay ovens almost identical to those depicted on walls of ancient tombs can still be found in some of the smaller villages of Egypt, Iran and Turkey. The ovens are fuelled with wood, corn kernels or even camel dung and, when they are hot, the flattened dough is baked against the sides of the walls.

Although the bread is flat, Middle Eastern bread is generally not unleavened, apart from rare exceptions, such as the

BELOW: The flat breads of the Middle East can be indistinguishable from each other. These khoubiz are very similar to the Egyptian aiysh.

Arabian crisp bread *ragayig*. The ancient Egyptians mastered the art of leavening bread and by the 12th century BC, 40 kinds of breads and pastries were available to upper-class Egyptians from their bakeries. Wheat has always been the preferred grain. It is indigenous to Turkey and the Middle East, and the first wheat to be cultivated came from this region.

AIYSH

Aiysh is the Egyptian word for "life" and these flat round loaves must be one of the oldest breads known to mankind. We know that as long ago as 1500 BC, *aiysh* was made and sold by Egyptian bakers and the same baking methods are still used today in some parts of the country. The bread is similar to pitta bread, but smaller and thicker. It should be made with wholemeal flour. This same bread is found throughout the Middle East. The shape varies and the size ranges from 15cm/6in to 30cm/12in rounds, or ovals of up to 38cm/15in. In Yemen the bread is known as *saluf*; in Jordan and Palestine as *shrak;* and as *aiysh shami* in Syria. The bread is delicious when freshly cooked, puffing up to leave a hollow centre and a soft crust.

KHOUBIZ (KHOBZ)

This bread from the Levant and Arabian peninsula, means simply "bread" in Arabian and is virtually identical to Egyptian *aiysh*. Flat and slightly leavened, it is made in rounds varying between 15cm/6in and 30cm/12in in diameter. Originally made with a finely ground wholemeal flour similar to chapati flour, it is now more often made using white flour.

DARBARI

These white breads from Iran can be oval, rectangular or round in shape, varying from small breads, about 10cm/4in long, to much larger breads measuring up to 30cm/12in. All are flattish breads and the loaves are often slashed four or five times like the French *fougasse* to give a fretwork effect. They may be brushed with oil before baking, and spiced versions with cumin or caraway seeds scattered on top are sometimes to be found.

MANKOUSH (MANNAEESH)

Spelt in many different ways, this is the typical Lebanese version of *khoubiz*. Here the bread is rolled into 13cm/5in rounds and indented slightly in the middle so that it is concave. It is then brushed with olive oil and *za'atar*, a blend of sesame seeds,

RIGHT: Barbari are sometimes called Persian flat breads.

unleavened. Like *lavash*, this is a large flat bread, which is quite crisp and brittle when cooked. Almost certainly the most ancient of all breads, predating even *aiysh* and *khoubiz*, *ragayig* is nevertheless still eaten today, cooked in the same way as *lavash* until it is crisp and sometimes further dried in the sun. *Nane lavash* is oval-shaped with a softer texture and is a cross between *lavash* and an Indian naan.

PIDEH

This is an Armenian version of the Turkish *pide*; it is always made using wholemeal flour. The rolled-out breads are scattered with sesame seeds before being baked in the oven.

thyme, marjoram and *sumac*, a spice made from the dried red berries of a bush native to Sicily and western Asia. This herb and spice blend has an unusual sour flavour, thanks mainly to the *sumac*.

LAVASH

Lavash is one of the largest of the Middle Eastern flat breads. It can be round or oval, is extremely thin and can be up to 60cm/2ft in diameter. The bread came originally from Armenia and Iran, although its popularity has spread and it is widely eaten all over the Middle East. The dough is often taken by villagers to the local bakery to be slowly baked in clay ovens called *furunu*. Alternatively, it is baked in a *sorj*, a dome-covered oven like an inverted

BELOW: Flat breads, such as this munkoush from the Lebanon cook quickly and are ideal in lands where fuel is scarce.

wok. Cooked in this way, the bread becomes brittle and crisp and is generally eaten straight away, torn in large pieces. *Lavash* can be unleavened or leavened, but its close relative, *ragayig*, is always

MOROCCAN AND TUNISIAN BREADS

There are several types of Moroccan bread, mostly variations on the same theme. The wheat flour dough, can be white, wholemeal or a blend of both, and may be enriched with olive or peanut oil. It may be leavened naturally, although yeasts are more commonly used these days. Either way, the loaf is almost always round and flattish and equally invariably, is made by wives and daughters at home. In the past, and even now among some families, the unbaked loaves are carried to the local bakery to be cooked.

MOROCCAN HOLIDAY BREAD

Cornmeal, together with pumpkin and sunflower seeds, makes this a tasty bread. It is baked for special occasions.

TUNISIAN KESRET

This version of the Arabian bread, *khoubiz*, is mainly distinguished by the fact that it is cooked in a tagine, a North African earthenware cooking pot.

MELLA

This round flat bread, made by Tunisian nomads and sometimes containing caraway seeds, is covered with sand before being placed on the embers of a fire.

MARRAKESH SPICED BREAD

Moroccan cuisine reveals a number of cultural influences. France's short but significant domination with its invasion in the middle of the 19th century is noticeable in a number of spheres. French is still an important language in Morocco and many dishes clearly owe their inspiration to French cuisine, albeit with spicy flavours that are entirely local. Marrakesh spiced bread owes much to the French brioche – made with a yeasted white dough and enriched with butter and sometimes eggs – yet it is very much a product of Morocco. Flower water, either orange or rose, gives it a strongly perfumed taste and it is also sugary sweet, especially when served with honey or jam.

JEWISH BREADS

You do not have to travel far to enjoy this rich selection of breads. Wherever there is a Jewish community, a huge range of their particular breads will be produced, both for daily eating and for festivals and celebrations. The other singular aspect of Jewish breads, in contrast to English or French breads, for example, is that by definition, they do not belong to one country or region. Jewish cuisine embraces an enormous spectrum of culinary traditions, ranging across eastern and central Europe, through the Mediterranean, the Middle East, north-east Africa and India.

Visit a Jewish delicatessen and you will find a surprising number of loaves bearing a close resemblance to the breads of Germany, Russia or eastern Europe. The harmonization of ideas that occurs when people become neighbours is particularly apparent with age-old traditions such as bread making, and cultures are decidedly richer for it.

CHALLAH
There are many variations on this spectacular festive bread with its deep brown crust and soft white crumb. Challah is traditionally made for the

ABOVE: Rich challah spirals

Sabbath or for other Jewish holidays and while it is most often seen plaited, it can be shaped into spirals or wreaths, or baked in a tin. The dough is made using eggs and vegetable oil, which gives it a soft texture somewhere between that of a brioche and a soft white loaf. It is normally slightly sweetened, with either sugar or honey; the sweeter loaves also being stuffed with raisins. The most popular *challahs*, however, are simply liberally sprinkled with poppy seeds, which is one of their most characteristic features.

In Orthodox Jewish families two loaves of *challah* are placed on the traditional embroidered tablecloth. A blessing is said over the bread, before it is broken and handed to members of the family. The Hebrew word for "blessing" is *brachah*, which derives from the Ashkenazi (eastern European) word for plaited bread. The two loaves represent the manna sent down by God to the Israelites after leaving Egypt.

Challah can be plaited with three, six or twelve strands of dough. At Rosh Hashanah, it is customary to have round *challahs*, often sweetened with honey and sometimes enriched with raisins or sultanas. On the eve of Yom Kippur, *challah* is baked in the shape of wings, a ladder or raised arms, symbolizing prayers being made to heaven.

ABOVE: A plaited challah

BOULKAS

These are small roll-sized *challahs*, shaped into rounds, plaits or spirals and made especially for weddings. However, they are often baked and sold by large bakeries for any occasion.

BAGELS

The bagel – "the roll with a hole" – is the customary bread at Bar Mitzvahs although nowadays they can be bought almost anywhere and enjoyed literally at any time of the year. Their unique feature, apart from the central hole, is that they are briefly immersed in boiling water, or steamed for a minute, before being finally baked. The process means that the dough puffs up in the water but does not rise any more during baking, producing the characteristic dense texture. Even savoury-style bagels contain some sugar or malt extract, and a little is also added to the water during boiling. The bagel is then glazed with egg or egg white before being baked to give it a glossy crust and the result is a noticeably sweet-flavoured bread with a compact crumb and a chewy crust.

Bagels are almost always yeast-leavened, but beyond that there are countless variations. They can be made with wort, may contain cheese and/or butter, or may be made with just

BELOW: Boulkas

BELOW: Mixed bagels

RIGHT: Shabbat bread

small, rather solid roll is basically a small dimpled bun, stuffed with fried onions. The *baily* earns its name from the city of Bailystok in Poland, which was home to many Jews before they were forced to flee due to persecution.

SUMSUMS

Sumsums are the traditional breads of the Syrian Jews and look similar to bagels, although these little rolls with a hole are not boiled before baking, but go straight into the oven after shaping. *Sumsums* are usually sprinkled with sesame seeds.

SHABBAT BREAKFAST BREAD

Known as *kubaneh*, this unique bread is always cooked overnight so it is ready for the Sabbath breakfast. The bread is from the Yemen, which has its own Jewish cuisine, and is a yeasted white dough, enriched with butter and sweetened with sugar or honey. The rolled-out dough is spread with more butter and then rolled

water and margarine. Like so many Jewish breads, the bagel seems to have originated in Europe – created, it is said, by a Polish Jew in the Middle Ages to celebrate winning a war. Centuries later, such culinary techniques were taken to New York where many Jewish immigrants settled at the turn of the 20th century. The best bagels in the world are considered to be found in New York bakeries.

Bagels are mostly eaten sliced into two flat rings. They can be plain or toasted, and are commonly spread with cream cheese, topped with lox (smoked salmon) and then eaten as a sandwich. There is, of course, no end of other fillings, kosher or not, and similarly there are countless variations. In a Jewish bakery, you are likely to find wholemeal, rye and Granary versions, along with bagels sprinkled with poppy, sesame, caraway and sunflower seeds, sea salt or chopped onion. Among the many sweet bagels, which are widely available pre-packed in supermarkets as well as bakeries, are cinnamon and raisin-flavoured treats.

BAILYS

These are almost as popular in North America as the bagel, and both come from the same Ashkenazi Jewish culture. The

LEFT: Plain bagels

RIGHT: Matzos

up in a spiral and then steamed in a covered baking dish in a very low oven for up to 12 hours. It can be served with sugar but is also popular Yemeni-style with spicy or garlic chutneys.

MATZO

Matzo is a piece of unleavened bread that is served in Jewish households during Passover, Feast of the Unleavened Bread. The flat, brittle bread is made and baked with great speed and under strict dietary regulations by Jewish bakers to ensure that the flour and water mixture does not start to ferment, even by accident.

Passover is the most important holiday in the Jewish calendar and celebrates the Hebrews' deliverance from slavery in Egypt. *Matzo* is a reminder of how, in their escape from the Egyptians, the Hebrews had no time to let their bread rise. Leavened bread therefore became a prohibited food during the eight days of Passover although, paradoxically, the holiday is otherwise a time of celebration and good food.

Matzo is sometimes served at the table but more commonly the bread is ground into meal and used for cakes, biscuits and dumplings during Passover (see next entry).

PASSOVER ROLLS

Since leavened bread is forbidden during Passover, Ashkenazi Jews found intriguing ways of making breads without normal flour, which even without yeast will start a natural fermentation. The trick was to use *matzos*, flat and brittle breads, that have been ground to a fine meal.

Passover rolls, which are popular among Jewish communities in Paris and other parts of Europe, are almost identical to little choux buns, made with water, butter, *matzo* meal and eggs, and baked in the oven until golden. They are normally split and filled with cream cheese or cream.

LATKES

These small potato pancakes are thought to have originated in the Ukraine, where *kartoflani placke* were a popular dish at Christmas, served with goose. The dish was apparently adopted by the large Jewish population of the area, and is now traditionally served on the feast of Chanukah.

JEWISH RYE BREAD

There are many varieties of Jewish rye bread, most of which originated in Eastern Europe, where rye is such a popular grain. The sourdough starter for this well-known rye is made using the crusts of previous rye breads. It is then combined with white and rye flour and caraway seeds.

MANDEL BREAD (MANDELBROT)

This is a strange kind of hybrid – part loaf, part teabread and part biscuit. The word *mandelbrot* is Yiddish for "almond bread", and the dough is fashioned into a rough loaf shape before being baked. It is not a yeasted bread but is risen using self-raising flour or baking powder and, being enriched with eggs, flavoured with lemon and vanilla and studded with almonds, it is more like a biscuit than an ordinary bread. After baking it is cut into thick diagonal slices and baked again, which transforms the loaf/teabread into chunky biscuits. Mandel breads were once extremely popular among many Jewish people throughout the world, served with wine or other drinks. However, their popularity has declined over the years and while still baked by some Jewish bakers, they are difficult to find nowadays outside Israel and North America.

RIGHT: Jewish or seeded rye

BREADS OF THE AMERICAS

The United States of America yields a fabulous potpourri of breads. The thousands of people from Ireland, Italy, Germany and Scandinavia who emigrated to America at the turn of the century had little to take with them save the customs and traditions they held most dear. Baking bread would have been one of the very first tasks for the wife once a home had been established and, understandably, the breads she baked were the breads of her own country – a reminder of home and perhaps a promise of a better future.

Thriving communities were gradually established. Norwegians and other Scandinavians settled in many of the North Central states, such as Wisconsin, Minnesota and Iowa; German immigrants also settled around the Great Lakes, while in New York and in other large cities along the Eastern Seaboard, Italians and Jews made their home.

Grain, of course, was no problem in this "Land of Plenty". The United States were already world producers of grain, particularly wheat, but also rye, barley and oats. German and Eastern-European rye breads, country breads from Italy and a vast range of Jewish loaves were produced by the many

RIGHT: Hamburger buns can normally be distinguished by their sesame seed topping.

bakeries that sprang up to serve their own communities. Added to this, of course, were the established American loaves, themselves versions of breads brought to the New World by the early settlers, while in the South people moving north from Mexico continued to make their customary corn breads and tortillas. If indigenous breads can be said to exist in the United States, they are the breads made by Native Americans – whose bread making traditions were kept alive by people of American Indian descent in North and South Dakota and other central states.

ALL-AMERICAN BREADS

While some breads are mainly popular in, for example, north-eastern, southern or south-western states, certain loaves are extremely well known throughout the whole of the United States. Some of these, such as anadama bread, are best known by reputation. These loaves are sold occasionally by small bakeries as a curiosity, but they are more widely known from recipe books as the breads handed down

by generations. Other breads, however, are the standard loaves, sold in various shapes and sizes in every supermarket and convenience store. The best are, as ever, those made by craft bakeries.

As a general rule, you will find that standard American loaves – as opposed to those made by local Italian or French bakers, for example – have a more tender and softer crumb. This is because most American loaves contain fat in the form of milk and/or melted butter.

BURGER BUN

Burgers are almost an American way of life, which makes it all the more surprising that shop-bought burger buns can be sadly disappointing. While good burger buns do exist, many of the shop-bought burger buns are not dissimilar to those found outside America – white, squashy and with a smattering of sesame seeds on top. Perhaps their very blandness is considered a necessity to contrast with the beef and relishes inside, but any American burger *aficionado* will tell you that, on the contrary, the bun is an integral part of the eating experience. The best burger buns are made with a simple dough but, unlike the commercial supermarket variety, do not contain the emulsifiers that give the impression you are eating soft foam. The answer, as with so many breads, is to find a good baker. Italian, French and Jewish bakers are all likely to make their own versions, using the same dough as for their standard country breads and thus producing a bun with a pleasant texture and fine flavour.

GRAHAM BREAD

There is a wide variety of American wholemeal loaves, among which Graham bread is probably king – the name being synonymous with healthy eating. The bread is named after a 19th-century doctor, Dr Sylvester Graham,

RIGHT: Graham bread

who was a keen advocate of using the whole grain for milling flour, recognizing the benefits of bran in the diet. Graham flour, Graham bread and Graham crackers are all named after him, the best and most authentic flour being stoneground and coarsely milled wholemeal flour.

BASIC WHITE BREAD

This is a simple, well-flavoured tin loaf with a slightly chewy crust and a close but soft texture.

CORNELL BREAD

This light-textured wheat germ bread is mainly of historic interest since, although it is a nutritious loaf, it has long than happy antecedents and is rarely made these days. In the 1930s Cornell University pioneered a high-protein loaf, made with wheat germ, white and soya flours, sugar and milk for patients who lived in mental hospitals. Gradually, other public institutions, such as schools and hospitals, started producing the loaf. When, in the early 1940s, during World War II, meat was either rationed or extremely expensive, people looked for a high-protein alternative and the Cornell loaf became recommended eating. The bread clearly never recovered from such damning acclaim – even the most wonderful bread is, for most, a poor substitute to meat – and for that war generation, the scarcity and poor food that the Cornell loaf represented, meant that it became deeply unfashionable. A pity really, as recipes suggest that it is not at all bad.

BROWN AND WHOLEMEAL BREAD

There are many variations of wholemeal (wholewheat) bread. Wholewheat bread is widely available, normally in a loaf shape. There are also variations of brown bread, containing a blend of wholemeal and white flour. Wheat germ may also be added – you will need to ask or read the side of the packet to be sure. Cracked wheat bread has a delicious nutty flavour and crunchy texture, and is a good, nutritious loaf. It is usually round, although short batons and loaves are also available. It is made using milk or buttermilk, together with honey, molasses or brown sugar. The most nutritious breads are made with stoneground wholemeal flour, although white flour with added wheat germ and/or cracked wheat is still a healthy alternative with a good texture

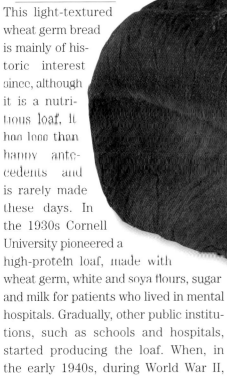

ABOVE: Basic white bread has a soft, close texture.

ABOVE: American seven-grain (top), wholewheat (round) and cracked wheat loaves

and flavour. Seven-grain bread is another healthy loaf. It contains seven grains: normally wheat, rye and corn; and then four of the following – brown rice, buckwheat, soya, oats, barley, millet, sunflower seeds, sesame seeds or flaxseed. As you might expect, it is a dense, sturdy loaf and is popular with health-food enthusiasts.

PULLMAN LOAF

This white loaf is named after the Pullman railway coach, the box shape of which is exactly that of the bread. The bread is similar to *pain de mie*, the French sandwich loaf. It is made in a rectangular tin, rather longer than a standard loaf tin, sometimes with a sliding lid so that the crust is soft on all sides. Like *pain de mie*, it is used for sandwiches and toasting and is normally white, made American-style with butter or other fat.

SWIRL BREAD

This very attractive loaf is widely available throughout the United States. It is made by using two doughs: one of white flour, the other using a wholemeal flour to which molasses is added. The doughs are rolled out after their first rising and the wholemeal rectangle is placed on top of the white one. The two are then rolled up together. When cut, each slice of bread has a swirl pattern.

BEER BREAD

Beer and butter are the ingredients that make this a most unusual bread. It comes from Georgia and is raised by

LEFT: The Pullman loaf is used for sandwiches

RIGHT: Swirl bread: molasses gives the dough an intense colour.

using self-raising flour or baking powder. A whole can of beer is poured into the flour mixture to make a thick batter, which is then poured into a round or rectangular loaf tin in which 50g/2oz/¼ cup butter has been melted. Once the loaf is cooked, it is turned upside down and the butter trickles through the bread. The result is a moist and beautifully flavoured loaf.

TOMATO BREAD

With bakers from so many nationalities, it is not surprising to find loaves in the United States that are reminiscent of other breads of the world. Tomato bread may remind you of Italian or even some Greek breads, yet here the bread has been thoroughly naturalized, the pretty, pale pink colouring coming from tomato juice, which gives the bread a definite but not overpowering taste of tomato.

SUN-DRIED TOMATO BREAD

Sun-dried tomato bread is similar to tomato bread but contains pieces of sun-dried tomatoes. It has a rustic appearance. The shape is usually a free-form round, which may be slashed across the top and dusted with flour before baking. Sun-dried tomato bread is popular served with pasta or soup.

DILL BREAD

Dill is a popular ingredient in American breads and there are several well-known dill loaves. The dilly casserole bread is a favourite among home bakers but it can sometimes be found in delicatessens and specialist shops. As well as dill, it contains cottage cheese and has a distinctive and pleasant sour flavour. As the name suggests, it is baked in a casserole. Another dill loaf, but quite unlike the dilly casserole loaf, is the sour dill rye, which is made from a blend of wheat and rye flours, and is strongly flavoured with dillweed, caraway seeds and dill pickle brine.

CHOCOLATE BREAD

Chocolate breads are well known in the USA; bakers across the land all make their own favourite. One such

ABOVE: Dill bread

LEFT: Rustic, Italian-style sun-dried tomato bread

BELOW: Triticale bread

chocolate loaf is called *babka*. This is a Russian-style bread that has many variations and comes in all sorts of extraordinary shapes. The dough, which is enriched with eggs and butter, can be plain or rich with bittersweet chocolate, and it is also sometimes filled with almond paste, raisins, nuts and more roughly chopped chocolate so that the centre is moist and soft and deliciously rich.

TRITICALE BREAD

Triticale (pronounced so as to rhyme with "daily") is a grain that has been developed using modern gene manipulation techniques and is a hybrid of rye, durum and red winterwheat. This probably sounds more alarming than it is – farmers and agriculturists have been cross-breeding wheat and other cereals for hundreds of years in order to improve both yields and resistance to disease. The triticale grain is particularly high in protein, but low in gluten. When making dough the flour is blended with at least an equal amount of wheat flour, either white or wholemeal. The bread has a sweet and nutty flavour, that is reminiscent of rye yet without its characteristic density.

OATMEAL BREAD

For the early settlers in America, oats were one of the easier cereals to grow and oatmeal would have been used for oatcakes, cooked over a griddle, or, if wheat was available, added in varying proportions to flour to make loaves. Since oatmeal contains no gluten, only small quantities can be used if attempting to make anything that resembles a loaf. Wheat flour and occasionally rye flour form the basis of the dough, but oatmeal adds a pleasant flavour and texture.

BANANA BREAD

Teabreads are immensely popular throughout the USA and all sorts of fruits and vegetables are used for flavouring them. The breads are mostly made using baking powder and the mixture has more the consistency of a cake than a dough. Consequently most American teabreads are baked in tins, after which they are

OPPOSITE: Babka, a Russian-style chocolate loaf, comes in all shapes and sizes.

ABOVE: Oatmeal bread has a good texture and flavour.

turned out and thickly sliced to serve with tea or with morning coffee. Bananas are a favourite teabread ingredient.

LEMON BREAD

Lemon bread is as popular as all the other teabreads. It is a finer flavoured and more textured loaf than most teabreads. Lemon in the form of rind or extract is often added to other teabreads, but is wonderful when given a starring role.

RIGHT: Plaited Cheddar cheese bread that is flavoured with beer.

ABOVE: Lemon bread and banana bread

CHEDDAR CHEESE BREAD

There are all sorts of flavoured breads in the United States and cheese is a favourite ingredient. Grated cheese can be kneaded into the dough to give it a rich, soft flavour, or else sprinkled on top to melt into the crust. Cheddar cheese bread is a simple but tasty yeast-leavened loaf that is almost always made with white flour. It is excellent with soups and barbecues, and is delicious toasted. A plaited cheese loaf is sometimes made using beer rather than milk or water.

NORTH-EAST AMERICAN BREADS

This is the area of the original 13 colonies, founded by the Pilgrim Fathers. The Dutch came, too, as well as other pilgrims seeking religious freedom. Among these people were the Amish, whose communities can today be found in Ohio and Indiana but most famously in Pennsylvania. New York is the epicentre of this region and here can be found a breathtaking range of breads from countries all over the world. But the most famous of all New York's bread, notwithstanding the Italian ciabattas, Irish soda breads, and baguettes and *pain de campagne* from France, are the Jewish breads. New York has the biggest community of Jews outside Israel and the city is distinguished for having the best bagels in the world. National breads can be found under their own separate heading, but the following are a selection of breads that have evolved from the recipes settlers adapted to the cereals and climate they found in the New World.

ANADAMA BREAD

The anecdote behind this bread is so good that few bread books can resist it, although it is not generally a bread found in most bakers or supermarkets. The bread dates back to colonial times and is unusual since it is one of the rare cornmeal breads made with yeast. The story goes that an irritable New England woodsman had a wife by the name of Anna, who fed him nothing but a cornmeal and molasses mush for supper. One evening, having had more than he could take, he grabbed some flour and yeast off the shelf, mixed it into the mush and put it in the oven to bake, muttering "Anna, damn her" over and over again. Thus the name, "anadama" came about. The loaf is made with yellow cornmeal and wheat flour in varying proportions and is normally baked in a round cake tin.

BOSTON BROWN BREAD

The Pilgrims who arrived in Massachusetts and other New England states must have quickly found that rye, rather than wheat, flourished better in the cold snowy winters and damp summers of their new home. This bread is one of the best known of the old breads – made with rye blended with cornmeal and white flour, which was a common practice in poorer families where corn was easily available but wheat was not. The bread is steamed – these days normally in large coffee cans, but presumably originally in ceramic pudding moulds. The advantage was that the bread could be made without the need for an oven, another sign that this was a bread of poor people, who strived to make do with the resources they had. The bread is often sweetened with molasses and/or buttermilk, which gives it a distinctive sour/sweet flavour, and is a favourite to eat with Boston baked beans.

BAKED BROWN BREAD/DUTCH OVEN BREAD

This is similar in many ways to Boston brown bread: it is made using rye flour, cornmeal and wheat flour, with molasses and buttermilk. The difference is in the baking. Unlike Boston brown bread, which is steamed, this loaf is baked in the oven. It was originally baked in a Dutch oven, a round type of pot set over a fire. Today, it is normally cooked in a covered casserole. The bread is placed in a cold oven and then baked until firm.

NEW ENGLAND BUTTERMILK ROLLS

These small, yeast and soda risen breads are light and flaky with a delightful soft crumb, thanks to the buttermilk from which they are made.

EGG HARBOUR BREAD

The bread is made by the Amish, a Mennonite people of Swiss and Dutch origin, who fled their own countries in the 18th century due to religious persecution in Europe. They migrated first to Pennsylvania, where their descendants are called Pennsylvania Dutch, and then moved to Ohio and other Midwest states. Everything about their life and lifestyle is plain and simple. This white bread from a village on the shores of Lake Michigan is typical – a plain white yeasted dough that is allowed six risings before being baked, which gives a beautifully textured loaf with a soft crumb. Old-order Amish bread is made by the families in northern Indiana. The bread is

RIGHT: New England buttermilk rolls are light and flaky.

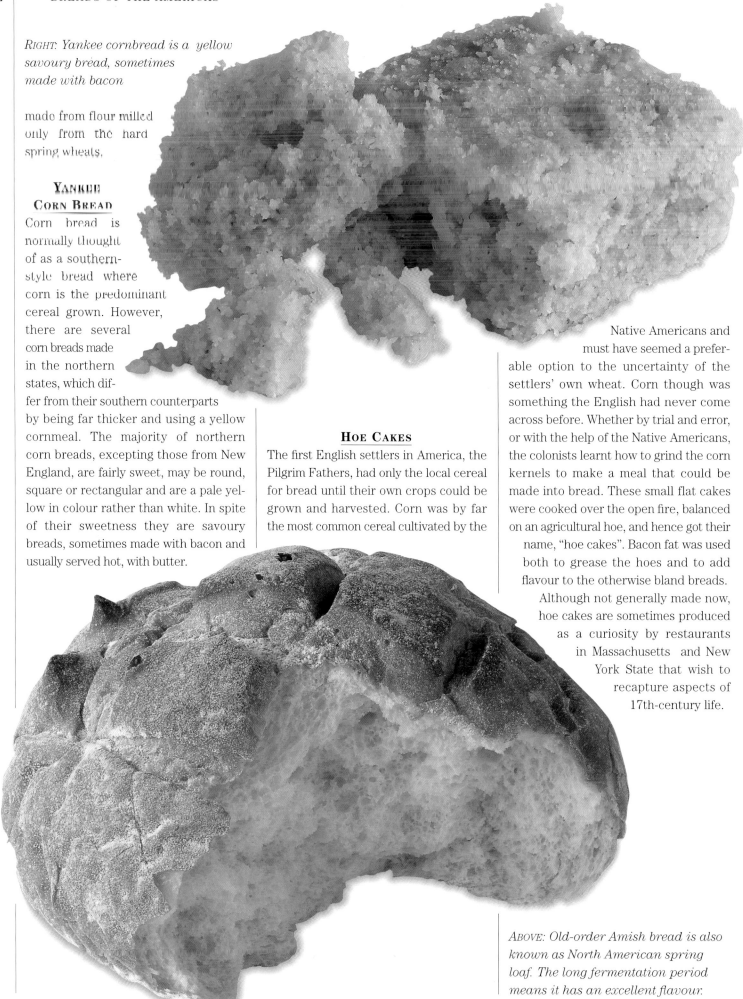

RIGHT: Yankee cornbread is a yellow savoury bread, sometimes made with bacon

made from flour milled only from the hard spring wheats.

YANKEE CORN BREAD

Corn bread is normally thought of as a southern-style bread where corn is the predominant cereal grown. However, there are several corn breads made in the northern states, which differ from their southern counterparts by being far thicker and using a yellow cornmeal. The majority of northern corn breads, excepting those from New England, are fairly sweet, may be round, square or rectangular and are a pale yellow in colour rather than white. In spite of their sweetness they are savoury breads, sometimes made with bacon and usually served hot, with butter.

HOE CAKES

The first English settlers in America, the Pilgrim Fathers, had only the local cereal for bread until their own crops could be grown and harvested. Corn was by far the most common cereal cultivated by the Native Americans and must have seemed a preferable option to the uncertainty of the settlers' own wheat. Corn though was something the English had never come across before. Whether by trial and error, or with the help of the Native Americans, the colonists learnt how to grind the corn kernels to make a meal that could be made into bread. These small flat cakes were cooked over the open fire, balanced on an agricultural hoe, and hence got their name, "hoe cakes". Bacon fat was used both to grease the hoes and to add flavour to the otherwise bland breads. Although not generally made now, hoe cakes are sometimes produced as a curiosity by restaurants in Massachusetts and New York State that wish to recapture aspects of 17th-century life.

ABOVE: Old-order Amish bread is also known as North American spring loaf. The long fermentation period means it has an excellent flavour.

MIDWEST AND NORTH CENTRAL AMERICAN BREADS

These are the heartlands of America, stretching from the dairy farms of Wisconsin to the prairies of Wyoming. Here in middle America, great store is set by family life with family meals being a central part. These states were settled mainly by Scandinavians, Germans and Slavs who brought with them the traditions of their homeland. Sourdough ryes and mixed-grain loaves are therefore among the most common breads available.

BELOW: Seeded rye (left) and old Milwaukee rye

SALT-RISING BREAD

There are several recipes in American cookbooks for salt-rising breads, but it is thought that the bread was originally made by pioneers crossing the Midwest and western prairies. The starter dough would have been carried in crocks, as the horse- or oxen-drawn wagons made their way across the plains. "Salt-rising" refers to the practice of keeping the active starter in a bowl nestling in a bed of salt, which is easy to warm and retains its heat for a long time. The starter would provide the leaven for fresh bread, which would have been made and baked in makeshift ovens each time the wagon train stopped.

Although an authentic bread of the prairies, nowadays this bread is a speciality of some of the East Coast bakers. The 19th-century sourdough loaf is known for its delicious and delicate crumb, yet also renowned for the difficulty in actually getting it to work. Several bakeries have succeeded with the bread, but the starter, made from scalded milk, sugar and cornmeal, is a notoriously tricky one to prepare. Once the starter begins to ferment, milk, white flour, fat, sugar and salt are added to make a sponge. This adds another potential complication as salt is never usually added to a starter or sponge because it tends to inhibit the yeast. Given the right conditions of warmth and humidity, however, the sponge should rise and fall, after which the remaining flour is added and the dough made into bread in the usual fashion.

LEFT: Heavy sour rye bread

RYE BREAD

There are many rye breads in the Midwest states of Wisconsin, Ohio, Minnesota, Iowa and Nebraska. Pumpernickel is commonly sold, as is a crusty rye bread made using rye and wheat flour but often with butter added, which is a feature of many American breads. Like most traditional ryes, Old Milwaukee rye is a sourdough loaf, made with molasses and flavoured in typical Germanic style with caraway seeds. The bread may be shaped into round loaves or fashioned into long, slender ones.

SEEDED RYE

Seeded rye bread is often known as Jewish rye and is popular not only in the Midwest, but as far east as New York.

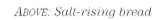
ABOVE: Salt-rising bread

HEAVY SOUR RYE BREAD

This is known as "corn bread" from the cornmeal that is sprinkled on the baking sheet, but is otherwise a rye sourdough made with a proportion of wheat flour. It is normally liberally sprinkled with caraway seeds. The bread is frequently sold by weight and can be recognized by its sides, which are liberally sprinkled with cornmeal, and its top, which is scattered with caraway seeds.

WEST COAST AMERICAN BREADS

In California, fashions come and go so quickly that it is surprising to find that some of the most traditional American breads are not only still being produced but are ever more popular – in the delicatessens, the restaurants and on the dinner party circuit. Many influences have come to play a part. The Pacific Coast was the end of the journey for pioneers hoping to find opportunity and freedom: Hispanics, from the south, gravitated towards the cities of Los Angeles and San Francisco, while Europeans settled all over the region, each culture establishing its own favourite styles of cooking and enthusiastically sampling others.

SAN FRANCISCAN SOURDOUGH

San Franciscan sourdough is probably the best-known American bread outside the United States, and is one that can be truly said to be all-American. It is a round, wheat, oven-baked loaf, with a star slash or a cross-hatched pattern on top. These breads, like the salt-rising breads, were brought to the West Coast by pioneers who crossed the prairies and plains of middle America in search of gold. The trip took the early pioneers five or six months and was extremely hazardous. The Forty-Niners – the men who took part in the 1849 Gold Rush – gave their camps names like Hell's Half Acre and Hangtown, which gives an idea of what life must have been like. Provisions for the journey included sacks of flour, together with a small piece of leavening kept back from the last batch of dough, so that bread could be baked en route. The leavening was stored in a crock inside a sack of flour.

The word "sourdough" refers quite simply to the bread's flavour. The bread has the same sharp/sour taste of yogurt or buttermilk.

It is said that it is impossible to make San Franciscan sourdough outside the city itself. The climate of San Francisco, with

LEFT: Perhaps America's best-known bread, the San Franciscan sourdough

its warmth and humidity, is particularly conducive to sourdough breads, and the bacterium, which feeds on the flour and water mixture, is unique to that area. However, home-bakers often attempt approximations, while professional bakeries all over California produce their own versions, including the *Berkeley sourdough*, which is a baguette shaped loaf.

MONKEY BREAD

This bread goes under a variety of names, including bubble loaf or poppy seed bubble loaf. The bread normally comprises seven or eight small dough balls baked in a ring mould so that when it is baked the bread does look like lots of bubbles. The little balls are dipped into melted butter and then sprinkled with poppy seeds or currants, raisins, nuts and/or sugar and cinnamon before being baked.

SOUTH-WEST AMERICAN BREADS

Texas, New Mexico and Arizona all border Mexico and their cuisine, including the bread, shows all the influences of its southern neighbour. Food can be spicy and very hot, and tortillas and other corn breads are as common as breads made with wheat.

JALAPEÑO CORN BREAD

This is a typical Tex-Mex-style bread, made with a blend of cornmeal and white flour. Hot jalapeño chillies are kneaded into the dough, and some loaves may contain whole corn kernels and cheese, too. The bread can be baked in loaf tins or shaped into rounds and oven bottom-baked and it has a unique, snappy flavour.

SOPAIPILLAS

These small, puffy breads are a speciality of New Mexico. They are made by mixing together flour, baking powder and salt, adding water to make a dough and then incorporating some vegetable fat, as when making puff pastry. The dough is then rolled out extremely thinly and cut into small squares, which are deep fried until puffy. If made professionally in a restaurant or by a baker, the corners can then be snipped off and filled with honey. Otherwise honey or syrup can simply be poured over the breads. A savoury alternative uses refried beans.

HOBO BREAD

Hobo bread is so-called, not because it is a favourite among tramps and vagrants, but because it is traditionally eaten outdoors. It is a sweet bread, rich with sultanas and nuts, that has been baked in a coffee can so that it is shaped like a long cylinder. Its popularity as an outdoor bread is probably due to the fact that the bread keeps well for several months. It is normally stored in the can in which it is cooked.

BREADS OF THE SOUTHERN STATES

This region includes Mississippi, Alabama and Georgia among others. Corn is cultivated in many of these states and the popularity of corn breads is well known, many people preferring the flat and rather mealy flavour of the corn to the wheat breads popular in the north.

NEW ORLEANS BREAD

New Orléans has many visible French influences – including its name, after Orléans in France – and not least its excellent breads. *Pain perdu* (French toast) is a favourite breakfast for many New Orléans citizens. New Orléans' French bread is softer than the real French version. It is sometimes known as feather bread and is very light. It has the same open texture as the French baguette, but has added fat and sugar, which makes it slightly richer and sweeter.

SPOON BREAD

This corn confection is part bread, part dessert, known as spoon bread for the simple reason that it has to be eaten with a spoon. It is the consistency of custard and is puffy and creamy when cooked. It is then liberally doused in corn syrup or honey and is very sweet. The bread is made with cornmeal, a little white flour, eggs, milk and baking powder. One story suggests that the bread was created when too much liquid was added to a corn bread batter and the baked bread had to be spooned out of the tin. Be that as it may, the Virginians insist that this event happened in one of their kitchens and thus claim spoon bread as their own. In Virginia, you will find this served both as a dessert and as a savoury course, made with bacon, cheese and garlic.

SOUTHERN CORN BREAD

There are numerous corn breads in the southern states. Convenience stores and supermarkets sell the more standard-type loaves, but in the home people still make their own breads, and since corn bread is best eaten as soon as possible, these are going to be the most tasty. Corn breads only rarely use yeast, and are relatively quick and easy to make. Southerners like white cornmeal for their breads, rather than the yellow meal preferred in the north and the breads are generally much thinner. Wheat flour is added to these breads in varying proportions, but in southern corn bread neither wheat flour nor fat is added, so that the corn flavour is predominant.

Other breads, such as rich corn bread, are made using cream, milk, butter and eggs. Corn pone is thought to be directly inspired by the Native Americans. It is a small, moist loaf, which is made from finely ground cornmeal along with buttermilk and lard.

NATIVE AMERICAN FRY-BREAD

People have lived in America for thousands of years, developing into various local populations of Native Americans who made bread from both wheat and corn for special occasions and for everyday eating. Hoe cakes made by early English settlers may well be adaptations or even pure copies of the breads made by the local people. Nowadays, there are reservations for Native Americans in various American states such as Oklahoma, and several of the more northern states. Their breads vary a little in size but are surprisingly similar across the continent, being small flat breads made from a flour and water dough that is rolled thinly and cut into diamonds, circles or squares. In North and South Dakota on the Sioux reservation, the breads are called "fry-breads" and are made for powwows – ceremonies or inter-tribal gatherings featuring much feasting and dancing.

SALLY LUNN

This famous bread from Bath in England is said to have been brought to America by the English settlers. It is well known all over the United States but has become a popular speciality bread in the South, where it is served for lunch or tea. The American version was originally made in a Turk's-head mould, but is now less elaborate, baked in a tube tin. There are also miniature versions baked in *petit four* tins, and muffin-size versions made in muffin tins.

CRANBERRY NUT BREAD

This loaf is a bread enriched with eggs and butter, and is famous for the bright red berries that speckle the loaf. Cranberries are in season during November which is why the bread is often associated with Thanksgiving and Christmas. Cranberry nut bread is commonly given as a gift at this time and is popular for its tart taste, which is often accentuated with the flavour of orange.

ZUCCHINI BREAD

Courgettes, or zucchini as they are known in the USA, are hugely popular, not only as a side vegetable, but for use in cakes, muffins and bread. The sweet bread, made with coarsely grated courgettes, sweet spices and sugar, and enriched with eggs and oil, can be iced or served as a dessert cake.

ABOVE: Southern corn bread is made from white cornmeal.

CARIBBEAN AND MEXICAN BREADS

HARD-DOUGH BREAD

This fairly heavy tin or plaited white loaf is almost the standard Caribbean bread. It is the most popular bread for the islanders and is becoming increasingly popular in those parts of Britain or the United States with a sizeable Afro-Caribbean population. It has a dense, chewy texture and like many West Indian breads, has a distinctly sweet flavour.

JOHNNY CAKES

Johnny cakes do not seem to have a single origin. There are recipes for them in a number of cookbooks from the USA as well as those from the Caribbean. Most agree however that the word is a corruption of "journey cake" – a bread that can be packed up and given to travellers for their day's journey. In Jamaica, in corroboration of this, johnny cakes can be bought freshly made from roadside stalls all over the island. Just as there is apparently no definitive ancestry, there is equally no single recipe for johnny cakes. Recipes suggest they can be made from cornmeal, wheat flour or a mixture of both. Some contain eggs and milk, while

ABOVE: Johnny cakes are a famous Jamaican bread.

the Jamaican johnny cake is made with butter or lard and coconut oil. Here the dough is shaped into balls and fried in oil. Other johnny cakes have a batter-like consistency. Cooked on a griddle or in a pan, they are served as a flat bread.

BULLA BUNS

These are spicy, round discs. They resemble muffins in appearance but are dense, dark and spicy, flavoured with allspice and rich with raisins and molasses.

CARIBBEAN BUN

A spicy teabread, this is liberally flavoured with allspice and is packed with fruit. The round buns are dark in colour and look sticky, thanks to the molasses which gives them an intense bitter/sweet flavour. Beyond the Caribbean, the buns are often available from ethnic markets and shops in larger cities and come either in small bun sizes or as a larger loaf.

TORTILLAS

Although other wheat loaves are available, tortillas are rightly known as the bread of Mexico. Freshly made and still warm, these flat breads are an essential part of every Mexican meal. Tortillas are

ABOVE: Hard-dough bread

also used in an enormous number of Mexican dishes, wrapped round meat, fish, vegetables or cheese and eaten for street food as well as snacks, suppers and elegant dinners.

There are basically two types of tortilla. Maize tortillas are made using a type of cornmeal called *masa harina*, literally meaning dough flour. These are the older of the two, having been made and eaten by native people for literally thousands of years. Until the arrival of the Spanish in the 16th century, there was no wheat in Mexico, but in northern parts of the country where wheat flourished, wheat flour (called just flour) became the preferred choice for tortillas.

HAWAIIAN BREADS

In this delightful tropical paradise, there is a fabulous amalgamation of cultures and cuisines: along with the indigenous Hawaiians, there are Chinese, Japanese, Portuguese and people of Filipino origin.

HAWAIIAN BREAD

This is a perfect tropical bread, made with fresh coconut and macadamia nuts, which give it a delicious crunchy texture. The yeast-leavened white dough is enriched with eggs, butter and milk.

PORTUGUESE SWEET BREAD

Towards the end of the last century, Portuguese immigrants came to Hawaii to work in the sugar fields. Over the years their bread has acquired a character that is part Portuguese and part Hawaiian. The dough is usually yeast-leavened and enriched with eggs and butter. It is also made with condensed rather than fresh milk since the latter was once a scarce commodity on an island given over entirely to fields of sugar cane. Currants and raisins also go into the doughs, as well as being used for decoration. It may be baked in a round in a coil, but is more usually plaited and sprinkled with coarse granulated sugar.

BELOW: Bulla buns

BREAD OF THE DEAD

Should you visit Mexico around the 2nd of November, All Souls' Day, you may find this famous and traditional bread, called *Pan de Muerto*. It is made as part of the celebrations in memory of the deceased but paradoxically, it is not a sad day, but a fiesta. Everyone visits their relatives' graves, bringing a picnic, wearing bright colourful clothes and carrying candies and flowers along with the special bread. The bread itself comes in various forms but most often seems to be a white, yeast-risen dough, flavoured with orange and sometimes with spices. It can be a simple round or a plaited loaf coiled into a circle. The bread is then decorated with pieces of dough formed into teardrops, bones or bunches of flowers.

ABOVE: Tortillas

WEST INDIAN ROTIS

West Indian *rotis* are huge and used, as they would be in India, for mopping up stews and curries, such as curried goat. Like Indian *rotis*, they are made with chapati flour, a very fine wholemeal flour, and are cooked on a griddle. *Rotis* are best eaten warm and if you do find them in Caribbean shops, they should be sprinkled with a little water, then heated in a hot oven.

ABOVE: Spicy Caribbean bun

INDIAN BREADS

There are principally two types of Indian bread, although all share the characteristic of being flat and oval or round. In Punjab and Kashmir in the north-west and in Pakistan, Afghanistan and Bangladesh there are the naan-style breads. Their defining feature is that naans, unlike the *chapatis* and *parathas* of the south, are leavened and when cooked become light and puffy, unlike the southern breads that are unleavened and much flatter.

The north Indian breads have much in common with many of the Middle Eastern breads – they are large and flat and used as a vehicle for other foods. Recipes for naans and many breads from Syria, Egypt, Iraq and Iran are almost interchangeable. The main difference is the way in which the breads are baked.

BHAKRIS

Bhakris are flat unleavened breads made from *jowar* flour, and sometimes known as *jowar rotis*. *Jowar* is widely grown in central and southern India. The tiny green seeds from the plant can be roasted and eaten as they are, or can be milled into flour. The dough is moulded and patted flat by hand and then baked on a griddle. *Bhakris* can be plain or baked with sesame seeds, and are served with butter as a snack.

CHAPATIS

Also unleavened, chapatis are now widely known throughout Britain thanks to the popularity of Indian food. While once a more exotic request from a restaurant menu, chapatis are now almost common-place, although the commercially available product is a rather poor imitation of the real thing. In India the chapati is popular in central and southern parts of the country, served with meals and used with the fingers to scoop up food and sauces. These authentic chapatis are made with *atta* (chapati flour), which is a very fine wholemeal flour.

ROTLAS

There are many variations of chapatis, called *rotlas*, *rotis*, and *dana rotis* to name but a few. They are all unleavened breads, made using wholemeal flour, to which ghee, oil, celery seeds and/or fresh coriander might be added. They are rolled out until thin and cooked like chapatis.

PARATHAS

Parathas are a richer and flakier version of chapatis. The chapati dough is spread with ghee, folded and then cooked over a *tava* (griddle) until puffy.

POORIS (PURIS)

These are puffier still and are available (and worth eating) only from a restaurant or by making them yourself, since they need to be eaten as soon as possible after cooking. They are normally made using a chapati dough. Small balls of dough are rolled out into 2.5cm/1in rounds and deep fried on both sides.

NAAN

The naan, unlike the chapatis of the south, is a leavened bread. The leaven varies from region to region and probably from home to home, according to the cook's preferred method. Yeast or a sourdough method can be used; others prefer using a chemical raising agent, such as bicarbonate of soda or self-raising flour. Yogurt, however, is the main ingredient that differentiates naans from its many Middle Eastern counterparts. It plays a part in fermenting the dough and some naan are made entirely using a yogurt fermentation. It is this fermentation that gives the bread its characteristic light and puffy texture and soft crust. The flavour comes

BELOW: Parathas are cooked with ghee and therefore have a golden appearance. Chapatis are cooked without any fat or oil and are thus flatter. They do not have the golden crust.

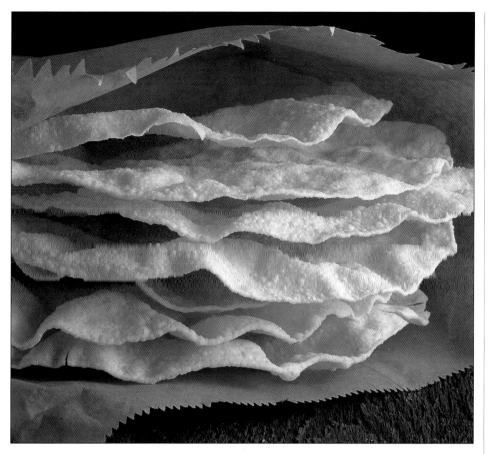

LEFT: *Poppadoms are popular everywhere with Indian food.*

teardrop shape. As the dough bakes, it scorches and puffs up to give a bread that is both crisp and soft in parts.

GOAN BATCH BREAD

In Goa, until recently part of Portuguese India, there is a white loaf called *pio*, possibly a corruption of *pao*, the Portuguese word for bread.

POPPADOMS

These thin crisp discs are widely available outside India, either ready-cooked or ready-to-cook. In India they are commonly served with vegetarian meals. Poppadoms are sold in markets and by street vendors: plain or flavoured with spices or seasoned with black or red pepper. The dough is generally made from dried pulses, but can also be made from potatoes or sago. It is then rolled thinly and left to dry in the sun. Poppadoms can be cooked by either deep frying or placing under a hot grill. Either way they brown in seconds and need close attention while cooking.

partly from the soured yogurt and partly, without doubt, from the *tandoor*, in which breads are traditionally cooked. A *tandoor* is a clay oven sunk into the ground and the flattened dough is baked against the blisteringly hot walls of the oven. The pull of gravity produces the

RIGHT:
*Naans can be
plain or stuffed.*

AUSTRALIAN BREADS

Australia, like other countries with large immigrant communities, has a wealth of wonderful breads whose origins lie in far off lands, plus one bread which is indigenous to the country, the famous damper. Once baked in the bush, in the embers of campfires, damper is today a favourite "barbie" food, and is almost as popular outside Australia as it originally was in the Outback.

In recent years there has been something of a revolution in Australian cooking, with some of the world's most innovative chefs producing delicious dishes based on the fine fresh ingredients for which the country is famous. Part of this revolution has been a back-to-basics approach, with more cooks seeking to get away from bland, mass-produced meals in favour of "real" food.

This is certainly true of baked goods. There has been a move away from the handy yet often horrid "cotton wool" breads, which once stacked every supermarket bakery shelf, and a return to real bread, with texture and taste.

Australian versions of Italian breads, such as focaccia, ciabatta, olive Toscano, *casalinga* and *bassotto*, and flat, Turkish

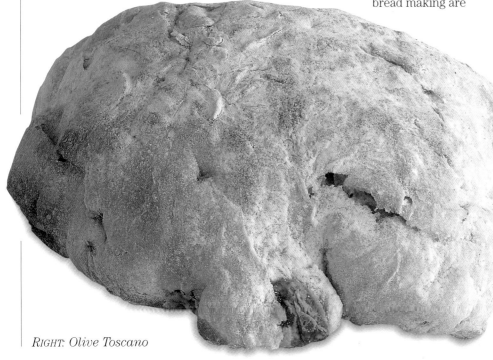

Above: The colourful and unusual vegetable il gianfornaio

bread are becoming increasingly popular, as is the brightly coloured *il gianfornaio*, which is a mosaic of red, green, yellow and orange doughs, each flavoured with a different coloured vegetable.

Leading the revolution in Australian bread making are small wood-burning bakeries, such as New Norcia in Western Australia. New Norcia is a monastic town, some 83 miles (133km) north-east of Perth. The wood-fired oven that had produced bread for the Benedictine Monks for over a century was shut down in 1989. Four years later it was fired again, and now produces – and sells – a wide range of breads, from a simple old-fashioned white loaf to their popular zucchini (courgette) bread. The monks also bake their own focaccia, an olive bread and an olive, rosemary and sun-dried tomato bread.

The breads proved so popular that a second wood-fired bakery was opened, this time in the city of Perth. Here the range is even more extensive, and includes several sourdoughs such as raisin and walnut sourdough, San Franciscan sourdough and both a light rye and a dark rye sourdough. Their unusual fig and fennel sourdough is very popular.

Supermarkets, too, have become much more adventurous, and the range of what are loosely termed "Continental breads" includes mixed grain and rye loaves with flavourings as diverse as

RIGHT: Olive Toscano

ABOVE: Ciabatta

sunflower seed and pineapple, walnut and fruit, and herb and tomato.

Many Australians bake their own bread, whether in ovens or bread-making machines, and the range of bread mixes available is almost as interesting as the variety of breads on sale in bakeries.

AUSTRALIAN SOURDOUGH

There are a number of sourdoughs made by craft bakers. Some are made to French recipes, using a similar recipe to that used

for the French *pain de campagne*. Potato sourdoughs, made with a potato starter, are similar to San Franciscan sourdoughs.

OLIVE TOSCANO

Like the Italian *pane Toscano*, this is a crusty, close-textured, and slightly chewy bread, made without any salt. Olive Toscano has green olives added to the dough, which add flavour and contrast well with the salt-free crumb.

DAMPER BREAD

Damper bread is the most famous and probably the only traditional bread of Australia. Like the United States' Native

LEFT: Potato sourdough

ABOVE: Bassotto

American bread, it is designed to be made in the open country – in this case, in the bush. The dough, made from wheat flour and water, and sometimes flavoured with spices, is patted into cakes and baked either on hot stones or under a pot. The name "damper" comes from the fact that the fire was damped down so that the embers were just the right heat for

RIGHT: Flat Turkish bread has become one of Australia's favourite breads.

DR ALLINSON

This bread is based on the original recipe that Dr Allinson developed in the 19th century. It is a yeast-leavened bread made of organic stoneground wholemeal flour and canola (a type of cereal) and is rolled in sesame seeds before being baked in a deep-sided loaf tin.

cooking the bread. Damper bread was also sometimes made by wrapping the dough around sticks and baking it over the fire – the same method as was used for a traditional South African bread called stick bread. The sticks are removed after cooking and the holes in the bread filled with either cheese or butter.

RIGHT: Densely textured rye bread (left) and farmer rye are generally available from bakeries in the larger Australian cities.

TURKISH BREAD

Turkish bread is one of the most popular breads in Australia, particularly in Sydney. The same as Turkish *ekmet*, it too can come in varying sizes, from small rounds to large ovals. The best breads are made according to traditional Turkish methods, and are baked in wood-burning stoves.

RYE BREAD

There are various rye breads available in the cities; farmer rye is a small dense loaf, while a lite rye has a much lighter flavour and texture with a hint of malt. *Black rye* is strictly for rye lovers, and is made to an old European recipe, using a rye sourdough starter, blended with stoneground rye and wheat flour.

LEFT: Dr Allinson bread is made from organic flour and is rolled in sesame seeds before being baked in a loaf tin.

CHINESE BREADS

While for the people of southern China rice is the staple food, in the wheat-growing region of the north, bread is eaten in lieu of rice.

French-style baked loaves and rolls are becoming increasingly popular throughout the country (especially in the cities), but the traditional breads are almost always steamed. Some *dim sum* breads are fried or baked on a griddle.

MAN TO

Man to are widely eaten throughout the north of China. The small, steaming hot buns are sold everywhere – in restaurants and teahouses, on street stalls and by itinerant sellers. They are eaten sometimes as snacks, but more commonly as the traditional accompaniment to a meal, in the same way as those in the southwest of the country eat rice. They are made from white flour, yeast and sugar and then formed into small balls and steamed in wicker baskets for about 20 minutes. *Man to* have the consistency of many of the steamed *dim sum* dumplings. They can also be added to soups and other dishes.

CHICKEN BUNS (GEE BAO)

These are little steamed buns filled with a mixture of chicken and oyster sauce, and served as *dim sum*.

SPRING ONION BREAD (CHUNG YAU BENG)

From Hong Kong comes this extraordinary pan-fried bread, made uniquely using a hot roux (a cooked flour and butter paste) that is worked into a similar dough made with cold water. The complicated process involves spreading each piece of dough with a hot oil and flour roux, and then finally rolling it up with spring onions. This is not a recipe for the faint hearted, but if you are lucky you may be offered these treats at a restaurant. The ring-shaped breads are fried in oil and have a delicious crisp outside while inside you bite into layers of soft dough around the spring onions.

SWEET BUNS (HWA JWEN)

These sweet steamed buns are a popular snack food.

PEONY BUNS

These pretty buns are often served as a sweetmeat in Hong Kong. Like *chung yau beng* they are made from two types of dough, the first made by mixing three parts wheat flour with one part root flour, and adding lard, sugar and water. A second dough, made simply from cornflour and lard, is then prepared. Both doughs are divided into 12 balls and the more elaborate dough is wrapped around the simpler one. Each ball is then rolled to a round and spread with lotus seed paste before being shaped once more into a ball. A star-shape is cut in the top of each bun and they are then deep-fried until they are crisp. The points of the star on each bun open out to create the peony shape for which the buns are named.

LEFT: Pineapple (left) and cocktail pork man to (steamed buns)

JAPANESE BREADS

There is no tradition of breadmaking in Japan. Rice was, and still is, the staple food and, until relatively recently, bread was completely unknown to all but the most travelled of the Japanese. Japan, unlike other countries in Asia, was virtually untouched by European influences until around the middle of the last century when a new philosophy was adopted and the country began to court positively the governments of Europe. Many Japanese were sent to France, Britain, Holland and Germany to see what could be learnt from the West in terms of seafaring, technology and government. Foodstuffs were probably not high on the agenda, but inevitably these Japanese visitors would have been struck by the concept of baking a food made from the flour of a grain. Recipes were taken back to Japan and very gradually more and more people acquired a liking for bread so that by the middle of this century, a few Japanese bakeries sprang up, making

RIGHT: Melon (left) and melon and milk chocolate rolls have a soft crumb.

breads often in the image of favourite breads from Britain and France but with their own special character.

DOUBLE SOFT WHITE

This is a typical and extremely popular Japanese loaf, which is simply the Japanese version of an English white loaf. Indeed it is often known as "English bread" and in shape is like a tin loaf. However, the flour used by Japanese bakers is particularly soft and dense and the bread has more the texture of a soft milk bread, with a similar soft smooth

LEFT: Double soft white is about the most popular Japanese bread

crust. The bread is normally cut into thick slices and then lightly toasted and eaten with butter or, more conventionally in Japan, with a spread or fruit conserve.

JAPANESE FRENCH BREAD

This is simply a French baguette, but again made with the very soft Japanese flour, so that the crumb is slightly denser and the crust less fragile than that on an authentic baguette. It can be used for sandwiches or eaten by itself with butter or a spread.

MELON BREAD

A flavoured bread, this one is popular in Britain among Japanese expatriots. The breads can be loaf-shaped but are more commonly made as rolls. Melon and milk chocolate rolls contain chunks of chocolate and are a popular tea-time bread.

JAPANESE CREAM BREAD

These small soft rolls contain cream and are consequently very soft, not unlike an English bridge roll. Like the soft white bread, these rolls are eaten at tea time with a conserve or even with butter.

RIGHT: Japanese cream bread: these small soft rolls are enriched with cream.

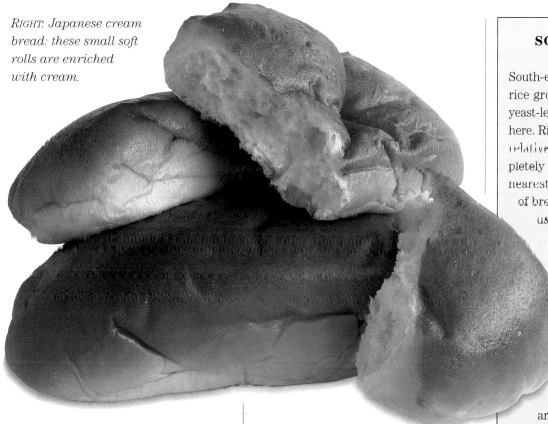

JAPANESE RAISIN BREAD

A simple white fruit bread, this may be tin-baked or baked in the oven so that it is evenly crusty.

JAPANESE CREAM FAIRY-TALE ROLLS

These popular tea-time rolls are filled with cream and sometimes with a mixture of chocolate and cream.

RED BEAN ROLLS

Red bean rolls are a delicious combination of ideas and flavours from countries with very different culinary back-grounds. From the outside these little bread rolls look similar to large English muffins – soft white breads with a thin, chewy crust. Inside though, these little rolls have a delicious sweet filling that is typically Japanese – red bean paste with its distinctive sweet and sour flavour. Red bean rolls are an extremely popular treat at tea time.

JAPANESE CURRY BREAD

Like red bean rolls, these are a delicious "East meets West" dish. The breads are deep fried and have a curry-flavoured filling of potatoes, with a hint of meat.

SOUTH-EAST ASIAN BREADS

South-east Asia is part of the largest rice growing area of the world and yeast-leavened breads are not typical here. Rice is the staple food and until relatively recently bread was completely unknown. Rice cakes are the nearest thing to the Western idea of bread. Flat and sticky, they are usually sweetened and eaten as delicacies and sweets.

However, bread is not unheard of in South-east Asia. Western influences mean that there is now an established appetite for American and European foods and bread is becoming more popular. In Indonesia, flour mills are now springing up and much of the flour is used for bread making. One favourite white bread is called *roti tawar*. Another bread, *panada*, shows a more adventurous spirit, combining wheat flour with coconut milk. These light, sweet rolls sometimes have vegetable or meat fillings.

LEFT: Japanese Curry bread

BREAD RECIPES OF THE WORLD

There are few things more pleasurable than the aroma and taste of freshly cooked home-made bread. This collection of recipes includes savoury and sweet classics from around the world, as well as a good selection of lesser-known specialities. A wide variety of flours, all of which are readily available, has been used to create distinctive breads which reflect the different flavours of the regions. These recipes aim to take the mystery out of bread making and inspire you to try baking many different and delicious breads.

BRITISH BREADS

The range of British breads is extensive and includes a variety of shapes with picturesque names, including the bloomer, cob, split tin, cottage loaf and ornamental harvest loaf. The textures and tastes are influenced by different ingredients and cooking methods. Irish soda bread, as its name suggests, is leavened with bicarbonate of soda instead of yeast, while in Scotland, where bannocks and oatcakes are cooked on a girdle or griddle, grains such as barley and oatmeal contribute to the country-fresh flavours. Doughs enriched with dried fruits, such as Welsh bara brith and Cornish saffron bread, are delicious regional specialities.

GRANARY COB

450g/1lb/4 cups Granary or malthouse flour
10ml/2 tsp salt
15g/½ oz fresh yeast
300ml/½ pint/1¼ cups lukewarm water or milk and water mixed

FOR THE TOPPING
30ml/2 tbsp water
2.5ml/½ tsp salt
wheat flakes or cracked wheat, to sprinkle

MAKES 1 ROUND LOAF

Cob is an old word meaning "head". If you make a slash across the top of the dough, the finished loaf, known as a Danish cob, will look like a large roll. A Coburg cob has a cross cut in the top before baking.

1 Lightly flour a baking sheet. Sift the flour and salt together in a large bowl and make a well in the centre. Place in a very low oven for 5 minutes to warm.

2 Mix the yeast with a little of the water or milk mixture then blend in the rest. Add the yeast mixture to the centre of the flour and mix to a dough.

3 Turn out on to a lightly floured surface and knead for about 10 minutes until smooth and elastic. Place in a lightly oiled bowl, cover with lightly oiled clear film and leave to rise, in a warm place, for 1¼ hours, or until doubled in bulk.

4 Turn the dough out on to a lightly floured surface and knock back. Knead for 2–3 minutes, then roll into a ball, making sure the dough looks like a plump round cushion, otherwise it will become too flat. Place in the centre of the prepared baking sheet. Cover with an inverted bowl and leave to rise, in a warm place, for 30–45 minutes.

5 Mix the water and salt and brush over the bread. Sprinkle with wheat flakes or cracked wheat.

6 Meanwhile, preheat the oven to 230°C/450°F/Gas 8. Bake for 15 minutes, then reduce the oven temperature to 200°C/400°F/Gas 6 and bake for a further 20 minutes, or until the loaf is firm to the touch and sounds hollow when tapped on the base. Cool on a wire rack.

GRANT LOAVES

This quick and easy recipe was created by Doris Grant and was included in her cookbook, published in the 1940s – the dough requires no kneading and takes only a minute to mix. The loaves should keep moist for several days.

1.4kg/3lb/12 cups wholemeal bread flour
15ml/1 tbsp salt
15ml/1 tbsp easy-blend dried yeast
1.2 litres/2 pints/5 cups warm water (35–38°C)
15ml/1 tbsp muscovado sugar

MAKES 3 LOAVES

1 Thoroughly grease 3 loaf tins, each about 21 × 11 × 6cm/8½ × 4½ × 2½ in and set aside in a warm place. Sift the flour and salt together in a large bowl and warm slightly to take off the chill.

2 Sprinkle the dried yeast over 150ml/ ¼ pint/⅔ cup of the water. After a couple of minutes stir in the sugar. Leave for 10 minutes.

COOK'S TIP
Muscovado sugar gives this bread a rich flavour. An unrefined cane sugar, it is dark and moist.

3 Make a well in the centre of the flour and stir in the yeast mixture and remaining water. The dough should be slippery. Mix for about 1 minute, working the sides into the middle.

4 Divide among the prepared tins, cover with oiled clear film and leave to rise, in a warm place, for 30 minutes, or until the dough has risen by about a third to within 1cm/½ in of the top of the tins.

5 Meanwhile, preheat the oven to 200°C/ 400°F/Gas 6. Bake for 40 minutes, or until the loaves are crisp and sound hollow when tapped on the base. Turn out on to a wire rack to cool.

POPPY-SEEDED BLOOMER

*675g/1½ lb/6 cups unbleached white
bread flour
10ml/2 tsp salt
15g/½ oz fresh yeast
430ml/15fl oz/1⅞ cups water*

*FOR THE TOPPING
2.5ml/½ tsp salt
30ml/2 tbsp water
poppy seeds, for sprinkling*

MAKES 1 LARGE LOAF

*This satisfying white bread, which is the British version of the chunky baton
loaf found throughout Europe, is made by a slower rising method and with
less yeast than usual. It produces a longer-keeping loaf with a fuller flavour.
The dough takes about 8 hours to rise, so you'll need to start this bread
early in the morning.*

1 Lightly grease a baking sheet. Sift the flour and salt together into a large bowl and make a well in the centre.

2 Mix the yeast and 150ml/¼ pint/⅔ cup of the water in a jug or bowl. Mix in the remaining water. Add to the centre of the flour. Mix, gradually incorporating the surrounding flour, until the mixture forms a firm dough.

COOK'S TIP
The traditional cracked, crusty appearance of this loaf is difficult to achieve in a domestic oven. However, you can get a similar result by spraying the oven with water before baking. If the underneath of the loaf is not very crusty at the end of baking, turn the loaf over on the baking sheet, switch off the heat and leave in the oven for a further 5–10 minutes.

VARIATION
For a more rustic loaf, replace up to half the flour with wholemeal bread flour.

3 Turn out on to a lightly floured surface and knead the dough very well, for at least 10 minutes, until smooth and elastic. Place the dough in a lightly oiled bowl, cover with lightly oiled clear film and leave to rise, at cool room temperature, about 15–18°C/60–65°F, for 5–6 hours, or until doubled in bulk.

4 Knock back the dough, turn out on to a lightly floured surface and knead it thoroughly and quite hard for about 5 minutes. Return the dough to the bowl, and re-cover. Leave to rise, at cool room temperature, for a further 2 hours or slightly longer.

5 Knock back again and repeat the thorough kneading. Leave the dough to rest for 5 minutes, then roll out on a lightly floured surface into a rectangle 2.5cm/1in thick. Roll the dough up from one long side and shape it into a square-ended thick baton shape about 33 × 13cm/13 × 5in.

6 Place it seam side up on a lightly floured baking sheet, cover and leave to rest for 15 minutes. Turn the loaf over and place on the greased baking sheet. Plump up by tucking the dough under the sides and ends. Using a sharp knife, cut 6 diagonal slashes on the top.

7 Leave to rest, covered, in a warm place, for 10 minutes. Meanwhile preheat the oven to 230°C/450°F/Gas 8.

8 Mix the salt and water together and brush this glaze over the bread. Sprinkle with poppy seeds.

9 Spray the oven with water, bake the bread immediately for 20 minutes, then reduce the oven temperature to 200°C/400°F/Gas 6; bake for 25 minutes more, or until golden. Transfer to a wire rack to cool.

COTTAGE LOAF

*675g/1½ lb/6 cups unbleached white
bread flour
10ml/2 tsp salt
20g/¾ oz fresh yeast
400ml/14fl oz/1⅔ cups lukewarm
water*

MAKES 1 LARGE ROUND LOAF

COOK'S TIPS

• To ensure a good-shaped cottage loaf
the dough needs to be firm enough to
support the weight of the top ball.
• Do not over-prove the dough on
the second rising or the loaf may
topple over – but even if it does it will
still taste good.

*Snipping the top and bottom sections of the dough at 5cm/2in intervals not
only looks good but also helps the loaf to expand in the oven.*

1 Lightly grease 2 baking sheets. Sift the
flour and salt together into a large bowl
and make a well in the centre.

2 Mix the yeast in 150ml/¼ pint/⅔ cup
of the water until dissolved. Pour into
the centre of the flour with the
remaining water and mix to a firm dough.

3 Knead on a lightly floured surface for
10 minutes until smooth and elastic.
Place in a lightly oiled bowl, cover with
lightly oiled clear film and leave to rise,
in a warm place, for about 1 hour, or
until doubled in bulk.

4 Turn out on to a lightly floured surface
and knock back. Knead for 2–3 minutes
then divide the dough into two-thirds
and one-third; shape each to a ball.

5 Place the balls of dough on the prepared
baking sheets. Cover with inverted bowls
and leave to rise, in a warm place, for
about 30 minutes (see Cook's Tips).

6 Gently flatten the top of the larger
round of dough and, with a sharp knife,
cut a cross in the centre, about 4cm/
1½ in across. Brush with a little water
and place the smaller round on top.

7 Carefully press a hole through the
middle of the top ball, down into the
lower part, using your thumb and first
two fingers of one hand. Cover with
lightly oiled clear film and leave to rest
in a warm place for about 10 minutes.
Preheat the oven to 220°C/ 425°F/Gas 7
and place the bread on the lower shelf.
It will finish expanding as the oven heats
up. Bake for 35–40 minutes, or until
golden brown and sounding hollow
when tapped. Cool on a wire rack.

CHEESE AND ONION LOAF

Almost a meal in itself, this hearty bread tastes delicious as an accompaniment to salads and cold meats, or with soup.

1 Lightly grease a 25 × 10cm/10 × 4in loaf tin. Melt 25g/1oz/2 tbsp of the butter in a heavy-based frying pan and sauté the onion until it is soft and light golden. Set aside to cool.

2 Sift the flour into a large bowl and stir in the yeast, mustard, salt and pepper. Stir in three-quarters of the grated cheese and the onion. Make a well in the centre. Add the milk and water; blend to a soft dough. Turn out on to a lightly floured surface and knead for 10 minutes until smooth and elastic.

3 Place the dough in a lightly oiled bowl, cover with lightly oiled clear film and leave to rise, in a warm place, for 45–60 minutes, or until doubled in bulk.

4 Turn the dough out on to a lightly floured surface, knock back, and knead gently. Divide into 20 equal pieces and shape into small rounds. Place half in the prepared tin and brush with some melted butter. Top with the remaining rounds of dough and brush with the remaining butter.

5 Cover with oiled clear film and leave to rise for 45 minutes, until the dough reaches the top of the tin. Meanwhile, preheat the oven to 190°C/375°F/Gas 5.

6 Sprinkle the remaining cheese over the top. Bake for 40–45 minutes or until risen and golden brown. Cool on a wire rack.

1 onion, finely chopped
45g/1¾oz/3½ tbsp butter
450g/1lb/4 cups unbleached white bread flour
6g/¼oz sachet easy-blend dried yeast
5ml/1 tsp mustard powder
175g/6oz/1½ cups grated mature Cheddar cheese
150ml/¼ pint/⅔ cup lukewarm milk
150ml/¼ pint/⅔ cup lukewarm water
salt and ground black pepper

MAKES 1 LARGE LOAF

COOK'S TIP
If you prefer, use 20g/¾ oz fresh yeast instead of the easy-blend yeast. Mix the fresh yeast with the milk until dissolved, then add to the flour.

SPLIT TIN

*500g/1¼lb/5 cups unbleached white
bread flour, plus extra for dusting
10ml/2 tsp salt
15g/½oz fresh yeast
300ml/½ pint/1¼ cups lukewarm
water
60ml/4 tbsp lukewarm milk*

MAKES 1 LOAF

*As its name suggests, this homely loaf is so called because of the centre split.
Some bakers mould the dough in two loaves – they join together whilst
proving but retain the characteristic crack after baking.*

1 Lightly grease a 900g/2lb loaf tin
(18.5 × 11.5cm/7¼ × 4½in). Sift the
flour and salt together into a large bowl
and make a well in the centre. Mix the
yeast with half the lukewarm water in a
jug, then stir in the remaining water.

2 Pour the yeast mixture into the centre
of the flour and using your fingers, mix
in a little flour. Gradually mix in more of
the flour from around the edge of the
bowl to form a thick, smooth batter.

3 Sprinkle a little more flour from
around the edge over the batter and
leave in a warm place to "sponge".
Bubbles will appear in the batter after
about 20 minutes. Add the milk and
remaining flour; mix to a firm dough.

4 Place on a lightly floured surface and
knead for about 10 minutes until smooth
and elastic. Place in a lightly oiled bowl,
cover with lightly oiled clear film and
leave to rise, in a warm place, for 1–1¼
hours, or until nearly doubled in bulk.

5 Knock back the dough and turn out on
to a lightly floured surface. Shape it into
a rectangle, the length of the tin. Roll up
lengthways, tuck the ends under and
place seam side down in the prepared
tin. Cover and leave to rise, in a warm
place, for about 20–30 minutes, or until
nearly doubled in bulk.

6 Using a sharp knife, make one deep
central slash the length of the bread;
dust with flour. Leave for 10–15 minutes.

7 Meanwhile, preheat the oven to 230°C/
450°F/Gas 8. Bake for 15 minutes, then
reduce the oven temperature to 200°C/
400°F/Gas 6. Bake for 20–25 minutes
more, or until the bread is golden and
sounds hollow when tapped on the base.
Turn out on to a wire rack to cool.

WELSH CLAY POT LOAVES

These breads are flavoured with chives, sage, parsley and garlic. You can use any selection of your favourite herbs. For even more flavour, try adding a little grated raw onion and grated cheese to the dough.

115g/4oz/1 cup wholemeal bread flour
350g/12oz/3 cups unbleached white
bread flour
7.5ml/1½ tsp salt
15g/½ oz fresh yeast
150ml/¼ pint/⅔ cup lukewarm milk
120ml/4fl oz/½ cup lukewarm water
70g/2oz/¼ tbsp butter, melted
15ml/1 tbsp chopped fresh chives
15ml/1 tbsp chopped fresh parsley
5ml/1 tsp chopped fresh sage
1 garlic clove, crushed
beaten egg, for glazing
fennel seeds, for sprinkling (optional)

MAKES 2 LOAVES

COOK'S TIP
To prepare and seal new clay flower pots, clean them thoroughly, oil them inside and outside and bake them three or four times. Preheat the oven to about 200°C/400°F/Gas 6 and bake for 30–40 minutes. Try to do this while you are baking other foods.

1 Lightly grease 2 clean 14cm/5½ in diameter, 11cm/4½ in high clay flower pots. Sift the flours and salt together into a large bowl and make a well in the centre. Blend the yeast with a little of the milk until smooth, then stir in the remaining milk. Pour the yeast liquid into the centre of the flour and sprinkle over a little of the flour from around the edge. Cover the bowl and leave in a warm place for 15 minutes.

2 Add the water, melted butter, herbs and garlic to the flour mixture and blend together to form a dough. Turn out on to a lightly floured surface and knead for about 10 minutes until the dough is smooth and elastic.

3 Place in a lightly oiled bowl, cover with lightly oiled clear film and leave to rise, in a warm place, for 1¼–1½ hours, or until doubled in bulk.

4 Turn the dough out on to a lightly floured surface and knock back. Divide in two. Shape and fit into the prepared flower pots. They should about half fill the pots. Cover with oiled clear film and leave to rise for 30–45 minutes, in a warm place, or until the dough is 2.5cm/1in from the top of the pots.

5 Meanwhile, preheat the oven to 200°C/400°F/Gas 6. Brush the tops with beaten egg and sprinkle with fennel seeds, if using. Bake for 35–40 minutes or until golden. Turn out on to a wire rack to cool.

HARVEST FESTIVAL SHEAF

This is one of the most visually stunning breads. Celebratory loaves can be seen in various forms in churches and at some bakers throughout Britain around the September harvest.

900g/2lb/8 cups unbleached white bread flour
15ml/1 tbsp salt
15g/½oz fresh yeast
75ml/5 tbsp lukewarm milk
400ml/14fl oz/1⅔ cups cold water

FOR THE TOPPING
1 egg
15ml/1 tbsp milk

MAKES 1 LARGE LOAF

1 Lightly grease a large baking sheet, at least 38 × 33cm/15 × 13in. Sift the flour and salt together into a large bowl and make a well in the centre.

2 Cream the yeast with the milk in a jug. Add to the centre of the flour with the water and mix to a stiff dough. Turn out on to a lightly floured surface and knead for about 10–15 minutes until smooth and elastic.

3 Place in a lightly oiled bowl, cover with lightly oiled clear film and leave to rise, at room temperature, for about 2 hours, or until doubled in bulk.

4 Turn the dough out on to a lightly floured surface, knock back and knead for about 1 minute. Cover and leave to rest for 10 minutes.

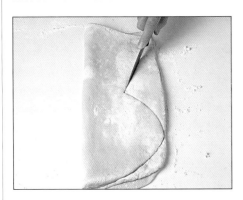

5 Divide the dough in two. Roll out one piece to a 35 × 24cm/14 × 10in oblong. Fold loosely in half lengthways. Using a sharp knife, cut out a half mushroom shape for the sheaf (leave the folded edge uncut). Make the stalk "base" about 18cm/7in long.

6 Place the dough on the prepared baking sheet and open out. Prick all over with a fork and brush with water to prevent a skin from forming. Reserve 75g/3oz of the trimmings for the tie. Cover and set aside. Divide the remaining dough in two pieces and mix the rest of the trimmings with one half. Cover and set aside. Beat together the egg and milk for the glaze.

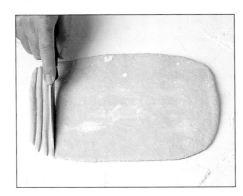

7 Roll out the remaining dough on a lightly floured surface to a rectangle, 28 × 18cm/11 × 7in, and cut into 30–35 thin strips 18cm/7in long. Place side by side lengthways on the base, as close as possible, to represent wheat stalks. Brush with some glaze.

8 Take the larger piece of reserved dough and divide into four. Divide each piece into about 25 and shape into oblong rolls to make about 100 wheat ears. Make each roll pointed at one end.

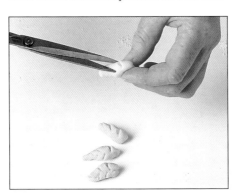

9 Holding one roll at a time, snip along each side towards the centre, using scissors, to make wheat ear shapes.

10 Preheat the oven to 220°C/425°F/Gas 7. Arrange the ears around the outer edge of the top of the mushroom shape, overlapping on to the baking sheet. Repeat a second row lower down, placing the row between the first ears. Repeat until they are all used. Brush with some glaze as you proceed to prevent the dough from drying out.

11 Divide the smaller piece of reserved dough into 6 pieces and roll each to a 43cm/17in strip. Make 2 plaits each with 3 strips. Place across the wheat stalks to make a tied bow. Brush with some glaze. Prick between the wheat ears and stalks using a sharp knife and bake the sheaf for 15 minutes.

12 Reduce the oven temperature to 180°C/350°F/Gas 4. Brush the bread with the remaining glaze and bake for a further 30–35 minutes, or until golden and firm. Leave to cool on the baking sheet.

COOK'S TIPS
• Check the bread occasionally while baking, and cover the ends with foil after the first 15 minutes if they start to over-brown.
• Harvest loaves are often baked for display, rather than for eating. If you'd like to do this, then leave the baked loaf in the oven, reduce the temperature to very low, 120°C/250°F/Gas ½, for several hours until the dough dries out.

SCOTTISH MORNING ROLLS

450g/1lb/4 cups unbleached plain white flour, plus extra for dusting
10ml/2 tsp salt
20g/¾ oz fresh yeast
150ml/¼ pint/⅔ cup lukewarm milk
150ml/¼ pint/⅔ cup lukewarm water
30ml/2 tbsp milk, for glazing

MAKES 10 ROLLS

These rolls are best served warm, as soon as they are baked. In Scotland they are a firm favourite for breakfast with a fried egg and bacon.

1 Grease 2 baking sheets. Sift the flour and salt together into a large bowl and make a well in the centre. Mix the yeast with the milk, then mix in the water. Add to the centre of the flour and mix together to form a soft dough.

2 Knead the dough lightly in the bowl, then cover with lightly oiled clear film and leave to rise, in a warm place, for 1 hour, or until doubled in bulk. Turn the dough out on to a lightly floured surface and knock back.

3 Divide the dough into 10 equal pieces. Knead lightly and, using a rolling pin, shape each piece to a flat oval 10 × 7.5cm/4 × 3in or a flat round 9cm/3½ in.

4 Transfer to the prepared baking sheets, spaced well apart, and cover with oiled clear film. Leave to rise, in a warm place, for about 30 minutes.

5 Meanwhile, preheat the oven to 200°C/ 400°F/Gas 6. Press each roll in the centre with the three middle fingers to equalise the air bubbles and to help prevent blistering. Brush with milk and dust with flour. Bake for 15–20 minutes or until lightly browned. Dust with more flour and cool slightly on a wire rack. Serve warm.

SHAPED DINNER ROLLS

These professional-looking rolls are perfect for entertaining. You can always make double the amount of dough and freeze half, tightly wrapped. Just thaw, glaze and bake as required.

450g/1lb/4 cups unbleached white
bread flour
10ml/2 tsp salt
2.5ml/½ tsp caster sugar
6g/¼oz sachet easy-blend dried yeast
50g/2oz/¼ cup butter or margarine
250ml/8fl oz/1 cup lukewarm milk
1 egg

FOR THE TOPPING
1 egg yolk
15ml/1 tbsp water
poppy seeds and sesame seeds,
for sprinkling

MAKES 12 ROLLS

1 Lightly grease 2 baking sheets. Sift the flour and salt together into a large bowl and stir in the sugar and yeast. Add the butter or margarine and rub in until the mixture resembles fine breadcrumbs.

3 Turn the dough out on to a lightly floured surface, knock back and knead for 2–3 minutes. Divide the dough into 12 equal pieces and shape into rolls as described in steps 4–8.

5 *To make trefoils:* divide each piece of dough into three and roll into balls. Place the three balls together in a triangular shape.

6 *To make batons:* shape each piece of dough into an oblong and slash the surface of each with diagonal cuts just before baking.

7 *To make cottage rolls:* divide each piece of dough into two-thirds and one-third and shape into rounds. Place the small one on top of the large one and make a hole through the centre with the handle of a wooden spoon.

8 *To make knots:* shape each piece of dough into a long roll and tie a single knot, pulling the ends through.

9 Place the dinner rolls on the prepared baking sheets, spacing them well apart, cover the rolls with oiled clear film and leave to rise, in a warm place, for about 30 minutes, or until doubled in bulk.

10 Meanwhile, preheat the oven to 220°C/425°F/Gas 7. Mix the egg yolk and water together for the glaze and brush over the rolls. Sprinkle some with poppy seeds and some with sesame seeds. Bake for 15–18 minutes or until golden. Lift the rolls off the sheet using a palette knife and transfer to a wire rack to cool.

2 Make a well in the centre. Add the milk and egg to the well and mix to a dough. Knead on a lightly floured surface for 10 minutes until smooth and elastic. Place in a lightly oiled bowl, cover with lightly oiled clear film and leave to rise, in a warm place, for 1 hour, or until doubled in bulk.

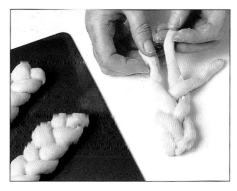

4 *To make plaits:* divide each piece of dough into three equal pieces. Working on a lightly floured surface, roll each piece to a sausage, keeping the lengths and widths even. Pinch 3 strips together at one end, then plait them neatly but not too tightly. Pinch the ends together and tuck under the plait.

IRISH SODA BREAD

225g/8oz/2 cups unbleached
plain flour
225g/8oz/2 cups wholemeal flour, plus
extra for dusting
5ml/1 tsp salt
10ml/2 tsp bicarbonate of soda
10ml/2 tsp cream of tartar
40g/1½ oz/3 tbsp butter or lard
5ml/1 tsp caster sugar
350–375ml/12–13fl oz/1½–1⅔ cups
buttermilk

MAKES 1 ROUND LOAF

VARIATION
Shape into two small loaves and bake
for 25–30 minutes.

*Soda bread can be prepared in minutes and is excellent served warm, fresh
from the oven. You can use all plain white flour, if preferred, to create a bread
with a finer texture.*

1 Preheat the oven to 190°C/375°F/Gas 5.
Lightly grease a baking sheet. Sift the
flour and salt into a large bowl.

2 Add the bicarbonate of soda and
cream of tartar, then rub in the butter or
lard. Stir in the sugar.

3 Pour in sufficient buttermilk to mix to
a soft dough. Do not over-mix or the
bread will be heavy and tough. Shape
into a round on a lightly floured surface.

4 Place on the prepared baking sheet
and mark a cross using a sharp knife,
cutting deep into the dough.

5 Dust lightly with wholemeal flour and
bake for 35–45 minutes or until well
risen and the bread sounds hollow when
tapped on the base. Serve warm.

CORNISH SAFFRON BREADS

Often called saffron cake, this light, delicately spiced bread contains strands of saffron and is made in a loaf tin. Whatever the name, the flavour and texture are superb.

300ml/½ pint/1¼ cups milk
2.5ml/½ tsp saffron strands
400g/14oz/3½ cups unbleached white bread flour
25g/1oz fresh yeast
50g/2oz/½ cup ground almonds
2.5ml/½ tsp grated nutmeg
2.5ml/½ tsp ground cinnamon
50g/2oz/¼ cup caster sugar
2.5ml/½ tsp salt
75g/3oz/6 tbsp butter, softened
50g/2oz/⅓ cup sultanas
50g/2oz/¼ cup currants

FOR THE GLAZE
30ml/2 tbsp milk
15ml/1 tbsp caster sugar

MAKES 2 LOAVES

1 Lightly grease two 900g/2lb loaf tins. Heat half the milk until almost boiling.

2 Place the saffron strands in a small heatproof bowl and pour over the milk. Stir gently, then leave to infuse for 30 minutes.

3 Heat the remaining milk in the same pan until it is just lukewarm.

4 Place 50g/2oz/½ cup flour in a small bowl, crumble in the yeast and stir in the lukewarm milk. Mix well, then leave for about 15 minutes until the yeast starts to ferment.

5 Mix the remaining flour, ground almonds, spices, sugar and salt together in a large bowl and make a well in the centre. Add the saffron infusion, yeast mixture and softened butter to the centre of the flour and mix to a very soft dough.

6 Turn out on to a lightly floured surface and knead for 5 minutes until smooth and elastic. Place in a lightly oiled bowl, cover with lightly oiled clear film and leave to rise, in a warm place, for 1½–2 hours, or until doubled in bulk.

7 Turn the dough out on to a lightly floured surface, knock back, and knead in the sultanas and currants. Divide in two and shape into two loaves. Place in the prepared tins. Cover with oiled clear film and leave to rise, in a warm place, for 1½ hours, or until the dough reaches the top of the tins.

8 Meanwhile, preheat the oven to 220°C/425°F/Gas 7. Bake the loaves for 10 minutes, then reduce the oven temperature to 190°C/375°F/Gas 5 and bake for 15–20 minutes or until golden.

9 While the loaves are baking, make the glaze. Heat the milk and sugar in a small saucepan, stirring until the sugar has dissolved. As soon as the loaves come out of the oven, brush them with the glaze, leave in the tins for 5 minutes, then turn out on to a wire rack to cool.

*225g/8oz/2 cups unbleached
plain flour
225g/8oz/2 cups unbleached white
bread flour
10ml/2 tsp salt
600ml/1 pint/2½ cups milk and
water mixed
30ml/2 tbsp sunflower oil
15ml/1 tbsp caster sugar
15g/½ oz fresh yeast
2.5ml/½ tsp bicarbonate of soda
120ml/4fl oz/½ cup lukewarm water*

MAKES ABOUT 20 CRUMPETS

COOK'S TIP
If the batter does not produce the
characteristic bubbles, add a little
more water before cooking the next
batch of crumpets.

CRUMPETS

*Home-made crumpets are less doughy and not as heavy as most supermarket
versions. Serve them lightly toasted, oozing with butter.*

1 Lightly grease a griddle or heavy-based frying pan and 4 × 8cm/3¼in plain pastry cutters or crumpet rings.

2 Sift the flours and salt together into a large bowl and make a well in the centre. Heat the milk and water mixture, oil and sugar until lukewarm. Mix the yeast with 150ml/¼ pint/⅔ cup of this liquid.

3 Add the yeast mixture and remaining liquid to the centre of the flour and beat vigorously for about 5 minutes until smooth and elastic. Cover with lightly oiled clear film and leave to rise, in a warm place, for about 1½ hours, or until the mixture is bubbly and about to fall.

4 Dissolve the soda in the lukewarm water and stir into the batter. Re-cover and leave to rise for 30 minutes.

5 Place the cutters or crumpet rings on the griddle and warm over a medium heat. Fill the cutters or rings a generous 1cm/½in deep. Cook over a gentle heat for 6–7 minutes. The tops should be dry, with a mass of tiny holes.

6 Carefully remove the cutters or rings and turn the crumpets over. Cook for 1–2 minutes or until pale golden. Repeat with remaining batter. Serve warm.

*450g/1lb/4 cups unbleached white
bread flour
7.5ml/1½ tsp salt
350–375ml/12–13fl oz/1½–1⅔ cups
lukewarm milk
2.5ml/½ tsp caster sugar
15g/½oz fresh yeast
15ml/1 tbsp melted butter or olive oil
rice flour or semolina, for dusting*

MAKES 9 MUFFINS

COOK'S TIPS
• Muffins should be cut around the
outer edge only using a sharp knife
and then torn apart. If toasting, toast
the whole muffins first and then split
them in half.
• If you'd like to serve the muffins
warm, transfer them to a wire rack to
cool slightly before serving.

ENGLISH MUFFINS

*Perfect served warm, split open and buttered for afternoon tea; or try these
favourites toasted, split and topped with ham and eggs for brunch.*

1 Generously flour a non-stick baking sheet. Very lightly grease a griddle. Sift the flour and salt together into a large bowl and make a well in the centre. Blend 150ml/¼ pint/⅔ cup of the milk, sugar and yeast together. Stir in the remaining milk and butter or oil.

2 Add the yeast mixture to the centre of the flour and beat for 4–5 minutes until smooth and elastic. The dough will be soft but just hold its shape. Cover with lightly oiled clear film and leave to rise, in a warm place, for 45–60 minutes, or until doubled in bulk.

3 Turn out the dough on a well floured surface and knock back. Roll out to about 1cm/½in thick. Using a floured 7.5cm/3in plain cutter, cut out 9 rounds.

4 Dust with rice flour or semolina and place on the prepared baking sheet. Cover and leave to rise, in a warm place, for about 20–30 minutes.

5 Warm the griddle over a medium heat. Carefully transfer the muffins in batches to the griddle. Cook slowly for about 7 minutes on each side or until golden brown. Transfer to a wire rack to cool.

LARDY CAKE

450g/1lb/4 cups unbleached white
bread flour
5ml/1 tsp salt
15g/½ oz/1 tbsp lard
25g/1oz/2 tbsp caster sugar
20g/¾ oz fresh yeast
300ml/½ pint/1¼ cups lukewarm
water

For the Filling
75g/3oz/6 tbsp lard
75g/3oz/6 tbsp soft light
brown sugar
115g/4oz/½ cup currants,
slightly warmed
75g/3oz/½ cup sultanas, slightly
warmed
25g/1oz/3 tbsp mixed chopped peel
5ml/1 tsp mixed spice

For the Glaze
10ml/2 tsp sunflower oil
15–30ml/1–2 tbsp caster sugar

Makes 1 Large Loaf

This special rich fruit bread was originally made throughout many counties of England for celebrating the harvest. Using lard rather than butter or margarine makes an authentic lardy cake.

1 Grease a 25 × 20cm/10 × 8in shallow roasting tin. Sift the flour and salt into a large bowl and rub in the lard. Stir in the sugar and make a well in the centre.

2 In a bowl, cream the yeast with half of the water, then blend in the remainder. Add to the centre of the flour and mix to a smooth dough.

3 Turn out on to a lightly floured surface and knead for about 10 minutes until smooth and elastic. Place in a lightly oiled bowl, cover with lightly oiled clear film and leave to rise, in a warm place, for 1 hour, or until doubled in bulk.

4 Turn the dough out on to a lightly floured surface and knock back. Knead for 2 3 minutes. Roll into a rectangle about 5mm/¼ in thick.

5 Using half the lard for the filling, cover the top two-thirds of the dough with flakes of lard. Sprinkle over half the sugar, half the dried fruits and peel and half the mixed spice. Fold the bottom third up and the top third down, sealing the edges with the rolling pin.

6 Turn the dough by 90 degrees. Repeat the rolling and cover with the remaining lard, fruit and peel and mixed spice. Fold, seal and turn as before. Roll out the dough to fit the prepared tin. Cover with lightly oiled clear film and leave to rise, in a warm place, for 30–45 minutes, or until doubled in size.

7 Meanwhile, preheat the oven to 200°C/400°F/Gas 6. Brush the top of the lardy cake with sunflower oil and sprinkle with caster sugar.

8 Score a criss-cross pattern on top using a sharp knife, then bake for 30–40 minutes until golden. Turn out on to a wire rack to cool slightly. Serve warm, cut into slices or squares.

MALTED CURRANT BREAD

This spiced currant bread makes a good tea or breakfast bread, sliced and spread with a generous amount of butter. It also makes superb toast.

50g/2oz/3 tbsp malt extract
30ml/2 tbsp golden syrup
50g/2oz/¼ cup butter
450g/1lb/4 cups unbleached white bread flour
5ml/1 tsp mixed spice
20g/¾oz fresh yeast
175ml/6fl oz/¾ cup lukewarm milk
175g/6oz/1 cup currants, slightly warmed

FOR THE GLAZE
30ml/2 tbsp milk
30ml/2 tbsp caster sugar

MAKES 2 LOAVES

COOK'S TIP
When you are making more than one loaf, the easiest way to prove them is to place the tins in a lightly oiled large polythene bag.

1 Lightly grease two 450g/1lb loaf tins. Place the malt extract, golden syrup and butter in a saucepan and heat gently until the butter has melted. Set aside to cool completely.

2 Sift the flour and mixed spice together into a large bowl and make a well in the centre. Cream the yeast with a little of the milk, then blend in the remaining milk. Add the yeast mixture and cooled malt mixture to the centre of the flour and blend together to form a dough.

3 Turn out the dough on to a lightly floured surface and knead for about 10 minutes until smooth and elastic. Place in a lightly oiled bowl, cover with lightly oiled clear film and leave to rise, in a warm place, for 1½–2 hours, or until doubled in bulk.

4 Turn the dough out on to a lightly floured surface, knock back, then knead in the currants. Divide the dough in two and shape into two loaves. Place in the prepared tins. Cover with oiled clear film and leave to rise, in a warm place, for 2–3 hours, or until the dough reaches the top of the tins.

5 Meanwhile, preheat the oven to 200°C/400°F/Gas 6. Bake for 35–40 minutes or until golden. While the loaves are baking heat the milk and sugar for the glaze in a small saucepan. Turn out the loaves on to a wire rack, then invert them, so that they are the right way up. Immediately brush the glaze evenly over the loaves and leave to cool.

115g/4oz/1 cup barley flour
50g/2oz/½ cup unbleached plain flour
or wholemeal flour
2.5ml/½ tsp salt
2.5ml/½ tsp cream of tartar
25g/1oz/2 tbsp butter or margarine
175ml/6fl oz/¾ cup buttermilk
2.5ml/½ tsp bicarbonate of soda

MAKES 1 ROUND LOAF

COOK'S TIPS
• If you cannot locate buttermilk,
then use soured milk instead. Stir
5ml/1 tsp lemon juice into
175ml/6 fl oz/¾ cup milk and set aside
for an hour to sour.
• If you find the earthy flavour of
barley flour too strong, reduce it to
50g/2oz/¼ cup and increase the plain
white flour to 115g/4oz/1 cup.
Alternatively, replace half the barley
flour with fine oatmeal.

BARLEY BANNOCK

*Bannocks are flat loaves about the size of a dinner plate. They are
traditionally baked on a griddle or girdle (which is the preferred name in
Scotland). Barley flour adds a wonderfully earthy flavour to the bread.*

1 Wipe the surface of a griddle with a little vegetable oil. Sift the flours, salt and cream of tartar together into a large bowl. Add the butter or margarine and rub into the flour until it resembles fine breadcrumbs.

3 On a floured surface pat the dough out to form a round about 2cm/¾in thick. Mark the dough into 4 wedges, using a sharp knife, if you prefer.

2 Mix the buttermilk and bicarbonate of soda together. When the mixture starts to bubble add to the flour. Mix together to form a soft dough. Do not over-mix the dough or it will toughen.

4 Heat the griddle until hot. Cook the bannock on the griddle for about 8–10 minutes per side over a gentle heat. Do not cook too quickly or the outside will burn before the centre is cooked. Cool the bannock slightly on a wire rack and eat while still warm.

SCOTTISH OATCAKES

*The crunchy texture of these tempting oatcakes makes them difficult to resist.
Serve with butter and slices of a good mature cheese.*

*115g/4oz/1 cup medium or
fine oatmeal*
1.5ml/¼ tsp salt
pinch of bicarbonate of soda
*15ml/1 tbsp melted butter
or lard*
45–60ml/3–4 tbsp hot water

MAKES 8 OATCAKES

VARIATIONS
• Oatcakes are traditionally cooked
on the griddle, but they can also
be cooked in the oven at 180°C/
350°F/Gas 4 for about 20 minutes, or
until pale golden in colour.
• Small round oatcakes can be
stamped out using a 7.5cm/3in plain
cutter, if preferred.

1 Very lightly oil a griddle or heavy-based frying pan. Mix the oatmeal, salt and soda together in a bowl.

3 On an oatmeal-dusted surface roll each piece of dough out as thinly as possible into a round about 15cm/6in across and 5mm/¼in thick.

4 Cut each round into 4 quarters or farls. Heat the griddle over a medium heat until warm. Transfer 4 farls, using a spatula or fish slice, to the griddle and cook over a low heat for 4–5 minutes. The edges may start to curl.

2 Add the melted butter or lard and sufficient hot water to make a dough. Lightly knead on a surface dusted with oatmeal until it is smooth. Cut the dough in half.

5 Using the spatula or slice, carefully turn the farls over and cook for about 1–2 minutes. If preferred the second side can be cooked under a preheated grill until crisp, but not brown. Transfer to a wire rack to cool. Repeat with the remaining farls.

WELSH BARA BRITH

20g/¾ oz fresh yeast
210ml/7fl oz/scant 1 cup lukewarm
milk
450g/1lb/4 cups unbleached white
bread flour
75g/3oz/6 tbsp butter or lard
5ml/1 tsp mixed spice
2.5ml/½ tsp salt
50g/2oz/⅓ cup light brown sugar
1 egg, lightly beaten
115g/4oz/⅔ cup seedless raisins,
slightly warmed
75g/3oz/scant ½ cup currants,
slightly warmed
40g/1½ oz/¼ cup mixed chopped peel
15–30ml/1–2 tbsp clear honey,
for glazing

MAKES 1 LARGE ROUND LOAF

This rich, fruity bread – the name literally means "speckled bread" – is a speciality from North Wales. The honey glaze makes a delicious topping.

1 Grease a baking sheet. In a jug, blend the yeast with a little of the milk, then stir in the remainder. Set aside for 10 minutes.

2 Sift the flour into a large bowl and rub in the butter or lard until the mixture resembles breadcrumbs. Stir in the mixed spice, salt and sugar and make a well in the centre.

3 Add the yeast mixture and beaten egg to the centre of the flour and mix to a rough dough.

4 Turn out the dough on to a lightly floured surface and knead for about 10 minutes until smooth and elastic. Place in a lightly oiled bowl, cover with lightly oiled clear film and leave to rise, in a warm place, for 1½ hours, or until doubled in bulk.

5 Turn out the dough on to a lightly floured surface, knock back, and knead in the dried fruits and peel. Shape into a round and place on the prepared baking sheet. Cover with oiled clear film and leave to rise, in a warm place, for 1 hour, or until the dough doubles in size.

6 Meanwhile, preheat the oven to 200°C/400°F/Gas 6. Bake for 30 minutes or until the bread sounds hollow when tapped on the base. If the bread starts to over-brown, cover it loosely with foil for the last 10 minutes. Transfer the bread to a wire rack, brush with honey and leave to cool.

VARIATIONS
• The bara brith can be baked in a 1.5–1.75 litre/2½–3 pint/6¼–7½ cup loaf tin or deep round or square cake tin, if you prefer.
• For a more wholesome loaf, replace half the white flour with wholemeal bread flour.

SALLY LUNN

Sally Lunn is traditionally served warm sliced into three layers horizontally, spread with clotted cream or butter and re-assembled. It looks fantastic.

1 Lightly butter a 15cm/6in round cake tin, 7.5cm/3in deep. Dust lightly with flour, if not a non-stick finish. Melt the butter in a small saucepan and then stir in the milk or cream and sugar. The mixture should be tepid. Remove from the heat, add the yeast and blend thoroughly until the yeast has dissolved. Leave for 10 minutes, or until the yeast starts to work.

2 Sift the flour and salt together into a large bowl. Stir in the lemon rind and make a well in the centre. Add the yeast mixture to the centre of the flour and mix together to make a soft dough just stiff enough to form a shape.

3 Turn out the dough on to a lightly floured surface and knead for about 10 minutes until smooth and elastic. Shape into a ball and place in the prepared tin. Cover with lightly oiled clear film and leave to rise, in a warm place, for 1¼–1½ hours.

4 When the dough has risen almost to the top of the tin, remove the clear film.

5 Meanwhile, preheat the oven to 220°C/ 425°F/Gas 7. Bake for 15–20 minutes or until light golden. While the loaf is baking, heat the milk and sugar for the glaze in a small saucepan until the sugar has dissolved, then bring to the boil. Brush the glaze over the bread.

6 Leave to cool in the tin for 10 minutes, or until the bread comes away from the side easily, then cool slightly on a wire rack before slicing and filling.

25g/1oz/2 tbsp butter
150ml/¼ pint/⅔ cup milk or double cream
15ml/1 tbsp caster sugar
15g/½oz fresh yeast
275g/10oz/2½ cups unbleached white bread flour
2.5ml/½ tsp salt
finely grated rind of ½ lemon

FOR THE GLAZE
15ml/1 tbsp milk
15ml/1 tbsp caster sugar

MAKES 1 ROUND LOAF

FRENCH BREADS

Although best known for the baguette, France has many more breads to offer, from specialities like fougasse or pain aux noix – which introduce cheese and walnuts – to rustic crusty breads like pain de campagne rustique, pain polka and that old fashioned rye bread, pain bouillie. Enriched doughs are popular with the French and include the rich, buttery yet light classic breakfast treats of croissants and brioche. Perfect with a cup of coffee!

FRENCH BAGUETTES

500g/1¼ lb/5 cups unbleached white bread flour
115g/4oz/1 cup fine French plain flour
10ml/2 tsp salt
15g/½ oz fresh yeast
525ml/18fl oz/2¼ cups lukewarm water

MAKES 3 LOAVES

VARIATION
If you make baguettes regularly you may want to purchase baguette frames to hold and bake the breads in, or long *bannetons* in which to prove this wonderful bread.

Baguettes are difficult to reproduce at home as they require a very hot oven and steam. However, by using less yeast and a triple fermentation you can produce a bread with a superior taste and far better texture than mass-produced baguettes. These are best eaten on the day of baking.

1 Sift the flours and salt together into a large bowl. Add the yeast to the water in another large bowl and stir to dissolve. Gradually beat in half the flour mixture to form a batter. Cover with clear film and leave at room temperature for about 3 hours, or until nearly trebled in size and starting to collapse.

2 Add the remaining flour a little at a time, beating with your hand. Turn out on to a lightly floured surface and knead for 8–10 minutes to form a moist dough. Place in a lightly oiled bowl, cover with lightly oiled clear film and leave to rise, in a warm place, for about 1 hour.

3 When the dough has almost doubled in bulk, knock it back, turn out on to a lightly floured surface and divide into 3 equal pieces. Shape each into a ball and then into a rectangle measuring about 15 × 7.5cm/6 × 3in.

4 Fold the bottom third up lengthways and the top third down and press down to make sure the pieces of dough are in contact. Seal the edges. Repeat two or three more times until each loaf is an oblong. Leave to rest in between folding for a few minutes, if necessary, to avoid tearing the dough.

5 Gently stretch each piece of dough lengthways into a 33–35cm/13–14in long loaf. Pleat a floured dish towel on a baking sheet to make 3 moulds for the loaves. Place the breads between the pleats of the towel, to help hold their shape while rising. Cover with lightly oiled clear film and leave to rise, in a warm place, for about 45–60 minutes.

6 Meanwhile, preheat the oven to maximum, at least 230°C/450°F/Gas 8. Roll the loaves on to a baking sheet, spaced well apart. Using a sharp knife, slash the top of each loaf several times with long diagonal slits. Place at the top of the oven, spray the inside of the oven with water and bake for 20–25 minutes, or until golden. Spray the oven twice more during the first 5 minutes of baking. Transfer to a wire rack to cool.

PAIN POLKA

This attractive, deeply cut, crusty bread is made by using a little of the previous day's dough as a starter. However, if you do not have any you can make a starter dough, the details for which are given.

FOR THE STARTER
225g/8oz/1 cup 6 15 hours-old
French baguette dough
or 7g/¼ oz fresh yeast
120ml/4fl oz/½ cup lukewarm water
115g/4oz/1 cup unbleached
white flour

FOR THE DOUGH
7g/¼ oz fresh yeast
280ml/scant ½ pint/scant 1¼ cups
lukewarm water
450g/1lb/4 cups unbleached white
bread flour, plus extra
for dusting
15ml/1 tbsp salt

MAKES 1 LOAF

COOK'S TIP
The piece of previously made dough can be kept covered in the fridge for up to 2 days, or frozen for up to one month. Just let it come back to room temperature and allow it to rise for an hour before using.

1 Lightly flour a baking sheet. If you have leftover bread dough, proceed to step 3. Make the starter. Mix the yeast with the water, then gradually stir in sufficient flour to form a batter. Beat vigorously, then gradually add the remaining flour and mix to a soft dough.

2 Knead for 5 minutes. Place in a bowl, cover with oiled clear film, and leave at room temperature for 4–5 hours, or until well risen and starting to collapse.

3 In a bowl, mix the yeast for the dough with half of the water, then stir in the remainder. Add the previously made dough or starter (*left*) and knead to dissolve the dough. Gradually add the flour and salt and mix to a dough. Turn out on to a lightly floured surface and knead for 8–10 minutes until the dough is smooth and elastic.

4 Place the dough in a lightly oiled bowl, cover with lightly oiled clear film and leave to rise, in a warm place, for about 1½ hours, or until doubled in bulk.

5 Turn out the dough on to a lightly floured surface, knock back and shape into a round ball. Flatten slightly and place on the prepared baking sheet.

6 Cover with lightly oiled clear film and leave to rise, in a warm place, for 1 hour, or until almost doubled in size.

7 Dust the top of the loaf with flour and, using a sharp knife, cut the top fairly deeply in a criss-cross pattern. Leave to rest for 10 minutes. Meanwhile, preheat the oven to 230°C/450°F/Gas 8.

8 Bake for 25–30 minutes, or until browned. Spray the inside of the oven with water as soon as the bread goes into the oven, and 3 times during the first 10 minutes of baking. Transfer to a wire rack to cool.

CROISSANTS

*350g/12oz/3 cups unbleached white
bread flour
115g/4oz/1 cup fine French
plain flour
5ml/1 tsp salt
25g/1oz/2 tbsp caster sugar
15g/½ oz fresh yeast
225ml/scant 8fl oz/scant 1 cup
lukewarm milk
1 egg, lightly beaten
225g/8oz/1 cup butter*

*FOR THE GLAZE
1 egg yolk
15ml/1 tbsp milk*

MAKES 14 CROISSANTS

COOK'S TIP

Make sure that the block of butter
and the dough are about the same
temperature when combining, to
ensure the best results.

*Golden layers of flaky pastry, puffy, light and flavoured with butter is how the
best croissants should be. Serve warm on the day of baking.*

3 Knock back, re-cover and chill in the
fridge for 1 hour. Meanwhile, flatten the
butter into a block about 2cm/¾in thick.
Knock back the dough and turn out on
to a lightly floured surface. Roll out into
a rough 25cm/10in square, rolling the
edges thinner than the centre.

4 Place the block of butter diagonally in
the centre and fold the corners of the
dough over the butter like an envelope,
tucking in the edges to completely
enclose the butter.

1 Sift the flours and salt together into a
large bowl. Stir in the sugar. Make a well
in the centre. Cream the yeast with
45ml/3 tbsp of the milk, then stir in the
remainder. Add the yeast mixture to the
centre of the flour, then add the egg and
gradually beat in the flour until it forms
a dough.

2 Turn out on to a lightly floured surface
and knead for 3–4 minutes. Place in a
large lightly oiled bowl, cover with
lightly oiled clear film and leave to rise,
in a warm place, for about 45 minutes–
1 hour, or until doubled in bulk.

5 Roll the dough into a rectangle about
2cm/¾in thick, approximately twice as
long as it is wide. Fold the bottom third
up and the top third down and seal the
edges with a rolling pin. Wrap in clear
film and chill for 20 minutes.

6 Repeat the rolling, folding and chilling
twice more, turning the dough by
90 degrees each time. Roll out on a
floured surface into a 63 × 33cm/25 ×
13in rectangle; trim the edges to leave a
60 × 30cm/24 × 12in rectangle. Cut in
half lengthways. Cut crossways into
14 equal triangles with 15cm/6in bases.

7 Place the dough triangles on 2 baking
sheets, cover with clear film and chill for
10 minutes.

8 To shape the croissants, place each
one with the wide end at the top, hold
each side and pull gently to stretch the
top of the triangle a little, then roll
towards the point, finishing with the
pointed end tucked underneath. Curve
the ends towards the pointed end to
make a crescent. Place on two baking
sheets, spaced well apart.

9 Mix together the egg yolk and milk
for the glaze. Lightly brush a little glaze
over the croissants, avoiding the cut
edges of the dough. Cover the croissants
loosely with lightly oiled clear film and
leave to rise, in a warm place, for about
30 minutes, or until they are nearly
doubled in size.

10 Meanwhile, preheat the oven to
220°C/425°F/Gas 7. Brush the croissants
with the remaining glaze and bake for
15–20 minutes, or until crisp and
golden. Transfer to a wire rack to cool
slightly before serving warm.

VARIATION

To make chocolate-filled
croissants, place a small square of
milk or plain chocolate or 15ml/1 tbsp
coarsely chopped chocolate at the
wide end of each triangle before
rolling up as in step 8.

PAIN BOUILLIE

This is an old-fashioned style of rye bread, made before sourdough starters were used. Rye flour is mixed with boiling water like a porridge and left overnight to ferment. The finished bread has a rich earthy flavour, with just a hint of caraway.

FOR THE PORRIDGE
225g/8oz/2 cups rye flour
450ml/3/4 pint/13/4 cups boiling water
5ml/1 tsp clear honey

FOR THE DOUGH
7g/1/4 oz fresh yeast
30ml/2 tbsp lukewarm water
5ml/1 tsp caraway seeds, crushed
10ml/2 tsp salt
350g/12oz/3 cups unbleached white bread flour
olive oil, for brushing

MAKES 2 LOAVES

1 Lightly grease a 23.5 × 13cm/9¼ × 5in loaf tin. Place the rye flour for the porridge in a large bowl. Pour over the boiling water and leave to stand for 5 minutes. Stir in the honey. Cover with clear film and leave in a warm place for about 12 hours.

2 Make the dough. Put the yeast in a measuring jug and blend in the water. Stir the mixture into the porridge with the crushed caraway seeds and salt. Add the white flour a little at a time, mixing first with a wooden spoon and then with your hands, until the mixture forms a firm dough.

3 Turn out on to a lightly floured surface and knead for 6–8 minutes until smooth and elastic. Return to the bowl, cover with lightly oiled clear film and leave to rise, in a warm place, for 1½ hours, or until doubled in bulk.

4 Turn out the dough on to a lightly floured surface and knock back. Cut into 2 equal pieces and roll each piece into a rectangle 38 × 12cm/15 × 4½in. Fold the bottom third up and the top third down and seal the edges. Turn over.

5 Brush one side of each piece of folded dough with olive oil and place side by side in the prepared tin, oiled edges next to each other. Cover with lightly oiled clear film and leave to rise, in a warm place, for 1 hour, or until the dough reaches the top of the tin.

6 Meanwhile, preheat the oven to 220°C/425°F/Gas 7. Brush the tops of the loaves with olive oil, and using a sharp knife, slash with one or two cuts. Bake for 30 minutes, then reduce the oven temperature to 190°C/375°F/Gas 5 and bake for a further 25–30 minutes. Turn out on to a wire rack to cool.

COOK'S TIP
Serve very thinly sliced, with a little butter, or as an accompaniment to cold meats and cheeses.

EPI

This pretty, wheat-ear shaped crusty loaf makes a good presentation bread. The recipe uses a piece of fermented French baguette dough as a starter, which improves the flavour and texture of the finished bread.

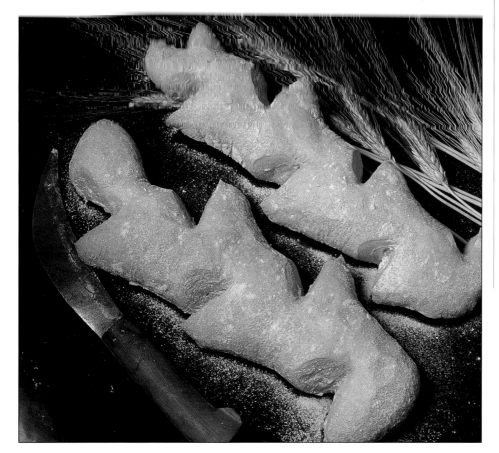

7g/¼ oz fresh yeast
275ml/9fl oz/generous 1 cup lukewarm water
115g/4oz/½ cup 6–10-hours-old French baguette dough
225g/8oz/2 cups unbleached white bread flour
55g/2oz/¼ cup fine French plain flour
5ml/1 tsp salt

MAKES 2 LOAVES

COOK'S TIP
You can use any amount up to 10 per cent of previously made French baguette dough for this recipe. The épi can also be shaped into a circle to make an attractive crown.

1 Sprinkle a baking sheet with flour. Mix the yeast with the water in a jug. Place the French bread dough in a large bowl and break up. Add a little of the yeast water to soften the dough. Mix in a little of the bread flour, then alternate the additions of yeast water and both flours until incorporated. Sprinkle the salt over the dough and knead in. Turn out the dough on to a lightly floured surface and knead for about 5 minutes until smooth and elastic.

2 Place in a lightly oiled bowl, cover with lightly oiled clear film and leave to rise, in a warm place, for about 1 hour, or until the dough has doubled in bulk.

3 Knock back the dough with your fist, then cover the bowl again with the oiled clear film and leave to rise, in a warm place, for about 1 hour.

4 Divide the dough into 2 equal pieces, place on a lightly floured surface and stretch each piece into a baguette.

5 Let the dough rest between rolling for a few minutes if necessary to avoid tearing. Pleat a floured dish towel on a baking sheet to make 2 moulds for the loaves. Place them between the pleats of the towel, cover with lightly oiled clear film and leave to rise, in a warm place, for 30 minutes.

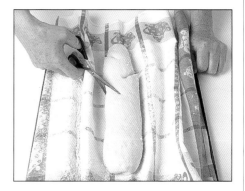

6 Meanwhile, preheat the oven to 230°C/450°F/Gas 8. Using scissors, make diagonal cuts halfway through the dough about 5cm/2in apart, alternating the cuts along the loaf. Gently pull the dough in the opposite direction.

7 Place on the prepared baking sheet and bake for 20 minutes, or until golden. Spray the inside of the oven with water 2–3 times during the first 5 minutes of baking. Transfer to a wire rack to cool.

PAIN DE CAMPAGNE RUSTIQUE

This superb country bread is made using a natural French chef starter to produce a rustic flavour and texture. In France, breads like this are often made three or four times the size of this loaf.

FOR THE CHEF
50g/2oz/¹/2 cup wholemeal bread flour
45ml/3 tbsp warm water

FOR THE 1ST REFRESHMENT
60ml/4 tbsp warm water
75g/3oz/³/4 cup wholemeal bread flour

FOR THE 2ND REFRESHMENT
120ml/4fl oz/¹/2 cup lukewarm water
115g/4oz/1 cup unbleached white bread flour
25g/1oz/¹/4 cup wholemeal bread flour

FOR THE DOUGH
150–175ml/5–6fl oz/²/3–³/4 cup lukewarm water
350g/12oz/3 cups unbleached white bread flour
10ml/2 tsp salt

MAKES 1 LOAF

COOK'S TIPS

• You will need to start making this bread about four days before you'd like to eat it.

• To make another loaf, keep the piece of starter dough (see step 6) in the fridge for up to three days. Use the reserved piece of starter dough for the 2nd refreshment in place of the *levain* in step 3, gradually mix in the water, then the flours and leave to rise as described.

1 To make the *chef*, place the flour in a small bowl, add the water and knead for 3–4 minutes to form a dough. Cover with clear film and leave the *chef* in a warm place for 2 days.

2 Pull off the hardened crust and discard, then remove 30ml/2 tbsp of the moist centre. Place in a large bowl and gradually mix in the water for the 1st refreshment. Gradually mix in the flour and knead for 3–4 minutes to form a dough or *levain*, then cover with clear film and leave in a warm place for 1 day.

3 Discard the crust from the *levain* and gradually mix in the water for the 2nd refreshment. Mix in the flours a little at a time, mixing well after each addition to form a firm dough. Cover with lightly oiled clear film and leave to rise, in a warm place, for about 10 hours, or until doubled in bulk.

4 Lightly flour a baking sheet. For the final stage in the preparation of the dough, gradually mix the water into the *levain* in the bowl, then gradually mix in the flour, then the salt. Turn out the dough on to a lightly floured surface and knead for about 5 minutes until smooth and elastic.

5 Place the dough in a large lightly oiled bowl, cover with lightly oiled clear film and leave to rise, in a warm place, for 1¹/2–2 hours, or until the dough has almost doubled in bulk.

6 Knock back the dough and cut off 115g/4oz/¹/2 cup. Set aside for making the next loaf. Shape the remaining dough into a ball – you should have about 350g/12oz/1¹/2 cups.

7 Line a 10cm/4in high, 23cm/9in round basket or large bowl with a dish towel and dust with flour.

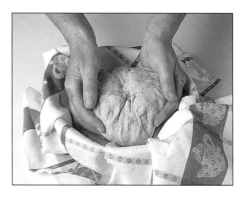

8 Place the dough ball seam side up in the prepared basket or bowl. Cover with lightly oiled clear film and leave to rise, in a warm place, for 2–3 hours, or until almost doubled in bulk.

9 Preheat the oven to 230°C/450°F/ Gas 8. Invert the loaf on to the prepared baking sheet and sprinkle with flour.

10 Slash the top of the loaf, using a sharp knife, four times at right angles to each other, to form a square pattern.

11 Sprinkle with a little more flour, if you like, then bake for 30–35 minutes, or until the loaf has browned and sounds hollow when tapped on the base. Transfer to a wire rack to cool.

*450g/1lb/4 cups unbleached white
bread flour
5ml/1 tsp salt
20g/³/4 oz fresh yeast
280ml/9fl oz/generous 1 cup
lukewarm water
15ml/1 tbsp extra virgin olive oil*

FOR THE FILLING
*50g/2oz/¹/3 cup Roquefort
cheese, crumbled
40g/1¹/2oz/¹/3 cup walnut
pieces, chopped
25g/1oz/2 tbsp drained, canned
anchovy fillets, soaked in milk and
drained again, chopped
olive oil, for brushing*

MAKES 2 LOAVES

VARIATIONS
• Replace the cheese with 15ml/1 tbsp
chopped fresh sage or thyme or
40g/1½oz/⅓ cup chopped pitted olives.
• To make a sweet fougasse, replace
15ml/1 tbsp of the water with orange
flower water. Include 50g/2oz/⅓ cup
chopped candied orange peel and
25g/1oz/2 tbsp sugar.

FOUGASSE

*A fougasse is a lattice-shaped, flattish loaf from the South of France. It can be
cooked as a plain bread or flavoured with cheese, anchovies, herbs, nuts or
olives. On Christmas Eve in Provence a fougasse flavoured with orange
flower water is part of a table centrepiece of thirteen desserts, used to
symbolize Christ and the Twelve Apostles.*

2 Place the dough in a lightly oiled bowl,
cover with lightly oiled clear film and
leave to rise, in a warm place, for about
1 hour, or until doubled in bulk.

3 Turn out on to a lightly floured surface
and knock back the dough. Divide into
2 equal pieces and flatten one piece of
dough. Sprinkle over the cheese and
walnuts and fold the dough over on
itself 2–3 times to incorporate. Repeat
with the remaining piece of dough, this
time incorporating the anchovies. Shape
each piece of flavoured dough into a ball.

4 Flatten each ball of dough and fold the
bottom third up and the top third down,
to make an oblong. Roll the cheese
dough into a rectangle measuring about
28 × 15cm/11 × 6in. Using a sharp knife,
make 4 diagonal cuts almost to the edge.
Pull and stretch the dough evenly, so
that it resembles a ladder.

5 Shape the anchovy dough into an oval
with a flat base, about 25cm/10in long.
Using a sharp knife, make 3 diagonal
slits on each side towards the flat base,
and pull to open the cuts. Transfer to
the prepared baking sheets, cover with
lightly oiled clear film and leave to rise,
in a warm place, for about 30–45
minutes, or until nearly doubled in bulk.

6 Meanwhile, preheat the oven to 220°C/
425°F/Gas 7. Brush both loaves with a
little olive oil and bake for 25 minutes,
or until golden. Transfer to a wire rack
to cool.

1 Lightly grease 2 baking sheets. Sift the
flour and salt together into a large bowl
and make a well in the centre. In a
measuring jug, cream the yeast with
60ml/4 tbsp of the water. Pour the yeast
mixture into the centre of the flour with
the remaining water and the olive oil
and mix to a soft dough. Turn out on to
a lightly floured surface and knead the
dough for 8–10 minutes until smooth
and elastic.

PAIN AUX NOIX

This delicious butter- and milk-enriched wholemeal bread is filled with walnuts. It is the perfect companion for cheese.

50g/2oz/¼ cup butter
350g/12oz/3 cups wholemeal bread flour
115g/4oz/1 cup unbleached white bread flour
15ml/1 tbsp light brown muscovado sugar
7.5ml/1½ tsp salt
20g/¾ oz fresh yeast
275ml/9fl oz/generous 1 cup lukewarm milk
175g/6oz/1½ cups walnut pieces

MAKES 2 LOAVES

3 Knead on a lightly floured surface for 6–8 minutes. Place in a lightly oiled bowl, cover with lightly oiled clear film and leave to rise, in a warm place, for 1 hour, or until doubled in bulk.

4 Turn out the dough on to a lightly floured surface and gently knock back. Press or roll out to flatten and then sprinkle over the nuts. Gently press the nuts into the dough, then roll it up. Return to the oiled bowl, re-cover and leave, in a warm place, for 30 minutes.

5 Turn out on to a lightly floured surface, divide in half and shape each piece into a ball. Place on the baking sheets, cover with lightly oiled clear film and leave to rise, in a warm place, for 45 minutes, or until doubled in bulk.

6 Meanwhile, preheat the oven to 220°C/425°F/Gas 7. Using a sharp knife, slash the top of each loaf 3 times. Bake for about 35 minutes, or until the loaves sound hollow when tapped on the base. Transfer to a wire rack to cool.

1 Lightly grease 2 baking sheets. Place the butter in a small saucepan and heat until melted and starting to turn brown, then set aside to cool. Mix the flours, sugar and salt in a large bowl and make a well in the centre. Cream the yeast with half the milk. Add to the centre of the flour with the remaining milk.

2 Pour the cool melted butter through a fine strainer into the centre of the flour so that it joins the liquids already there. Using your hand, mix the liquids together in the bowl and gradually mix in small quantities of the flour to make a batter. Continue until the mixture forms a moist dough.

450g/1lb/4 cups unbleached white
bread flour
10ml/2 tsp salt
15ml/1 tbsp caster sugar
50g/2oz/¹⁄4 cup butter, softened
15g/¹⁄2 oz fresh yeast
280ml/9fl oz/generous 1 cup
lukewarm milk, plus 15ml/1 tbsp
extra milk, for glazing

MAKES 12 ROLLS

VARIATION
These can also be made into long
rolls. To shape, flatten each ball of
dough and fold in half. Roll back and
forth, using your hand to form a
13cm/5in long roll, tapered at either
end. Just before baking, slash the tops
horizontally several times.

400g/14oz/3¹⁄2 cups unbleached white
bread flour
7.5ml/1¹⁄2 tsp salt
5ml/1 tsp caster sugar
15g/¹⁄2 oz fresh yeast
120ml/4fl oz/¹⁄2 cup lukewarm
milk
175ml/6fl oz/³⁄4 cup lukewarm
water

MAKES 10 ROLLS

PETIT PAINS AU LAIT

These classic French round milk rolls have a soft crust and a light, slightly
sweet crumb. They won't last long!

1 Lightly grease 2 baking sheets. Sift the
flour and salt together into a large bowl.
Stir in the sugar. Rub the softened
butter into the flour.

2 Cream the yeast with 60ml/4 tbsp of
the milk. Stir in the remaining milk.
Pour into the flour mixture and mix to a
soft dough.

3 Turn out on to a lightly floured surface
and knead for 8–10 minutes until
smooth and elastic. Place in a lightly
oiled bowl, cover with lightly oiled clear
film and leave to rise, in a warm place,
for 1 hour, or until doubled in bulk.

4 Turn out the dough on to a lightly
floured surface and gently knock back.
Divide into 12 equal pieces. Shape into
balls and space on the baking sheets.

5 Using a sharp knife, cut a cross in the
top of each roll. Cover with lightly oiled
clear film and leave to rise, in a warm
place, for about 20 minutes, or until
doubled in size.

6 Preheat the oven to 200°C/400°F/
Gas 6. Brush the rolls with milk and
bake for 20–25 minutes, or until golden.
Transfer to a wire rack to cool.

FRENCH DIMPLED ROLLS

A French and Belgian speciality, these attractive rolls are distinguished by
the split down the centre. They have a crusty finish while remaining soft and
light inside – they taste lovely, too.

3 Add the water and gradually mix in
the flour to form a fairly moist, soft
dough. Turn out on to a lightly floured
surface and knead for 8–10 minutes
until smooth and elastic. Place in a
lightly oiled bowl, cover with lightly
oiled clear film and leave to rise, at room
temperature, for about 1½ hours, or
until doubled in bulk.

4 Turn out on to a lightly floured surface
and knock back. Re-cover and leave to
rest for 5 minutes. Divide the dough into
10 pieces. Shape into balls by rolling the
dough under a cupped hand, then roll
until oval. Lightly flour the tops. Space
well apart on the baking sheets, cover
with lightly oiled clear film and leave to
rise, at room temperature, for about 30
minutes, or until almost doubled in size.

5 Lightly oil the side of your hand and
press the centre of each roll to make a
deep split. Re-cover and leave to rest for
15 minutes. Meanwhile, place a roasting
tin in the bottom of the oven and
preheat the oven to 230°C/450°F/Gas 8.
Pour 250ml/8fl oz/1 cup water into the
tin and bake the rolls for 15 minutes, or
until golden. Cool on a wire rack.

1 Lightly grease 2 baking sheets. Sift the
flour and salt into a large bowl. Stir in
the sugar and make a well in the centre.

2 Cream the yeast with the milk until
dissolved, then pour into the centre of
the flour mixture. Sprinkle over a little
of the flour from around the edge. Leave
at room temperature for 15–20 minutes,
or until the mixture starts to bubble.

KUGELHOPF

This inviting, fluted ring-shaped bread originates from Alsace, although Germany, Hungary and Austria all have their own variations of this popular recipe. Kugelhopf can be sweet or savoury; this version is richly flavoured with nuts, onion and bacon.

150g/5oz/²/₃ cup unsalted butter, softened
12 walnut halves
675g/1¹/₂lb/6 cups unbleached white bread flour
7.5ml/1¹/₂ tsp salt
20g/³/₄oz fresh yeast
300ml/10fl oz/1¹/₄ cups milk
115g/4oz smoked bacon, diced
1 onion, finely chopped
15ml/1 tbsp vegetable oil
5 eggs, beaten
freshly ground black pepper

MAKES 1 LOAF

VARIATION
If you wish to make a sweet kugelhopf replace the walnuts with whole almonds and the bacon and onion with 115g/4oz/1 cup raisins and 50g/2oz/¹/₃ cup mixed chopped peel. Add 50g/2oz/¼ cup caster sugar in step 2 and omit the black pepper.

1 Use 25g/1oz/2 tbsp of the butter to grease a 23cm/9in kugelhopf mould. Place 8 walnut halves around the base and chop the remainder.

2 Sift the flour and salt together into a large bowl and season with pepper. Make a well in the centre. In a jug, cream the yeast with 45ml/3 tbsp of the milk. Pour into the centre of the flour with the remaining milk. Mix in a little flour to make a thick batter. Sprinkle a little of the remaining flour over the top of the batter, cover with clear film and leave in a warm place for 20–30 minutes until the yeast mixture bubbles.

3 Meanwhile, fry the bacon and onion in the oil until the onion is pale golden.

4 Add the eggs to the flour mixture and gradually beat in the flour, using your hand. Gradually beat in the remaining softened butter to form a soft dough. Cover with lightly oiled clear film and leave to rise, in a warm place, for 45–60 minutes, or until almost doubled in bulk. Preheat the oven to 200°C/400°F/Gas 6.

5 Knock back the dough and gently knead in the bacon, onion and nuts. Place in the mould, cover with lightly oiled clear film and leave to rise, in a warm place, for about 1 hour, or until it has risen to the top of the mould.

6 Bake for 40–45 minutes, or until the loaf has browned and sounds hollow when tapped on the base. Cool in the mould for 5 minutes, then on a wire rack.

BRIOCHE

Rich and buttery yet light and airy, this wonderful loaf captures the essence of the classic French bread.

1 Sift the flour and salt together into a large bowl and make a well in the centre. Put the yeast in a measuring jug and stir in the milk.

2 Add the yeast mixture to the centre of the flour with the eggs and mix together to form a soft dough.

3 Using your hand, beat the dough for 4–5 minutes until smooth and elastic. Cream the butter and sugar together. Gradually add the butter mixture to the dough in small amounts, making sure it is incorporated before adding more. Beat until smooth, shiny and elastic.

350g/12oz/3 cups unbleached white bread flour
2.5ml/½ tsp salt
15g/½ oz fresh yeast
60ml/4 tbsp lukewarm milk
3 eggs, lightly beaten
175g/6oz/¾ cup butter, softened
25g/1oz/2 tbsp caster sugar

FOR THE GLAZE
1 egg yolk
15ml/1 tbsp milk

MAKES 1 LOAF

4 Cover the bowl with lightly oiled clear film and leave the dough to rise, in a warm place, for 1–2 hours or until doubled in bulk.

5 Lightly knock back the dough, then re-cover and place in the fridge for 8–10 hours or overnight.

6 Lightly grease a 1.6 litre/2¾ pint/ scant 7 cup brioche mould. Turn the dough out on to a lightly floured surface. Cut off almost a quarter and set aside. Shape the rest into a ball and place in the prepared mould. Shape the reserved dough into an elongated egg shape. Using two or three fingers, make a hole in the centre of the large ball of dough. Gently press the narrow end of the egg-shaped dough into the hole.

7 Mix together the egg yolk and milk for the glaze, and brush a little over the brioche. Cover with lightly oiled clear film and leave to rise, in a warm place, for 1½–2 hours, or until the dough nearly reaches the top of the mould.

8 Meanwhile, preheat the oven to 230°C/ 450°F/Gas 8. Brush the brioche with the remaining glaze and bake for 10 minutes. Reduce the oven temperature to 190°C/ 375°F/Gas 5 and bake for a further 20–25 minutes, or until golden. Turn out on to a wire rack to cool.

MEDITERRANEAN BREADS

*The warm, rich flavours of the Mediterranean find their way into the breads. Olive oil,
sun-dried tomatoes, olives, garlic and fresh herbs all feature in breads that are so delicious
that they are now widely enjoyed all over the world. Ciabatta, panini all'olio rolls, focaccia
and schiacciata are just a few examples. Spanish, Moroccan and Portuguese breads include
local grains like corn and barley, together with seeds such as sesame, sunflower and
pumpkin. Elaborate speciality breads are baked for religious festivals, the Greek
Easter bread – tsoureki – and the Christmas breads – christopsomo and
Twelfth Night bread – being some of the most spectacular.*

PUGLIESE

This classic Italian open-textured, soft-crumbed bread is moistened and flavoured with fruity olive oil. Its floured top gives it a true country feel.

For the Biga Starter
175g/6oz/1½ cups unbleached white bread flour
7g/¼ oz fresh yeast
90ml/6 tbsp lukewarm water

For the Dough
225g/8oz/2 cups unbleached white bread flour, plus extra for dusting
225g/8oz/2 cups unbleached wholemeal bread flour
5ml/1 tsp caster sugar
10ml/2 tsp salt
15g/½ oz fresh yeast
275ml/9fl oz/generous 1 cup lukewarm water
75ml/5 tbsp extra virgin olive oil

Makes 1 Large Loaf

VARIATION

Incorporate 150g/5oz/1 cup chopped black olives into the dough at the end of step 5 for extra olive flavour.

1 Sift the flour for the *biga* starter into a large bowl. Make a well in the centre. In a small bowl, cream the yeast with the water. Pour the liquid into the centre of the flour and gradually mix in the surrounding flour to form a firm dough.

2 Turn the dough out on to a lightly floured surface and knead for 5 minutes until smooth and elastic. Return to the bowl, cover with lightly oiled clear film and leave to rise, in a warm place, for 8–10 hours, or until the dough has risen well and is starting to collapse.

3 Lightly flour a baking sheet. Mix the flours, sugar and salt for the dough in a large bowl. Cream the yeast and the water in another large bowl, then stir in the *biga* and mix together.

4 Stir in the flour mixture a little at a time, then add the olive oil in the same way, and mix to a soft dough. Turn out on to a lightly floured surface and knead the dough for 8–10 minutes until smooth and elastic.

5 Place in a lightly oiled bowl, cover with lightly oiled clear film and leave to rise, in a warm place, for 1–1½ hours, or until doubled in bulk.

6 Turn out on to a lightly floured surface and knock back. Gently pull out the edges and fold under to make a round.

7 Transfer to the prepared baking sheet, cover with lightly oiled clear film and leave to rise, in a warm place, for 1–1½ hours, or until almost doubled in size.

8 Meanwhile, preheat the oven to 230°C/450°F/Gas 8. Lightly dust the loaf with flour and bake for 15 minutes. Reduce the oven temperature to 200°C/400°F/Gas 6 and bake for a further 20 minutes, or until the loaf sounds hollow when tapped on the base. Transfer to a wire rack to cool.

CIABATTA

This irregular-shaped Italian bread is so called because it looks like an old shoe or slipper. It is made with a very wet dough flavoured with olive oil; cooking produces a bread with holes and a wonderfully chewy crust.

1 Cream the yeast for the *biga* starter with a little of the water. Sift the flour into a large bowl. Gradually mix in the yeast mixture and sufficient of the remaining water to form a firm dough.

2 Turn out the *biga* starter dough on to a lightly floured surface and knead for about 5 minutes until smooth and elastic. Return the dough to the bowl, cover with lightly oiled clear film and leave in a warm place for 12–15 hours, or until the dough has risen and is starting to collapse.

3 Sprinkle 3 baking sheets with flour. Mix the yeast for the dough with a little of the water until creamy, then mix in the remainder. Add the yeast mixture to the *biga* and gradually mix in.

4 Mix in the milk, beating thoroughly with a wooden spoon. Using your hand, gradually beat in the flour, lifting the dough as you mix. Mixing the dough will take 15 minutes or more and form a very wet mix, impossible to knead on a work surface.

5 Beat in the salt and olive oil. Cover with lightly oiled clear film and leave to rise, in a warm place, for 1½–2 hours, or until doubled in bulk.

6 Using a spoon, carefully tip one-third of the dough at a time on to the prepared baking sheets, trying to avoid knocking back the dough in the process.

7 Using floured hands, shape into rough oblong loaf shapes, about 2.5cm/1in thick. Flatten slightly with splayed fingers. Sprinkle with flour and leave to rise in a warm place for 30 minutes.

8 Meanwhile, preheat the oven to 220°C/425°F/Gas 7. Bake for 25–30 minutes, or until golden brown and sounding hollow when tapped on the base. Transfer to a wire rack to cool.

FOR THE BIGA STARTER
7g/¼ oz fresh yeast
175–200ml/6–7fl oz/¾–scant 1 cup lukewarm water
350g/12oz/3 cups unbleached plain flour, plus extra for dusting

FOR THE DOUGH
15g/½ oz fresh yeast
400ml/14fl oz/1⅔ cups lukewarm water
60ml/4 tbsp lukewarm milk
500g/1¼ lb/5 cups unbleached white bread flour
10ml/2 tsp salt
45ml/3 tbsp extra virgin olive oil

MAKES 3 LOAVES

VARIATION
To make tomato-flavoured ciabatta, add 115g/4oz/1 cup chopped, drained sun-dried tomatoes in olive oil. Add with the olive oil in step 5.

*450g/1lb/4 cups unbleached white
bread flour
10ml/2 tsp salt
15g/1/2 oz fresh yeast
250ml/8fl oz/1 cup lukewarm water
60ml/4 tbsp extra virgin olive oil,
plus extra for brushing*

MAKES 16 ROLLS

1 Lightly oil 3 baking sheets. Sift the flour and salt together in a large bowl and make a well in the centre.

2 In a jug, cream the yeast with half of the water, then stir in the remainder. Add to the centre of the flour with the oil and mix to a dough.

3 Turn the dough out on to a lightly floured surface and knead for 8–10 minutes until smooth and elastic. Place in a lightly oiled bowl, cover with lightly oiled clear film and leave to rise, in a warm place, for about 1 hour, or until the dough has nearly doubled in bulk.

4 Turn on to a lightly floured surface and knock back. Divide into 12 equal pieces of dough and shape into rolls as described in steps 5, 6, 7 and 8.

5 For *tavalli* (twisted spiral rolls): roll each piece of dough into a strip about 30cm/12in long and 4cm/1½ in wide. Twist each strip into a loose spiral and join the ends of dough together to make a circle. Place on the prepared baking sheets, spaced well apart. Brush the *tavalli* lightly with olive oil, cover with lightly oiled clear film and leave to rise, in a warm place, for 20–30 minutes.

PANINI ALL'OLIO

The Italians adore interesting and elaborately shaped rolls. This distinctively flavoured bread dough, enriched with olive oil, can be used for making rolls or shaped as one large loaf.

6 For *filoncini* (finger-shaped rolls): flatten each piece of dough into an oval and roll to about 23cm/9in in length without changing the basic shape. Make it 5cm/2in wide at one end and 10cm/4in wide at the other. Roll up, starting from the wider end. Using your fingers, gently stretch the dough roll to 20–23cm/8–9in long. Cut in half. Place on the prepared baking sheets, spaced well apart. Brush the finger shapes with olive oil, cover with lightly oiled clear film and leave to rise, in a warm place, for 20–30 minutes.

7 For *carciofi* (artichoke-shaped rolls): shape each piece of dough into a ball and space well apart on the prepared baking sheets. Brush with olive oil, cover with lightly oiled clear film and leave to rise, in a warm place, for 20–30 minutes. Meanwhile, preheat the oven to 200°C/400°F/Gas 6. Using scissors, snip 4–5 5mm/1/4 in deep cuts in a circle on the top of each *carciofo*, then make 5 larger horizontal cuts around the sides. Bake the rolls for 15 minutes. Transfer to a wire rack to cool.

OLIVE BREAD

Black and green olives and good-quality fruity olive oil combine to make this strongly flavoured and irresistible Italian bread.

275g/10oz/2½ cups unbleached white bread flour
50g/2oz/½ cup wholemeal bread flour
6g/¼ oz sachet easy blend dried yeast
7.5ml/1½ tsp salt
250ml/9fl oz/scant 1 cup lukewarm water
15ml/1 tbsp extra virgin olive oil, plus extra, for brushing
115g/4oz/1 cup pitted black and green olives, coarsely chopped

MAKES 1 LOAF

1 Lightly grease a baking sheet. Mix the flours, yeast and salt together in a large bowl and make a well in the centre.

2 Add the water and oil to the centre of the flour and mix to a soft dough. Knead the dough on a lightly floured surface for 8–10 minutes until smooth and elastic. Place in a lightly oiled bowl, cover with lightly oiled clear film and leave to rise, in a warm place, for 1 hour, or until doubled in bulk.

3 Turn out on to a lightly floured surface and knock back. Flatten out and sprinkle over the olives. Fold up and knead to distribute the olives. Leave to rest for 5 minutes, then shape into an oval loaf. Place on the prepared baking sheet.

4 Make 6 deep cuts in the top of the loaf, and gently push the sections over. Cover with lightly oiled clear film and leave to rise, in a warm place, for 30–45 minutes, or until doubled in size.

VARIATIONS
• Increase the proportion of wholemeal flour to make the loaf more rustic.
• Add some hazelnuts or pine nuts.

5 Meanwhile, preheat the oven to 200°C/400°F/Gas 6. Brush the bread with olive oil and bake for 35 minutes. Transfer to a wire rack to cool.

20g/¾ oz fresh yeast
325–350ml/11–12fl oz/1¹⁄₃–1¹⁄₂ cups
lukewarm water
45ml/3 tbsp extra virgin olive oil
500g/1¹⁄₄ lb/5 cups unbleached white
bread flour
10ml/2 tsp salt
15ml/1 tbsp chopped fresh sage

For the Topping
60ml/4 tbsp extra virgin olive oil
4 garlic cloves, chopped
12 fresh sage leaves

Makes 2 Round Loaves

VARIATION
Flavour the bread with other herbs,
such as oregano, basil or rosemary
and top with chopped black olives.

1 Lightly oil 2 × 25cm/10in shallow
round cake tins or pizza pans. Cream
the yeast with 60ml/4 tbsp of the water,
then stir in the remaining water. Stir in
the oil.

2 Sift the flour and salt together into
a large bowl and make a well in the
centre. Pour the yeast mixture into the
well in the centre of the flour and mix to
a soft dough.

3 Turn out the dough on to a lightly
floured surface and knead for 8–10
minutes until smooth and elastic. Place
in a lightly oiled bowl, cover with lightly
oiled clear film or a large, lightly oiled
polythene bag, and leave to rise, in a
warm place, for about 1–1¹⁄₂ hours, or
until the dough has doubled in bulk.

FOCACCIA

*This simple dimple-topped Italian
flat bread is punctuated with olive
oil and the aromatic flavours of sage
and garlic to produce a truly
succulent loaf.*

4 Knock back the dough and turn out on
to a lightly floured surface. Gently knead
in the chopped sage. Divide the dough
into 2 equal pieces. Shape each into a
ball, roll out into 25cm/10in circles and
place in the prepared tins.

5 Cover with lightly oiled clear film and
leave to rise in a warm place for about
30 minutes. Uncover, and using your
fingertips, poke the dough to make deep
dimples over the entire surface. Replace
the clear film cover and leave to rise
until doubled in bulk.

6 Meanwhile, preheat the oven to 200°C/
400°F/Gas 6. Drizzle over the olive oil for
the topping and sprinkle each focaccia
evenly with chopped garlic. Dot the sage
leaves over the surface. Bake for 25–30
minutes, or until both loaves are golden.
Immediately remove the focaccia from
the tins and transfer them to a wire rack
to cool slightly. These loaves are best
served warm.

POLENTA BREAD

Polenta is widely used in Italian cooking. Here it is combined with pine nuts to make a truly Italian bread with a fantastic flavour.

50g/2oz/¹/₂ cup polenta
300ml/¹/₂ pint/1¹/₄ cups lukewarm water
15g/¹/₂ oz fresh yeast
2.5ml/¹/₂ tsp clear honey
225g/8oz/2 cups unbleached white bread flour
25g/1oz/2 tbsp butter
45ml/3 tbsp pine nuts
7.5ml/1¹/₂ tsp salt

FOR THE TOPPING
1 egg yolk
15ml/1 tbsp water
pine nuts, for sprinkling

MAKES 1 LOAF

1 Lightly grease a baking sheet. Mix the polenta and 250ml/8fl oz/1 cup of the water together in a saucepan and slowly bring to the boil, stirring continuously with a large wooden spoon. Reduce the heat and simmer for 2–3 minutes, stirring occasionally. Set aside to cool for 10 minutes, or until just warm.

2 In a small bowl, mix the yeast with the remaining water and honey until creamy. Sift 115g/4oz/1 cup of the flour into a large bowl. Gradually beat in the yeast mixture, then gradually stir in the polenta mixture to combine. Turn out on to a lightly floured surface and knead for 5 minutes until smooth and elastic.

3 Cover the bowl with lightly oiled clear film or a lightly oiled polythene bag. Leave the dough to rise, in a warm place, for about 2 hours, or until it has doubled in bulk.

4 Meanwhile, melt the butter in a small pan, add the pine nuts and cook over a medium heat, stirring, until pale golden. Set aside to cool.

5 Add the remaining flour and the salt to the polenta dough and mix to a soft dough. Knead in the pine nuts. Turn out on to a lightly floured surface and knead for 5 minutes until smooth and elastic.

6 Place in a lightly oiled bowl, cover with lightly oiled clear film and leave to rise, in a warm place, for 1 hour, or until doubled in bulk.

7 Knock back the dough and turn it out on to a lightly floured surface. Cut the dough into 2 equal pieces and roll each piece into a fat sausage about 38cm/15in long. Plait together and place on the prepared baking sheet. Cover with lightly oiled clear film and leave to rise, in a warm place, for 45 minutes. Meanwhile, preheat the oven to 200°C/400°F/Gas 6.

8 Mix the egg yolk and water and brush over the loaf. Sprinkle with pine nuts and bake for 30 minutes, or until golden and sounding hollow when tapped on the base. Cool on a wire rack.

PANE TOSCANO

This bread from Tuscany is made without salt and probably originates from the days when salt was heavily taxed. To compensate for the lack of salt, this bread is usually served with salty foods, such as anchovies and olives.

550g/1¼ lb/5 cups unbleached white
bread flour
350ml/12fl oz/1½ cups boiling water
ᴍᴇᴅɪᴇᴠᴀʟ ᴏʀɪɢɪɴᴀʟ
60ml/4 tbsp lukewarm water

MAKES 1 LOAF

COOK'S TIP
Salt controls the action of yeast in bread so the leavening action is more noticeable. Don't let this unsalted bread over-rise or it may collapse.

6 Fold the sides of the round into the centre and seal. Place seam side up on the prepared baking sheet. Cover with lightly oiled clear film and leave to rise, in a warm place, for 30–45 minutes, or until doubled in size.

7 Flatten the loaf to about half its risen height and flip over. Cover with a large upturned bowl and leave to rise, in a warm place, for 30 minutes.

8 Meanwhile, preheat the oven to 220°C/ 425°F/Gas 7. Slash the top of the loaf, using a sharp knife, if wished. Bake for 30–35 minutes, or until golden. Transfer to a wire rack to cool.

1 First make the starter. Sift 175g/6oz/ 1½ cups of the flour into a large bowl. Pour over the boiling water, leave for a couple of minutes, then mix well. Cover the bowl with a damp dish towel and leave for 10 hours.

2 Lightly flour a baking sheet. Cream the yeast with the lukewarm water. Stir into the starter.

3 Gradually add the remaining flour and mix to form a dough. Turn out on to a lightly floured surface and knead for 5–8 minutes until smooth and elastic.

4 Place in a lightly oiled bowl, cover with lightly oiled clear film and leave to rise, in a warm place, for 1–1½ hours, or until doubled in bulk.

5 Turn out the dough on to a lightly floured surface, knock back, and shape into a round.

SICILIAN SCROLL

A wonderful pale yellow, crusty-topped loaf, enhanced with a nutty flavour from the sesame seeds. It's perfect for serving with cheese.

450g/1lb/4 cups finely ground semolina
115g/4oz/1 cup unbleached white bread flour
10ml/2 tsp salt
20g/3/4 oz fresh yeast
360ml/12 1/2 fl oz/generous 1 1/2 cups lukewarm water
30ml/2 tbsp extra virgin olive oil
sesame seeds, for sprinkling

MAKES 1 LOAF

1 Lightly grease a baking sheet. Mix the semolina, white bread flour and salt together in a large bowl and make a well in the centre.

2 In a jug, cream the yeast with half the water, then stir in the remainder. Add the creamed yeast to the centre of the semolina mixture with the olive oil and gradually incorporate the semolina and flour to form a firm dough.

3 Turn out the dough on to a lightly floured surface and knead for 8–10 minutes until smooth and elastic. Place in a lightly oiled bowl, cover with lightly oiled clear film and leave to rise, in a warm place, for 1–1 1/2 hours, or until doubled in bulk.

4 Turn out on to a lightly floured surface and knock back. Knead gently, then shape into a fat roll about 50cm/20in long. Form into an "S" shape.

5 Carefully transfer the dough to the prepared baking sheet, cover with lightly oiled clear film and leave to rise, in a warm place, for 30–45 minutes, or until doubled in size.

6 Meanwhile, preheat the oven to 220°C/425°F/Gas 7. Brush the top of the scroll with water and sprinkle with sesame seeds. Bake for 10 minutes. Spray the inside of the oven with water twice during this time. Reduce the oven temperature to 200°C/400°F/Gas 6 and bake for a further 25–30 minutes, or until golden. Transfer to a wire rack to cool.

VARIATION

Although sesame seeds are the traditional topping on this delectable Italian bread, poppy seeds, or even crystals of sea salt, could be used instead.

PROSCIUTTO LOAF

*This savoury Italian bread from Parma is spiked with the local dried ham.
Just a small amount fills the loaf with marvellous flavour.*

1 Lightly grease a baking sheet. Sift the flour and salt together into a large bowl and make a well in the centre. Cream the yeast with 30ml/2 tbsp of the water, then gradually mix in the rest. Pour into the centre of the flour.

2 Gradually beat in most of the flour with a wooden spoon to make a batter. Beat gently to begin with and then more vigorously as the batter thickens. After most of the flour has been incorporated, beat in the remainder with your hand to form a moist dough.

3 Turn out on to a lightly floured surface and knead for 5 minutes until smooth and elastic. Place in a lightly oiled bowl, cover with lightly oiled clear film and leave to rise, in a warm place, for 1½ hours, or until doubled in bulk.

4 Turn out the dough on to a lightly floured surface, knock back and then knead for 1 minute. Flatten to a round, then sprinkle with half the prosciutto and pepper. Fold the dough in half and repeat with the remaining ham and pepper. Roll up, tucking in the sides.

350g/12oz/3 cups unbleached white
bread flour
7.5ml/1½ tsp salt
15g/½ oz fresh yeast
210ml/8fl oz/1 cup lukewarm water
40g/1½ oz prosciutto, torn into
small pieces
5ml/1 tsp freshly ground black pepper

MAKES 1 LOAF

VARIATIONS
• To make pesto bread, spread 45ml/
3 tbsp pesto over the flattened dough
in step 6, then continue as above.
• For sweet pepper bread, add
45ml/3 tbsp finely chopped roasted
yellow and red peppers instead of the
ham in step 4.

5 Place on the prepared baking sheet, cover with lightly oiled clear film and leave to rise, in a warm place, for about 30 minutes. On a lightly floured surface, roll into an oval, fold in half and seal the edges. Flatten and fold again. Seal and fold again to make a long loaf.

6 Roll into a stubby long loaf. Draw out the edges by rolling the dough under the palms of your hands. Place on the baking sheet, cover with lightly oiled clear film and leave to rise, in a warm place, for 45 minutes, or until the loaf has doubled in size. Meanwhile, preheat the oven to 200°C/400°F/Gas 6.

7 Slash the top of the loaf diagonally three or four times, using a sharp knife, and bake for 30 minutes, or until golden. Cool on a wire rack.

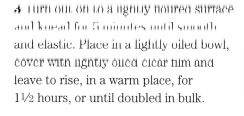

*225g/8oz/2 cups unbleached white
bread flour
7.5ml/1½ tsp salt
15g/½ oz fresh yeast
135ml/4½ fl oz/scant ⅔ cup lukewarm
water
30ml/2 tbsp extra virgin olive oil,
plus extra for brushing
sesame seeds, for coating*

MAKES 20 GRISSINI

COOK'S TIP

When baking the grissini turn them
over and change the position of the
baking sheets halfway through the
cooking time, so they brown evenly.

SESAME-STUDDED GRISSINI

*These crisp, pencil-like breadsticks are easy to make and far more delicious
than the commercially manufactured grissini. Once you start to nibble one, it
will be difficult to stop.*

1 Lightly oil 2 baking sheets. Sift the
flour and salt together into a large bowl
and make a well in the centre.

2 In a jug, cream the yeast with the
water. Pour into the centre of the flour,
add the olive oil and mix to a soft dough.
Turn out on to a lightly floured surface
and knead for 8–10 minutes until
smooth and elastic.

3 Roll the dough into a rectangle about
15 × 20cm/6 × 8in. Brush with olive oil,
cover with lightly oiled clear film and
leave to rise, in a warm place, for about
1 hour, or until doubled in bulk.

4 Preheat the oven to 200°C/400°F/
Gas 6. Spread out the sesame seeds.
Cut the dough in two 7.5 x 10cm/3 x 4in
rectangles. Cut each piece into ten
7.5cm/3in strips. Stretch each strip
gently until it is about 30cm/12in long.

5 Roll each grissini, as it is made, in the
sesame seeds. Place the grissini on the
prepared baking sheets, spaced well
apart. Lightly brush with olive oil. Leave
to rise, in a warm place, for 10 minutes,
then bake for 15–20 minutes. Transfer
to a wire rack to cool.

---

*175g/6oz/1½ cups unbleached
white flour
5ml/1 tsp salt
15ml/1 tbsp olive oil
105ml/7 tbsp lukewarm water*

MAKES 4 PIADINE

COOK'S TIPS

• If you don't have a griddle, a large
heavy-based frying pan will work
just as well. Keep the cooked
piadine warm while cooking
successive batches.
• Although not traditional in Italy,
these flat breads can also be flavoured
with herbs. Add 15ml/1 tbsp of dried
oregano. They also taste delicious
made with garlic- or chilli-flavoured
olive oil.

PIADINE

*These soft unleavened Italian breads, cooked directly on the hob, were
originally cooked on a hot stone over an open fire. They are best eaten while
still warm. Try them as an accompaniment to soups and dips.*

1 Sift the flour and salt together into a
large bowl; make a well in the centre.

2 Add the olive oil and water to the
centre of the flour and gradually mix in
to form a dough. Knead on a lightly
floured surface for 4–5 minutes until
smooth and elastic. Place in a lightly
oiled bowl, cover with oiled clear film
and leave to rest for 20 minutes.

3 Heat a griddle over a medium heat.
Divide the dough into 4 equal pieces and
roll each into an 18cm/7in round. Cover
until ready to cook.

4 Lightly oil the hot griddle, add 1 or 2
piadine and cook for about 2 minutes,
or until they are starting to brown. Turn
the piadine over and cook for a further
1–1½ minutes. Serve warm.

PANETTONE

This classic Italian bread can be found throughout Italy around Christmas. It is a surprisingly light bread even though it is rich with butter and dried fruit.

400g/14oz/3½ cups unbleached white bread flour
2.5ml/½ tsp salt
15g/½ oz fresh yeast
120ml/4fl oz/½ cup lukewarm milk
2 eggs
2 egg yolks
75g/3oz/6 tbsp caster sugar
150g/5oz/⅔ cup butter, softened
115g/4oz/⅔ cup mixed chopped peel
75g/3oz/½ cup raisins
melted butter, for brushing

MAKES 1 LOAF

COOK'S TIP
Once the dough has been enriched with butter, do not prove in too warm a place or the loaf will become greasy.

1 Using a double layer of greaseproof paper, line and butter a 15cm/6in deep cake tin or soufflé dish. Finish the paper 7.5cm/3in above the top of the tin.

2 Sift the flour and salt together into a large bowl. Make a well in the centre. Cream the yeast with 60ml/4 tbsp of the milk, then mix in the remainder.

3 Pour the yeast mixture into the centre of the flour, add the whole eggs and mix in sufficient flour to make a thick batter. Sprinkle a little of the remaining flour over the top and leave to "sponge", in a warm place, for 30 minutes.

4 Add the egg yolks and sugar and mix to a soft dough. Work in the softened butter, then turn out on to a lightly floured surface and knead for 5 minutes until smooth and elastic. Place in a lightly oiled bowl, cover with lightly oiled clear film and leave to rise, in a slightly warm place, for 1½–2 hours, or until doubled in bulk.

5 Knock back the dough and turn out on to a lightly floured surface. Gently knead in the peel and raisins. Shape into a ball and place in the prepared tin. Cover with lightly oiled clear film and leave to rise, in a slightly warm place, for about 1 hour, or until doubled.

6 Meanwhile, preheat the oven to 190°C/375°F/Gas 5. Brush the surface with melted butter and cut a cross in the top using a sharp knife. Bake for 20 minutes, then reduce the oven temperature to 180°C/350°F/Gas 4. Brush the top with butter again and bake for a further 25–30 minutes, or until golden. Cool in the tin for 5–10 minutes, then turn out on to a wire rack to cool.

PANE AL CIOCCOLATO

This slightly sweet chocolate bread from Italy is often served with creamy mascarpone cheese as a dessert or snack. The dark chocolate pieces add texture to this light loaf.

350g/12oz/3 cups unbleached white bread flour
25ml/1½ tbsp cocoa powder
2.5ml/½ tsp salt
25g/1oz/2 tbsp caster sugar
15g/½ oz fresh yeast
250ml/8fl oz/1 cup lukewarm water
25g/1oz/2 tbsp butter, softened
75g/3oz plain continental chocolate, coarsely chopped
melted butter, for brushing

MAKES 1 LOAF

1 Lightly grease a 15cm/6in round deep cake tin. Sift the flour, cocoa powder and salt together into a large bowl. Stir in the sugar. Make a well in the centre.

2 Cream the yeast with 60ml/4 tbsp of the water, then stir in the rest. Add to the centre of the flour mixture and gradually mix to a dough.

3 Knead in the softened butter, then knead on a floured surface until smooth and elastic. Place in a lightly oiled bowl, cover with lightly oiled clear film and leave to rise, in a warm place, for about 1 hour, or until doubled in bulk.

4 Turn out on to a lightly floured surface and knock back. Gently knead in the chocolate, then cover with lightly oiled clear film; leave to rest for 5 minutes.

5 Shape the dough into a round and place in the tin. Cover with lightly oiled clear film and leave to rise, in a warm place, for 45 minutes, or until doubled; the dough should reach the top of the tin.

6 Preheat the oven to 220°C/425°F/Gas 7. Bake for 10 minutes, then reduce the oven temperature to 190°C/375°F/Gas 5 and bake for a further 25–30 minutes. Brush the top with melted butter and leave to cool on a wire rack.

VARIATION
You can also shape this bread into one large, or two small rounds and bake on a lightly greased baking sheet. Reduce the baking time by about 10 minutes.

SCHIACCIATA

350g/12oz/3 cups unbleached white
bread flour
2.5ml/½ tsp salt
15g/½ oz fresh yeast
200ml/7fl oz/scant 1 cup lukewarm
water
60ml/4 tbsp extra virgin olive oil

FOR THE TOPPING
30ml/2 tbsp extra virgin olive oil,
for brushing
30ml/2 tbsp fresh rosemary leaves
coarse sea salt, for sprinkling

MAKES 1 LARGE LOAF

This Tuscan version of Italian pizza-style flat bread can be rolled to varying
thicknesses to give either a crisp or soft, bread-like finish.

2 Place in a lightly oiled bowl, cover with lightly oiled clear film and leave to rise, in a warm place, for about 1 hour, or until doubled in bulk.

1 Lightly oil a baking sheet. Sift the flour and salt into a large bowl and make a well in the centre. Cream the yeast with half the water. Add to the centre of the flour with the remaining water and olive oil and mix to a soft dough. Turn out the dough on to a lightly floured surface and knead for 10 minutes until smooth and elastic.

3 Knock back the dough, turn out on to a lightly floured surface and knead gently. Roll to a 30 × 20cm/12 × 8in rectangle and place on the prepared baking sheet. Brush with some of the olive oil for the topping and cover with lightly oiled clear film.

4 Leave to rise, in a warm place, for about 20 minutes, then brush with the remaining oil, prick all over with a fork and sprinkle with rosemary and sea salt. Leave to rise again in a warm place for 15 minutes.

5 Meanwhile, preheat the oven to 200°C/ 400°F/Gas 6. Bake for 30 minutes, or until light golden. Transfer to a wire rack to cool slightly. Serve warm.

PORTUGUESE CORN BREAD

*While the Spanish make a corn bread with barley flour, the Portuguese use
white bread flour and maize meal. This tempting version has a hard crust
with a moist, mouthwatering crumb. It slices beautifully and tastes wonderful
served simply with butter or olive oil, or with cheese.*

*20g/¾ oz fresh yeast
250ml/8fl oz/1 cup lukewarm water
225g/8oz/2 cups maize meal
450g/1lb/4 cups unbleached white
bread flour
150ml/¼ pint/⅔ cup lukewarm milk
30ml/2 tbsp olive oil
7.5ml/1½ tsp salt
polenta, for dusting*

MAKES 1 LARGE LOAF

VARIATION

Replace 50 per cent of the maize meal
with polenta for a rougher textured,
slightly crunchier loaf.

1 Dust a baking sheet with a little maize
meal. Put the yeast in a large bowl and
gradually mix in the lukewarm water
until smooth. Stir in half the maize meal
and 50g/2oz/½ cup of the flour and mix
to a batter, with a wooden spoon.

6 Turn out the dough on to a lightly
floured surface and knock back. Shape
into a round ball, flatten slightly and
place on the prepared baking sheet.
Dust with polenta, cover with a large
upturned bowl and leave to rise, in a
warm place, for about 1 hour, or until
doubled in size. Meanwhile, preheat the
oven to 230°C/450°F/Gas 8.

7 Bake for 10 minutes, spraying the
inside of the oven with water 2–3 times.
Reduce the oven temperature to 190°C/
375°F/Gas 5 and bake for a further
20–25 minutes, or until golden and
hollow sounding when tapped on the
base. Transfer to a wire rack to cool.

2 Cover the bowl with lightly oiled clear
film and leave the batter undisturbed in
a warm place for about 30 minutes, or
until bubbles start to appear on the
surface. Remove the clear film.

3 Stir the milk into the batter, then stir
in the olive oil. Gradually mix in the
remaining maize meal, flour and salt to
form a pliable dough.

4 Turn out the dough on to a lightly
floured surface and knead for about
10 minutes until smooth and elastic.

5 Place in a lightly oiled bowl, cover
with lightly oiled clear film and leave to
rise, in a warm place, for 1½–2 hours, or
until doubled in bulk.

PAN GALLEGO

350g/12oz/3 cups unbleached white bread flour
115g/4oz/1 cup wholemeal bread flour
10ml/2 tsp salt
20g/¾ oz fresh yeast
275ml/9fl oz/generous 1 cup lukewarm water
30ml/2 tbsp olive oil or melted lard
30ml/2 tbsp pumpkin seeds
30ml/2 tbsp sunflower seeds
15ml/1 tbsp millet
maize meal, for dusting

MAKES 1 LARGE LOAF

Here, a typical round bread with a twisted top from Galicia. The olive oil gives a soft crumb and the millet, pumpkin and sunflower seeds scattered through the loaf provide an interesting mix of textures.

COOK'S TIP
If wished, replace fresh yeast with a 6g/¼ oz sachet of easy-blend dried yeast. Stir into the flours in step 1. Continue as in the recipe.

1 Sprinkle a baking sheet with maize meal. Mix the flours and salt together in a large bowl.

2 In a bowl, mix the yeast with the water. Add to the centre of the flours with the olive oil or melted lard and mix to a firm dough. Turn out on to a lightly floured surface and knead for about 10 minutes until smooth and elastic. Place in a lightly oiled bowl, then cover with lightly oiled clear film and leave to rise, in a warm place, for about 1½–2 hours, or until doubled in bulk.

3 Knock back the dough and turn out on to a lightly floured surface. Gently knead in the pumpkin seeds, sunflower seeds and millet. Re-cover and leave to rest for 5 minutes.

4 Shape into a round ball; twist the centre to make a cap. Transfer to the prepared baking sheet and dust with maize meal. Cover with a large upturned bowl and leave to rise, in a warm place, for 45 minutes, or until doubled in bulk.

5 Meanwhile, place an empty roasting tin in the bottom of the oven. Preheat the oven to 220°C/425°F/Gas 7. Pour about 300ml/½ pint/1¼ cups cold water into the roasting tin. Lift the bowl off the risen loaf and immediately place the baking sheet in the oven, above the roasting tin. Bake the bread for 10 minutes.

6 Remove the tin of water and bake the bread for a further 25–30 minutes, or until well browned and sounding hollow when tapped on the base. Transfer to a wire rack to cool.

PAN DE CEBADA

This Spanish country bread has a close, heavy texture and is quite satisfying. It is richly flavoured, incorporating barley and maize flours.

FOR THE SOURDOUGH STARTER
175g/6oz/1½ cups maize meal
560ml/scant 1 pint/scant 2½ cups water
225g/8oz/2 cups wholemeal bread flour
150g/5oz/1¼ cups barley flour

FOR THE DOUGH
20g/¾ oz fresh yeast
45ml/3 tbsp lukewarm water
225g/8oz/2 cups wholemeal bread flour
15ml/1 tbsp salt
maize meal, for dusting

MAKES 1 LARGE LOAF

1 In a saucepan, mix the maize meal for the sourdough starter with half the water, then blend in the remainder. Cook over a gentle heat, stirring continuously, until thickened. Transfer to a large bowl and set aside to cool.

2 Mix in the wholemeal flour and barley flour. Turn out on to a lightly floured surface and knead for 5 minutes. Return to the bowl, cover with lightly oiled clear film and leave the starter in a warm place for 36 hours.

3 Dust a baking sheet with maize meal. In a small bowl, cream the yeast with the water for the dough. Mix the yeast mixture into the starter with the wholemeal flour and salt and work to a dough. Turn out on to a lightly floured surface and knead for 4–5 minutes until smooth and elastic.

4 Transfer the dough to a lightly oiled bowl, cover with lightly oiled clear film or an oiled polythene bag and leave, in a warm place, for 1½–2 hours to rise, or until nearly doubled in bulk.

5 Knock back the dough and turn out on to a lightly floured surface. Shape into a plump round. Sprinkle with a little maize meal.

6 Place the shaped bread on the prepared baking sheet. Cover with a large upturned bowl. Leave to rise, in a warm place, for about 1 hour, or until nearly doubled in bulk. Place an empty roasting tin in the bottom of the oven. Preheat the oven to 220°C/425°F/Gas 7.

7 Pour 300ml/½ pint/1¼ cups cold water into the roasting tin. Lift the bowl off the risen loaf and immediately place the baking sheet in the oven. Bake the bread for 10 minutes. Remove the tin of water, reduce the oven temperature to 190°C/375°F/Gas 5 and bake for about 20 minutes. Cool on a wire rack.

TWELFTH NIGHT BREAD

450g/1lb/4 cups unbleached white
bread flour
2.5ml/½ tsp salt
25g/1oz yeast
140ml/scant ¼ pint/scant ⅔ cup
mixed lukewarm milk
and water
75g/3oz/6 tbsp butter
75g/3oz/6 tbsp caster sugar
10ml/2 tsp finely grated
lemon rind
10ml/2 tsp finely grated
orange rind
2 eggs
15ml/1 tbsp brandy
15ml/1 tbsp orange flower water
silver coin or dried bean
(optional)
1 egg white, lightly beaten,
for glazing

FOR THE DECORATION
a mixture of candied and glacé
fruit slices
flaked almonds

MAKES 1 LARGE LOAF

COOK'S TIP
If you like, this bread can be baked
in a lightly greased 24cm/9½ in
ring-shaped cake tin or savarin
mould. Place the dough seam-side
down into the tin or mould and seal
the ends together.

1 Lightly grease a large baking sheet.
Sift the flour and salt together into a
large bowl. Make a well in the centre.

January 6th, Epiphany or the Day of the Three Kings, is celebrated in Spain as a time to exchange Christmas presents. Historically this date was when the Three Wise Men arrived bearing gifts. An ornamental bread ring is specially baked for the occasion. The traditional version contains a silver coin, china figure or dried bean hidden inside – the lucky recipient is declared King of the festival!

2 In a bowl, mix the yeast with the milk
and water until the yeast has dissolved.
Pour the yeast mixture into the centre
of the flour and stir in enough of the
flour from around the sides of the bowl
to make a thick batter.

3 Sprinkle a little of the remaining flour
over the top of the batter and leave to
"sponge", in a warm place, for about
15 minutes or until frothy.

4 Using an electric whisk or a wooden
spoon, beat the butter and sugar
together in a bowl until soft and creamy,
then set aside.

5 Add the citrus rinds, eggs, brandy and
orange flower water to the flour mixture
and use a wooden spoon to mix to a
sticky dough.

6 Using one hand, beat the mixture until
it forms a fairly smooth dough.
Gradually beat in the reserved butter
mixture and beat for a few minutes until
the dough is smooth and elastic. Cover
with lightly oiled clear film and leave to
rise, in a warm place, for about 1½
hours, or until doubled in bulk.

7 Knock back the dough and turn out on
to a lightly floured surface. Gently knead
for 2 or 3 minutes, incorporating the
lucky coin or bean, if using.

8 Using a rolling pin, roll out the dough
into a long strip measuring about 66 ×
13cm/26 × 5in.

9 Roll up the dough from one long side
like a Swiss roll to make a long sausage
shape. Place seam side down on the
prepared baking sheet and seal the ends
together. Cover with lightly oiled clear
film and leave to rise, in a warm place,
for 1–1½ hours, or until doubled in size.

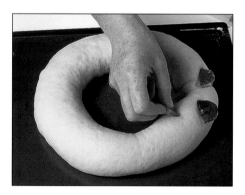

10 Meanwhile, preheat the oven to
180°C/350°F/Gas 4. Brush the dough
ring with lightly beaten egg white and
decorate with candied and glacé fruit
slices, pushing them slightly into the
dough. Sprinkle with almond flakes
and bake for 30–35 minutes, or until
risen and golden. Turn out on to a wire
rack to cool.

MALLORCAN ENSAIMADAS

*225g/8oz/2 cups unbleached white
bread flour*
2.5ml/½ tsp salt
50g/2oz/¼ cup caster sugar
15g/½ oz fresh yeast
75ml/5 tbsp lukewarm milk
1 egg
30ml/2 tbsp sunflower oil
50g/2oz/¼ cup butter, melted
icing sugar, for dusting

MAKES 16 ROLLS

*These spiral- or snail-shaped rolls are a popular Spanish breakfast treat.
Traditionally lard or* saim *was used to brush over the strips of sweetened
dough, but nowadays mainly butter is used to add a delicious richness.*

1 Lightly grease 2 baking sheets. Sift the flour and salt together into a large mixing bowl. Stir in the sugar and make a well in the centre.

2 Cream the yeast with the milk, pour into the centre of the flour mixture, then sprinkle a little of the flour mixture evenly over the top of the liquid. Leave in a warm place for about 15 minutes, or until frothy.

3 In a small bowl, beat the egg and sunflower oil together. Add to the flour mixture and mix to a smooth dough.

4 Turn out on to a lightly floured surface and knead for 8–10 minutes until smooth and elastic. Place in a lightly oiled bowl, cover with lightly oiled clear film and leave to rise, in a warm place, for 1 hour, or until doubled in bulk.

5 Turn out the dough on to a lightly floured surface. Knock back and divide the dough into 16 equal pieces. Shape each piece into a thin rope about 38cm/15in long. Pour the melted butter on to a plate and dip the ropes into the butter to coat.

6 On the baking sheets, curl each rope into a loose spiral, spacing well apart. Tuck the ends under to seal. Cover with lightly oiled clear film and leave to rise, in a warm place, for about 45 minutes, or until doubled in size.

7 Meanwhile, preheat the oven to 190°C/375°F/Gas 5. Brush the rolls with water and dust with icing sugar. Bake for 10 minutes, or until light golden brown. Cool on a wire rack. Dust again with icing sugar and serve warm.

PITTA BREAD

These Turkish breads are a firm favourite in both the eastern Mediterranean and the Middle East, and have crossed to England and the USA. This versatile soft, flat bread forms a pocket as it cooks, which is perfect for filling with vegetables, salads or meats.

225g/8oz/2 cups unbleached white bread flour
5ml/1 tsp salt
15g/¹/₂ oz fresh yeast
140ml/scant ¹/₄ pint/scant ²/₃ cup lukewarm water
10ml/2 tsp extra virgin olive oil

MAKES 6 PITTA BREADS

VARIATIONS
To make wholemeal pitta breads, replace half the white bread flour with wholemeal bread flour. You can also make smaller round pitta breads about 10cm/4in in diameter to serve as snack breads.

5 Roll out each ball of dough in turn to an oval about 5mm/¹/₄in thick and 15cm/6in long. Place on a floured dish towel and cover with lightly oiled clear film. Leave to rise at room temperature for about 20–30 minutes.

6 Meanwhile, preheat the oven to 230°C/450°F/Gas 8. Place 3 baking sheets in the oven to heat at the same time.

7 Place two pitta breads on each baking sheet and bake for 4–6 minutes, or until puffed up; they do not need to brown. If preferred, cook the pitta bread in batches. It is important that the oven has reached the recommended temperature before the pitta breads are baked. This ensures that they puff up.

8 Transfer the pittas to a wire rack to cool until warm, then cover with a dish towel to keep them soft.

1 Sift the flour and salt together into a bowl. Mix the yeast with the water until dissolved, then stir in the olive oil and pour into a large bowl.

2 Gradually beat the flour into the yeast mixture, then knead the mixture to make a soft dough.

3 Turn out on to a lightly floured surface and knead for 5 minutes until smooth and elastic. Place in a large clean bowl, cover with lightly oiled clear film and leave to rise, in a warm place, for about 1 hour, or until doubled in bulk.

4 Knock back the dough. On a lightly floured surface, divide it into 6 equal pieces and shape into balls. Cover with oiled clear film; let rest for 5 minutes.

CHRISTOPSOMO

A Byzantine cross flavoured with aniseed tops this Greek Christmas bread, which is also decorated with walnuts for good fortune. The fluffy, light, butter-enriched bread contains orange rind, cinnamon and cloves – all the lovely warm tastes associated with Christmas.

15g/1/2 oz fresh yeast
140ml/scant 1/4 pint/scant 2/3 cup lukewarm milk
450g/1lb/4 cups unbleached white bread flour
2 eggs
75g/3oz/6 tbsp caster sugar
2.5ml/1/2 tsp salt
75g/3oz/6 tbsp butter, softened
grated rind of 1/2 orange
5ml/1 tsp ground cinnamon
1.5ml/1/4 tsp ground cloves
pinch of crushed aniseed
8 walnut halves
beaten egg white, for glazing

MAKES 1 LOAF

COOK'S TIP
If you do not have any aniseed, flavour the dough with 5ml/1 tsp pastis, anisette or ouzo.

1 Lightly grease a large baking sheet. In a large bowl, mix the yeast with the milk until the yeast is dissolved, then stir in 115g/4oz/1 cup of the flour to make a thin batter. Cover with lightly oiled clear film and leave to "sponge" in a warm place for 30 minutes.

2 Beat the eggs and sugar until light and fluffy. Beat into the yeast mixture. Gradually mix in the remaining flour and salt. Beat in the softened butter and knead to a soft but not sticky dough. Knead on a lightly floured surface for 8–10 minutes until smooth and elastic. Place in a lightly oiled bowl, cover with lightly oiled clear film and leave to rise, in a warm place, for 1½ hours, or until doubled in bulk.

3 Turn out on to a lightly floured surface and gently knock back. Cut off about 50g/2oz of dough; cover and set aside. Gently knead the orange rind, ground cinnamon and cloves into the large piece of dough and shape into a round loaf. Place on the baking sheet.

4 Knead the aniseed into the remaining dough. Cut the dough in half and shape each piece into a 30cm/12in long rope. Cut through each rope at either end by one-third of its length. Place the two ropes in a cross on top of the loaf, then curl each cut end into a circle, in opposite directions.

5 Place a walnut half inside each circle. Cover the loaf with lightly oiled clear film and leave to rise for 45 minutes, or until doubled in size. Meanwhile, preheat the oven to 190°C/375°F/Gas 5. Brush the bread with the egg white and bake for 40–45 minutes, or until golden. Cool on a wire rack.

TSOUREKI

Topped with brightly coloured eggs, this plaited bread is an important part of the Greek Easter celebrations.

For the Eggs
3 eggs
1.5ml/¼ tsp bright red food colouring paste
15ml/1 tbsp white wine vinegar
5ml/1 tsp water
5ml/1 tsp olive oil

For the Dough
450g/1lb/4 cups unbleached white bread flour
2.5ml/½ tsp salt
5ml/1 tsp ground allspice
2.5ml/½ tsp ground cinnamon
2.5ml/½ tsp caraway seeds
20g/¾ oz fresh yeast
175ml/6fl oz/¾ cup lukewarm milk
50g/2oz/¼ cup butter
40g/1½oz/3 tbsp caster sugar
2 eggs

For the Glaze
1 egg yolk
5ml/1 tsp clear honey
5ml/1 tsp water

For the Decoration
50g/2oz/½ cup split almonds, slivered
edible gold leaf, optional

MAKES 1 LOAF

1 Lightly grease a baking sheet. Place the eggs in a pan of water and bring to the boil. Boil gently for 10 minutes. Meanwhile, mix the red food colouring, vinegar and water together in a shallow bowl. Remove the eggs from the boiling water, place on a wire rack for a few seconds to dry then roll in the colouring mixture. Return to the rack to cool and completely dry.

2 When cold, drizzle the olive oil on to absorbent kitchen paper, lift up each egg in turn and rub all over with the oiled paper.

3 To make the dough, sift the flour, salt, allspice and cinnamon into a large bowl. Stir in the caraway seeds.

4 In a jug, mix the yeast with the milk. In a bowl, cream the butter and sugar together, then beat in the eggs. Add the creamed mixture to the flour with the yeast mixture and gradually mix to a dough. Turn out the dough on to a lightly floured surface and knead until smooth and elastic.

5 Place in a lightly oiled bowl, cover with lightly oiled clear film and leave to rise, in a warm place, for about 2 hours, or until doubled in bulk.

6 Knock back the dough and knead for 2–3 minutes. Return to the bowl, re-cover and leave to rise again, in a warm place, for about 1 hour, or until doubled in bulk.

7 Knock back and turn out on to a lightly floured surface. Divide the dough into 3 equal pieces and roll each into a 38–50cm/15–20in long rope. Plait these together from the centre to the ends.

8 Place on the prepared baking sheet and push the dyed eggs into the loaf. Cover and leave to rise, in a warm place, for about 1 hour.

9 Meanwhile, preheat the oven to 190°C/375°F/Gas 5. Mix the egg yolk, honey and water together for the glaze, and brush over the loaf. Sprinkle with almonds and edible gold leaf, if using. Bake for 40–45 minutes, or until golden and sounding hollow when tapped on the base. Transfer to a wire rack to cool.

GREEK OLIVE BREAD

The flavours of the Mediterranean simply ooze from this decorative bread, speckled with black olives, red onions and herbs.

675g/1½ lb/6 cups unbleached white bread flour, plus extra for dusting
10ml/2 tsp salt
25g/1oz fresh yeast
350ml/12fl oz/1½ cups lukewarm water
75ml/5 tbsp olive oil
175g/6oz/1½ cups pitted black olives, roughly chopped
1 red onion, finely chopped
30ml/2 tbsp chopped fresh coriander or mint

MAKES 2 LOAVES

VARIATION
Make one large loaf and increase the baking time by about 15 minutes.

1 Lightly grease 2 baking sheets. Sift the flour and salt together into a large bowl and make a well in the centre.

2 In a jug, blend the yeast with half of the water. Add to the centre of the flour with the remaining water and the olive oil; mix to a soft dough.

3 Turn out the dough on to a lightly floured surface and knead for 8–10 minutes until smooth. Place in a lightly oiled bowl, cover with lightly oiled clear film and leave to rise, in a warm place, for 1 hour, or until doubled in bulk.

4 Turn out on to a lightly floured surface and knock back. Cut off a quarter of the dough, cover with lightly oiled clear film and set aside.

5 Roll out the remaining, large piece of dough to a round. Sprinkle the olives, onion and herbs evenly over the surface, then bring up the sides of the circle and gently knead together. Cut the dough in half and shape each piece into a plump oval loaf, about 20cm/8in long. Place on the prepared baking sheets.

6 Divide the reserved dough into 4 equal pieces and roll each to a long strand 60cm/24in long. Twist together and cut in half. Brush the centre of each loaf with water and place two pieces of twisted dough on top of each, tucking the ends underneath the loaves.

7 Cover with lightly oiled clear film and leave to rise, in a warm place, for about 45 minutes, or until the loaves are plump and nearly doubled in size.

8 Meanwhile, preheat the oven to 220°C/ 425°F/Gas 7. Dust the loaves lightly with flour and bake for 35–40 minutes, or until golden and sounding hollow when tapped on the base. Transfer to a wire rack to cool.

MOROCCAN HOLIDAY BREAD

*The addition of maize meal and a cornucopia of seeds gives this superb loaf
an interesting flavour and texture.*

*275g/10oz/2½ cups unbleached white
bread flour
50g/2oz/½ cup maize meal
5ml/1 tsp salt
20g/¾ oz fresh yeast
120ml/4fl oz/½ cup lukewarm water
120ml/4fl oz/½ cup lukewarm milk
15ml/1 tbsp pumpkin seeds
15ml/1 tbsp sesame seeds
30ml/2 tbsp sunflower seeds*

MAKES 1 LOAF

5 Turn out the dough on to a lightly
floured surface and knock back. Gently
knead the pumpkin and sesame seeds
into the dough. Shape into a round ball
and flatten slightly.

6 Place on the prepared baking sheet,
cover with lightly oiled clear film or slide
into a large, lightly oiled polythene bag
and leave to rise, in a warm place, for
45 minutes, or until doubled in bulk.

1 Lightly grease a baking sheet. Sift the
flours and salt into a large bowl.

2 Cream the yeast with a little of the
water in a jug. Stir in the remainder of
the water and the milk. Pour into the
centre of the flour and mix to a fairly
soft dough.

3 Turn out the dough on to a lightly
floured surface and knead for about
5 minutes until smooth and elastic.

4 Place in a lightly oiled bowl, cover
with lightly oiled clear film and leave to
rise, in a warm place, for about 1 hour,
or until doubled in bulk.

VARIATIONS
Incorporate all the seeds in the
dough in step 5 and leave the top of
the loaf plain. Alternatively, use
sesame seeds instead of sunflower
seeds for the topping and either
incorporate the sunflower seeds in the
loaf or leave them out.

7 Meanwhile, preheat the oven to 200°C/
400°F/Gas 6. Brush the top of the loaf
with water and sprinkle evenly with
the sunflower seeds. Bake the loaf for
30–35 minutes, or until it is golden and
sounds hollow when tapped on the base.
Transfer the loaf to a wire rack to cool.

NORTH EUROPEAN AND SCANDINAVIAN BREADS

The northern Europeans and Scandinavians make many different loaves, from the dense, dark German pumpernickel to a light Polish rye bread. Also from these northern climes come the famous Swedish crispbreads, Russian potato bread and blinis, a variety of sweet breads, lightly scented saffron buns and port-flavoured rye bread. Christmas breads are enriched with fruit, while Bulgaria has its own poppy-seeded circular bread for religious festivals.

SWISS BRAID

This plaited, attractively tapered loaf is known as zupfe *in Switzerland. Often eaten at the weekend, it is has a glossy crust and a wonderfully light crumb.*

350g/12oz/3 cups unbleached white bread flour
5ml/1 tsp salt
20g/¾ oz fresh yeast
30ml/2 tbsp lukewarm water
150ml/¼ pint/⅔ cup soured cream
1 egg, lightly beaten
50g/2oz/¼ cup butter, softened

FOR THE GLAZE
1 egg yolk
15ml/1 tbsp water

MAKES 1 LOAF

COOK'S TIP
If you prefer, use a 7g/¼ oz sachet of easy-blend yeast. Add directly to the flour with the salt, then add the warmed soured cream and water and mix together.

1 Lightly grease a baking sheet. Sift the flour and salt together into a large bowl and make a well in the centre. Mix the yeast with the water in a jug.

2 Gently warm the soured cream in a small pan until it reaches blood heat (35–38°C). Add to the yeast mixture and mix together.

3 Add the yeast mixture and egg to the centre of the flour and gradually mix to a dough. Beat in the softened butter.

4 Turn out on to a lightly floured surface and knead for 5 minutes until smooth and elastic. Place in a lightly oiled bowl, cover with lightly oiled clear film and leave to rise, in a warm place, for about 1½ hours, or until doubled in size.

5 Turn out on to a lightly floured surface and knock back. Cut in half and shape each piece of dough into a long rope about 35cm/14in in length.

6 To make the braid, place the two pieces of dough on top of each other to form a cross. Starting with the bottom rope, fold the top end over and place between the two bottom ropes. Fold the remaining top rope over so that all four ropes are pointing downwards. Starting from the left, plait the first rope over the second, and the third rope over the fourth.

7 Continue plaiting in this way to form a tapered bread. Tuck the ends underneath and place on the prepared baking sheet. Cover with lightly oiled clear film and leave to rise, in a warm place, for about 40 minutes.

8 Meanwhile, preheat the oven to 190°C/ 375°F/Gas 5. Mix the egg yolk and water for the glaze, and brush over the loaf. Bake the bread for 30–35 minutes, or until golden. Cool on a wire rack.

PRETZELS

*Pretzels or brezeln, as they are known in Germany, are said to be derived
from the Latin* bracellae *or arms, referring to the crossed "arms" of dough
inside the oval shape. This shape is also used for biscuits in Germany and
Austria, and in Alsace the pretzel shape is part of the wrought iron emblem of
quality that bakers display outside their shops.*

For the Yeast Sponge
7g/¼ oz fresh yeast
75ml/5 tbsp water
15ml/1 tbsp unbleached plain
white flour
For the Dough
7g/¼ oz fresh yeast
150ml/¼ pint/⅔ cup lukewarm water
75ml/5 tbsp lukewarm milk
400g/14oz/3½ cups unbleached white
bread flour
7.5ml/1½ tsp salt
25g/1oz/2 tbsp butter, melted

For the Topping
1 egg yolk
15ml/1 tbsp milk
sea salt or caraway seeds, for
sprinkling

MAKES 12 PRETZELS

4 Turn out the dough on to a lightly
floured surface. Divide the dough into
12 equal pieces and form into balls.
Take one ball of dough and cover the
remainder with a dish towel. Roll into a
thin stick 46cm/18in long and about
1cm/½ in thick in the middle and thinner
at the ends. Bend each end of the dough
stick into a horseshoe. Cross over and
place the ends on top of the thick part of
the pretzel. Repeat with the remaining
dough balls.

5 Place on the floured baking sheet to
rest for 10 minutes. Meanwhile, preheat
the oven to 190°C/375°F/Gas 5. Bring a
large saucepan of water to the boil, then
reduce to a simmer. Add the pretzels to
the simmering water in batches, about
2–3 at a time and poach for about
1 minute. Drain the pretzels on a dish
towel and place on the greased baking
sheets, spaced well apart.

1 Lightly flour a baking sheet. Also
grease 2 baking sheets. Cream the yeast
for the yeast sponge with the water,
then mix in the flour, cover with clear
film and leave to stand at room
temperature for 2 hours.

2 Mix the yeast for the dough with the
water until dissolved, then stir in the
milk. Sift 350g/12oz/3 cups of the flour
and the salt into a large bowl. Add the
yeast sponge mixture and the butter;
mix for 3–4 minutes. Turn out on to a
lightly floured surface and knead in the
remaining flour to make a medium firm
dough. Place in a lightly oiled bowl, cover
with lightly oiled clear film and leave to
rise, in a warm place, for 30 minutes, or
until almost doubled in bulk.

3 Turn out on to a lightly floured surface
and knock back the dough. Knead into a
ball, return to the bowl, re-cover and
leave to rise for 30 minutes.

6 Mix the egg yolk and milk together
and brush this glaze over the pretzels.
Sprinkle with sea salt or caraway seeds
and bake the pretzels for 25 minutes, or
until they are deep golden. Transfer to a
wire rack to cool.

PUMPERNICKEL

450g/1lb/4 cups rye flour
225g/8oz/2 cups wholemeal flour
115g/4oz/⅔ cup bulgur wheat
10ml/2 tsp salt
30ml/2 tbsp molasses
850ml/1 pint 8fl oz/3½ cups warm
water
15ml/1 tbsp vegetable oil

MAKES 2 LOAVES

COOK'S TIP
This bread improves on keeping. Keep
for at least 24 hours double-wrapped
inside a plastic bag or greaseproof
paper and foil before slicing.

*This famous German bread is extremely dense and dark, with an intense
flavour. It is baked very slowly and although cooked in the oven, it is more
like a steamed bread than a baked one.*

2 Mix the molasses with the warm water
and add to the flours with the vegetable
oil. Mix together to form a dense mass.

1 Lightly grease two 18 × 9cm/7 × 3½ in
loaf tins. Mix the rye flour, wholemeal
flour, bulgur wheat and salt together in a
large bowl.

3 Place in the prepared tins, pressing
well into the corners. Cover with lightly
oiled clear film and leave in a warm
place for 18–24 hours.

4 Preheat the oven to 110°C/225°F/
Gas ¼. Cover the tins tightly with foil.
Fill a roasting tin with boiling water and
place a rack on top.

5 Place the tins on top of the rack and
transfer very carefully to the oven. Bake
the loaves for 4 hours. Increase the oven
temperature to 160°C/325°F/Gas 3. Top
up the water in the roasting tin if
necessary, uncover the loaves and bake
for a further 30–45 minutes, or until the
loaves feel firm and the tops are crusty.

6 Leave to cool in the tins for 5 minutes,
then turn out on to a wire rack to cool
completely. Serve cold, very thinly
sliced, with cold meats.

German Sourdough Bread

This bread includes rye, wholemeal and plain flours for a superb depth of flavour. Serve it cut in thick slices, with creamy butter or a sharp cheese.

1 Mix the rye flour, warm water and caraway for the starter together in a large bowl with your fingertips, to make a soft paste. Cover with a damp dish towel and leave in a warm place for about 36 hours. Stir after 24 hours.

2 Lightly grease a baking sheet. In a measuring jug, blend the yeast for the dough with the lukewarm water. Add to the starter and mix thoroughly.

3 Mix the rye flour, wholemeal bread flour and unbleached white bread flour for the dough with the salt in a large bowl; make a well in the centre. Pour in the yeast liquid and gradually incorporate the surrounding flour to make a smooth dough.

4 Turn out the dough on to a lightly floured surface and knead for 8–10 minutes until smooth and elastic. Place in a lightly oiled bowl, cover with lightly oiled clear film and leave to rise, in a warm place, for 1½ hours, or until nearly doubled in bulk.

5 Turn out on to a lightly floured surface, knock back and knead gently. Shape into a round and place in a floured basket or *couronne*, with the seam up. Cover with lightly oiled clear film and leave to rise, in a warm place, for 2–3 hours.

6 Meanwhile, preheat the oven to 200°C/ 400°F/Gas 6. Turn out the loaf on to the prepared baking sheet and bake for 35–40 minutes. Cool on a wire rack.

For the Sourdough Starter
75g/3oz/¾ cup rye flour
80ml/3fl oz/⅓ cup warm water
pinch caraway seeds

For the Dough
15g/½ oz fresh yeast
315ml/11fl oz/1⅓ cups lukewarm water
275g/10oz/2½ cups rye flour
150g/5oz/1¼ cups wholemeal bread flour
150g/5oz/1¼ cups unbleached white bread flour
10ml/2 tsp salt

Makes 1 Loaf

COOK'S TIP
Proving the dough in a floured basket or *couronne* gives it its characteristic patterned crust, but is not essential. Make sure that you flour the basket well, otherwise the dough may stick.

STOLLEN

This German speciality bread, made for the Christmas season, is rich with rum-soaked fruits and is wrapped around a moist almond filling. The folded shape of the dough over the filling represents the baby Jesus wrapped in swaddling clothes.

75g/3oz/1/2 cup sultanas
50g/2oz/1/4 cup currants
45ml/3 tbsp rum
375g/13oz/31/4 cups unbleached white bread flour
2.5ml/1/2 tsp salt
50g/2oz/1/4 cup caster sugar
1.5ml/1/4 tsp ground cardamom
2.5ml/1/2 tsp ground cinnamon
40g/11/2 oz fresh yeast
120ml/4fl oz/1/2 cup lukewarm milk
50g/2oz/1/4 cup butter, melted
1 egg, lightly beaten
50g/2oz/1/3 cup mixed chopped peel
50g/2oz/1/3 cup blanched whole almonds, chopped
melted butter, for brushing
icing sugar, for dusting

FOR THE ALMOND FILLING
115g/4oz/1 cup ground almonds
50g/2oz/1/4 cup caster sugar
50g/2oz/1/2 cup icing sugar
2.5ml/1/2 tsp lemon juice
1/2 egg, lightly beaten

MAKES 1 LARGE LOAF

COOK'S TIP
You can dust the cooled stollen with icing sugar and cinnamon, or drizzle over a thin glacé icing.

1 Lightly grease a baking sheet. Preheat the oven to 180°C/350°F/Gas 4. Put the sultanas and currants in a heatproof bowl and warm for 3–4 minutes. Pour over the rum and set aside.

2 Sift the flour and salt together into a large bowl. Stir in the sugar and spices.

3 Mix the yeast with the milk until creamy. Pour into the flour and mix a little of the flour from around the edge into the milk mixture to make a thick batter. Sprinkle some of the remaining flour over the top of the batter, then cover with clear film and leave in a warm place for 30 minutes.

4 Add the melted butter and egg and mix to a soft dough. Turn out the dough on to a lightly floured surface and knead for 8–10 minutes until smooth and elastic. Place in a lightly oiled bowl, cover with lightly oiled clear film and leave to rise, in a warm place, for 2–3 hours, or until doubled in bulk.

5 Mix the ground almonds and sugars together for the filling. Add the lemon juice and sufficient egg to knead to a smooth paste. Shape into a 20cm/8in long sausage, cover and set aside.

6 Turn out the dough on to a lightly floured surface and knock back.

7 Pat out the dough into a rectangle about 2.5cm/1in thick and sprinkle over the sultanas, currants, mixed chopped peel and almonds. Fold and knead the dough to incorporate the fruit and nuts.

8 Roll out the dough into an oval about 30 × 23cm/12 × 9in. Roll the centre slightly thinner than the edges. Place the almond paste filling along the centre and fold over the dough to enclose it, making sure that the top of the dough doesn't completely cover the base. The top edge should be slightly in from the bottom edge. Press down to seal.

9 Place the loaf on the prepared baking sheet, cover with lightly oiled clear film and leave to rise, in a warm place, for 45–60 minutes, or until doubled in size.

10 Meanwhile, preheat the oven to 200°C/400°F/Gas 6. Bake the loaf for about 30 minutes, or until it sounds hollow when tapped on the base. Brush the top with melted butter and transfer to a wire rack to cool. Dust with icing sugar just before serving.

BUCHTY

*Popular in both Poland and Germany as breakfast treats, these are also
excellent split and toasted, and served with cured meats.*

*450g/1lb/4 cups unbleached white
bread flour
5ml/1 tsp salt
50g/2oz/¼ cup caster sugar
90g/3½oz/scant ½ cup butter
120ml/4fl oz/½ cup milk
20g/¾ oz fresh yeast
3 eggs, lightly beaten
40g/1½ oz/3 tbsp butter, melted
icing sugar, for dusting (optional)*

MAKES 16 ROLLS

COOK'S TIP
If you do not have a square tin use a
round one. Place 2 rolls in the centre
and the rest around the edge.

1 Grease a 20cm/8in square loose-
bottomed cake tin. Sift the flour and salt
together into a large bowl and stir in the
sugar. Make a well in the centre.

2 Melt 50g/2oz/¼ cup of the butter in a
small pan, then remove from the heat
and stir in the milk. Leave to cool until
lukewarm. Stir the yeast into the milk
mixture until it has dissolved.

3 Pour into the centre of the flour and
stir in sufficient flour to form a thick
batter. Sprinkle with a little of the
surrounding flour, cover and leave in a
warm place for 30 minutes.

4 Gradually beat in the eggs and
remaining flour to form a soft, smooth
dough. This will take about 10 minutes.
Cover with lightly oiled clear film and
leave to rise, in a warm place, for about
1½ hours, or until doubled in bulk.

5 Turn out the dough on to a lightly
floured surface and knock back. Divide
into 16 equal pieces and shape into
rounds. Melt the remaining butter, roll
the rounds in it to coat, then place,
slightly apart, in the tin. Cover with lightly
oiled clear film and leave to rise, in a warm
place, for about 1 hour, or until doubled.

6 Meanwhile, preheat the oven to 190°C/
375°F/Gas 5. Spoon any remaining
melted butter evenly over the rolls and
bake for 25 minutes, or until golden
brown. Turn out on to a wire rack to
cool. If serving buchty as a breakfast
bread, dust the loaf with icing sugar
before separating it into rolls.

POLISH RYE BREAD

This rye bread is made with half white flour which gives it a lighter, more open texture than a traditional rye loaf. Served thinly sliced, it is the perfect accompaniment for cold meats and fish.

1 Lightly grease a baking sheet. Mix the flours, caraway seeds and salt in a large bowl and make a well in the centre.

2 In a bowl or measuring jug, cream the yeast with the milk and honey. Pour into the centre of the flour, add the water and gradually incorporate the surrounding flour and caraway mixture until a dough forms.

3 Turn out the dough on to a lightly floured surface and knead for 8–10 minutes until smooth, elastic and firm. Place in a large, lightly oiled bowl, cover with lightly oiled clear film and leave to rise, in a warm place, for about 3 hours, or until doubled in bulk.

225g/8oz/2 cups rye flour
225g/8oz/2 cups unbleached white bread flour
10ml/2 tsp caraway seeds
10ml/2 tsp salt
20g/¾ oz fresh yeast
110ml/scant ¼ pint/scant ½ cup lukewarm milk
5ml/1 tsp clear honey
140ml/scant ¼ pint/scant ⅔ cup lukewarm water
wholemeal flour, for dusting

MAKES 1 LOAF

4 Turn out the dough on to a lightly floured surface and knock back. Shape into an oval loaf and place on the prepared baking sheet.

5 Dust with wholemeal flour, cover with lightly oiled clear film and leave to rise, in a warm place, for 1–1½ hours, or until doubled in size. Meanwhile, preheat the oven to 220°C/425°F/Gas 7.

6 Using a sharp knife, slash the loaf with two long cuts about 2.5cm/1in apart. Bake for 30–35 minutes, or until the loaf sounds hollow when tapped on the base. Transfer the loaf to a wire rack and set aside to cool.

HUNGARIAN SPLIT FARMHOUSE LOAF

—

A golden, fennel seed-encrusted loaf with a moist white crumb. It is equally delicious made into rolls – just reduce the baking time to 15–20 minutes.

*450g/1lb/4 cups unbleached white
bread flour
10ml/2 tsp salt
2.5ml/½ tsp fennel seeds, crushed
15ml/1 tbsp caster sugar
20g/¾ oz fresh yeast
275ml/9fl oz/1⅛ cups lukewarm water
25g/1oz/2 tbsp butter, melted*

*FOR THE TOPPING
1 egg white
pinch of salt
10ml/2 tsp fennel seeds, for sprinkling*

MAKES 1 LOAF

1 Lightly grease a baking sheet. Sift the white bread flour and salt together into a large bowl and stir in the crushed fennel seeds and caster sugar. Make a well in the centre.

2 Cream the yeast with a little water, stir in the rest, then pour into the centre of the flour. Stir in sufficient flour to make a runny batter. Sprinkle more of the flour on top, cover and leave in a warm place for 30 minutes, or until the sponge starts to bubble and rise.

3 Add the melted butter and gradually mix in with the remaining flour to form a dough. Turn out on to a lightly floured surface and knead for 8–10 minutes until smooth and elastic. Place in a lightly oiled bowl, cover with lightly oiled clear film and leave to rise, in a warm place, for 45–60 minutes, or until doubled in bulk.

4 Turn out on to a lightly floured surface and knock back. Shape into an oval and place on the prepared baking sheet. Cover with lightly oiled clear film and leave to rise, in a warm place, for 30–40 minutes, or until doubled in size.

5 Meanwhile, preheat the oven to 220°C/425°F/Gas 7. Mix the egg white and salt together, and brush this glaze over the loaf. Sprinkle with fennel seeds and then, using a sharp knife, slash along its length. Bake for 20 minutes, then reduce the oven temperature to 180°C/350°F/Gas 4 and bake for 10 minutes more, or until sounding hollow when tapped on the base. Transfer to a wire rack to cool.

GEORGIAN KHACHAPURI

These savoury buns are sold from street stalls as warm snacks. The sealed bread parcels envelop a meltingly delicious cheese filling; goat's cheese is typically used in Georgia.

1 Lightly grease a Yorkshire pudding tin with four 10cm/4in holes. Sift the flour and salt into a large bowl. Cream the yeast with the milk, add to the flour and mix to a dough. Knead in the butter, then knead on a lightly floured surface until smooth and elastic. Place in a lightly oiled bowl, cover with lightly oiled clear film and leave to rise, in a warm place, for 1–1½ hours, or until doubled in bulk.

2 Meanwhile, put the cheeses in a bowl and stir in the egg and softened butter for the filling. Season with plenty of salt and pepper.

VARIATIONS
- Use Red Leicester or Parmesan in place of the Cheddar.
- Make one large bread instead of the buns. Bake for 50–55 minutes.

225g/8oz/2 cups unbleached white bread flour
5ml/1 tsp salt
15g/½ oz fresh yeast
150ml/¼ pint/⅔ cup lukewarm milk
25g/1oz/2 tbsp butter, softened

FOR THE FILLING
225g/8oz/2 cups grated mature Cheddar cheese
225g/8oz Munster or Taleggio cheese, cut into small cubes
1 egg, lightly beaten
15ml/1 tbsp butter, softened
salt and freshly ground black pepper

FOR THE GLAZE
1 egg yolk
15ml/1 tbsp water

MAKES 4 BUNS

3 Turn the dough out onto a lightly floured surface and knead for 2–3 minutes. Divide into 4 equal pieces and roll each out into a 20cm/8in circle.

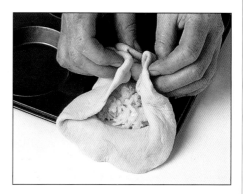

4 Place one dough circle in one hole of the Yorkshire pudding tin and fill with a quarter of the cheese filling. Gather the overhanging dough into the centre and twist to form a topknot. Repeat with the remaining dough and filling. Cover with lightly oiled clear film and leave to rise, in a warm place, for 20–30 minutes.

5 Meanwhile, preheat the oven to 180°C/350°F/Gas 4. Mix the egg yolk and water, and brush over the dough. Bake for 25–30 minutes, or until light golden. Cool for 2–3 minutes in the tin, then turn out on to a wire rack. Serve warm.

POPPY SEED ROLL

*A favourite sweet yeast bread in both Poland and Hungary, this has an
unusual filling of poppy seeds, almonds, raisins and citrus peel spiralling
through the dough.*

*350g/12oz/3 cups unbleached white
bread flour
2.5ml/½ tsp salt
25g/1oz/2 tbsp caster sugar
20g/¾ oz fresh yeast
120ml/4fl oz/½ cup lukewarm milk
1 egg, lightly beaten
50g/2oz/¼ cup butter, melted
15ml/1 tbsp toasted flaked almonds*

*FOR THE FILLING
115g/4oz/⅔ cup poppy seeds
50g/2oz/¼ cup butter
75g/3oz/6 tbsp caster sugar
75g/3oz/½ cup raisins
50g/2oz/½ cup ground almonds
50g/2oz/⅓ cup mixed chopped peel,
finely chopped
2.5ml/½ tsp ground cinnamon*

*FOR THE ICING
115g/4oz/1 cup icing sugar
15ml/1 tbsp lemon juice
10–15ml/2–3 tsp water*

MAKES 1 LARGE LOAF

1 Lightly grease a baking sheet. Sift the
flour and salt together into a large bowl.
Stir in the sugar. Cream the yeast with
the milk. Add to the flour with the egg
and melted butter and mix to a dough.

2 Turn out on to a lightly floured surface
and knead for 8–10 minutes until
smooth and elastic. Place in a lightly
oiled bowl, cover with lightly oiled clear
film and leave to rise, in a warm place,
for 1–1½ hours, or until doubled in size.

3 Meanwhile, pour boiling water over
the poppy seeds for the filling, then
leave to cool. Drain thoroughly in a fine
sieve. Melt the butter in a small pan, add
the poppy seeds and cook, stirring, for
1–2 minutes. Remove from the heat and
stir in the sugar, raisins, ground
almonds, mixed peel and cinnamon. Set
aside to cool.

4 Turn the dough out on to a lightly
floured surface, knock back and knead
lightly. Roll out into a rectangle 35 ×
25cm/14 × 10in. Spread the filling to
within 2cm/¾ in of the edges.

5 Roll up the dough, starting from one
long edge, like a Swiss roll, tucking in
the edges to seal. Place seam side down
on the prepared baking sheet. Cover
with lightly oiled clear film and leave to
rise, in a warm place, for 30 minutes, or
until doubled in size.

6 Meanwhile, preheat the oven to 190°C/
375°F/Gas 5. Bake for 30 minutes, or
until golden brown. Transfer to a wire
rack to cool until just warm.

7 Mix the icing sugar, lemon juice and
sufficient water together in a small
saucepan to make an icing stiff enough
to coat the back of a spoon. Heat gently,
stirring, until warm. Drizzle the icing
over the loaf and sprinkle the flaked
almonds over the top. Leave to cool
completely, then serve sliced.

RUSSIAN POTATO BREAD

*In Russia, potatoes are often used to replace some of the flour in bread
recipes. They endow the bread with excellent keeping qualities.*

225g/8oz potatoes, peeled
and diced
7g/¼ oz sachet easy-blend
dried yeast
350g/12oz/3 cups unbleached white
bread flour
115g/4oz/1 cup wholemeal bread
flour, plus extra for sprinkling
2.5ml/½ tsp caraway
seeds, crushed
10ml/2 tsp salt
25g/1oz/2 tbsp butter

MAKES 1 LOAF

1 Lightly grease a baking sheet. Add the
potatoes to a saucepan of boiling water
and cook until tender. Drain and reserve
150ml/¼ pint/⅔ cup of the cooking
water. Mash and sieve the potatoes and
leave to cool.

2 Mix the yeast, bread flours, caraway
seeds and salt together in a large bowl.
Add the butter and rub in. Mix the
reserved potato water and sieved
potatoes together. Gradually work this
mixture into the flour mixture to form a
soft dough.

3 Turn out on to a lightly floured surface
and knead for 8–10 minutes until
smooth and elastic. Place in a lightly
oiled bowl, cover with lightly oiled clear
film and leave to rise, in a warm place,
for 1 hour, or until doubled in bulk.

4 Turn out on to a lightly floured
surface, knock back and knead gently.
Shape into a plump oval loaf, about
18cm/7in long. Place on the prepared
baking sheet and sprinkle with a little
wholemeal bread flour.

5 Cover the dough with lightly oiled
clear film and leave to rise, in a warm
place, for 30 minutes, or until doubled in
size. Meanwhile, preheat the oven to
200°C/400°F/Gas 6.

6 Using a sharp knife, slash the top with
3–4 diagonal cuts to make a criss-cross
effect. Bake for 30–35 minutes, or until
golden and sounding hollow when
tapped on the base. Transfer to a wire
rack to cool.

VARIATION
To make a cheese-flavoured potato
bread, omit the caraway seeds and
knead 115g/4oz/1 cup grated Cheddar,
Red Leicester or a crumbled blue
cheese, such as Stilton, into the
dough before shaping.

*675g/1½ lb/6 cups unbleached white
bread flour*
10ml/2 tsp salt
25g/1oz fresh yeast
120ml/4fl oz/½ cup lukewarm milk
5ml/1 tsp clear honey
2 eggs
150ml/¼ pint/⅔ cup natural yogurt
50g/2oz/¼ cup butter, melted
beaten egg, for glazing
poppy seeds, for sprinkling

MAKES 1 LARGE LOAF

VARIATION
For a special finish, divide the dough
into 3 equal pieces, roll into long thin
strips and plait together, starting with
the centre of the strips. Once plaited,
shape into a circle and seal the ends
together. Make sure that the hole in
the centre is quite large, otherwise
the hole will fill in as the bread rises.

KOLACH

*Often prepared for religious celebrations and family feasts, this Bulgarian
bread gets its name from its circular shape – kolo, which means circle. It has
a golden crust sprinkled with poppy seeds and a moist crumb, which makes
this loaf a very good keeper.*

1 Grease a large baking sheet. Sift the
flour and salt together into a large bowl
and make a well in the centre.

2 Cream the yeast with the milk and
honey. Add to the centre of the flour
with the eggs, yogurt and melted butter.
Gradually mix into the flour to form a
firm dough.

3 Turn out on to a lightly floured surface
and knead for 8–10 minutes until
smooth and elastic. Place in a lightly
oiled bowl, cover with lightly oiled clear
film or slip into an oiled polythene bag.
Leave to rise, in a warm place, for
1½ hours, or until doubled in bulk.

4 Knock back the dough and turn out on
to a lightly floured surface. Knead lightly
and shape into a ball. Place seam side
down and make a hole in the centre with
your fingers.

5 Gradually enlarge the cavity, turning
the dough to make a 25cm/10in circle.
Transfer to the baking sheet, cover with
lightly oiled clear film and leave to rise,
in a warm place, for 30–45 minutes, or
until doubled in size.

6 Meanwhile, preheat the oven to 200°C/
400°F/Gas 6. Brush the loaf with beaten
egg and sprinkle with poppy seeds. Bake
for 35 minutes, or until golden. Cool on
a wire rack.

BLINIS

*Blinis are the celebrated leavened Russian pancakes. Traditionally served
with soured cream and caviar, they have a very distinctive flavour and a
fluffy, light texture.*

50g/2oz/½ cup buckwheat flour
*50g/2oz/½ cup unbleached
plain flour*
*2.5ml/½ tsp freshly ground
black pepper*
5ml/1 tsp salt
15g/½ oz fresh yeast
*200ml/7fl oz/scant 1 cup lukewarm
milk*
1 egg, separated

MAKES ABOUT 10 BLINIS

VARIATION
You can use all buckwheat flour,
which will give the blinis a
stronger flavour.

1 Mix the buckwheat flour, plain flour,
pepper and salt together in a large bowl.

2 In a small bowl, cream the yeast with
60ml/4 tbsp of the milk, then mix in the
remaining milk.

3 Add the egg yolk to the flour mixture
and gradually whisk in the yeast mixture
to form a smooth batter. Cover with
clear film and leave to stand in a warm
place for 1 hour.

4 Whisk the egg white until it forms soft
peaks and fold into the batter. Lightly oil
a heavy-based frying pan and heat it.

5 Add about 45ml/3 tbsp of the batter to
make a 10cm/4in round pancake. Cook
until the surface begins to dry out, then
turn the pancake over using a palette
knife and cook for 1–2 minutes. Repeat
with the remaining batter. Serve warm.

SUNSHINE LOAF

—

Scandinavia, Land of the Midnight Sun, has numerous breads based on rye.
This splendid table centrepiece is made with a blend of rye and white flours,
the latter helping to lighten the bread.

FOR THE STARTER
60ml/4 tbsp lukewarm milk
60ml/4 tbsp lukewarm water
7g/¹/4 oz fresh yeast
100g/3¾oz/scant 1 cup unbleached
white bread flour

FOR THE DOUGH
15g/¹/2 oz fresh yeast
500ml/17fl oz/generous 2 cups
lukewarm water
450g/1lb/4 cups rye flour
225g/8oz/2 cups unbleached white
bread flour
15ml/1 tbsp salt
milk, for glazing
caraway seeds, for sprinkling

MAKES 1 LARGE LOAF

VARIATION
This bread can be shaped into one
large round or oval loaf, if preferred.

1 Combine the milk and water for the
starter in a large bowl. Mix in the yeast
until dissolved. Gradually add the bread
flour, stirring it with a metal spoon.

2 Cover the bowl with clear film and
leave the mixture in a warm place for
3–4 hours, or until well risen, bubbly
and starting to collapse.

3 Mix the yeast for the dough with
60ml/4 tbsp of the water until creamy,
then stir in the remaining water.
Gradually mix into the starter to dilute
it. Gradually mix in the rye flour to form
a smooth batter. Cover with lightly oiled
clear film and leave in a warm place, for
3–4 hours, or until well risen.

4 Stir the bread flour and salt into the
batter to form a dough. Turn on to a
lightly floured surface and knead for
5 minutes until smooth and elastic.
Place in a lightly oiled bowl, cover with
lightly oiled clear film and leave to rise,
in a warm place, for about 1 hour, or
until doubled in bulk.

5 Knock back on a lightly floured
surface. Cut the dough into 5 equal
pieces. Roll one piece into a 50cm/20in
"sausage" and roll up into a spiral shape.

6 Cut the remaining pieces of dough in
half and shape each one into a 20cm/8in
rope. Place in a circle on a large baking
sheet, spaced equally apart, like rays of
the sun, and curl the ends round,
leaving a small gap in the centre. Place
the spiral shape on top. Cover with
lightly oiled clear film and leave to rise,
in a warm place, for 30 minutes.

7 Meanwhile, preheat the oven to 230°C/
450°F/Gas 8. Brush the bread with milk,
sprinkle with caraway seeds and bake
for 30 minutes, or until lightly browned.
Transfer to a wire rack to cool.

SAVOURY DANISH CROWN

*Filled with golden onions and cheese, this butter-rich bread ring is quite
irresistible and needs no accompaniment.*

1 Lightly grease a baking sheet. Sift the
flour and salt together into a large bowl.
Rub in 40g/1½ oz/3 tbsp of the butter.
Mix the yeast with the milk and water.
Add to the flour with the egg and mix to
a soft dough.

2 Turn out on to a lightly floured surface
and knead for 10 minutes until smooth
and elastic. Place in a lightly oiled bowl,
cover with lightly oiled clear film or slide
into an oiled polythene bag and leave to
rise, in a warm place, for about 1 hour,
or until doubled in bulk.

3 Knock back and turn out on to a
lightly floured surface. Roll out into an
oblong about 1cm/½ in thick.

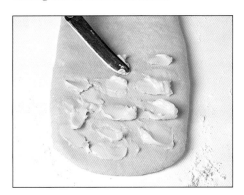

4 Dot half the remaining butter over the
top two-thirds of the dough. Fold the
bottom third up and the top third down
and seal the edges. Turn by 90 degrees
and repeat with the remaining butter.
Fold and seal as before. Cover the
dough with lightly oiled clear film and
leave to rest for about 15 minutes.

5 Turn by a further 90 degrees. Roll and
fold again without any butter. Repeat
once more. Wrap in lightly oiled clear
film and leave to rest in the fridge for
30 minutes.

6 Meanwhile, heat the oil for the filling.
Add the onions and cook for 10 minutes
until soft and golden. Remove from the
heat and stir in the breadcrumbs,
almonds, Parmesan and seasoning.

7 Add half the beaten egg to the
breadcrumb mixture and bind together.

8 Roll out the dough on a lightly floured
surface into a rectangle measuring 55 ×
23cm/22 × 9in. Spread with the filling to
within 2cm/¾ in of the edges, then roll
up like a Swiss roll from one long side.
Using a very sharp knife, cut in half
lengthways. Plait together with the cut
sides up and shape into a ring. Place on
the prepared baking sheet, cover with
lightly oiled clear film and leave to rise,
in a warm place, for 30 minutes.

9 Meanwhile, preheat the oven to 200°C/
400°F/Gas 6. Brush the remaining
beaten egg over the dough. Sprinkle
with sesame seeds and Parmesan
cheese and bake for 40–50 minutes, or
until golden. Transfer to a wire rack to
cool slightly if serving warm, or cool
completely to serve cold, cut into slices.

350g/12oz/3 cups unbleached white
bread flour
5ml/1 tsp salt
185g/6½ oz/generous ¾ cup butter,
softened
20g/¾ oz fresh yeast
200ml/7fl oz/scant 1 cup mixed
lukewarm milk and water
1 egg, lightly beaten

FOR THE FILLING
30ml/2 tbsp sunflower oil
2 onions, finely chopped
40g/1½ oz/¾ cup fresh breadcrumbs
25g/1oz/¼ cup ground almonds
50g/2oz/½ cup freshly grated
Parmesan cheese
1 egg, lightly beaten
salt and freshly ground black pepper

FOR THE TOPPING
15ml/1 tbsp sesame seeds
15ml/1 tbsp freshly grated
Parmesan cheese

MAKES 1 LARGE LOAF

DANISH JULEKAGE

In Scandinavia special slightly sweet holiday breads containing fragrant cardamom seeds are common. This exotic bread, enriched with butter and a selection of glacé and dried fruits or "jewels", is traditionally served over the Christmas period with hot spiced punch.

25g/1oz fresh yeast
75ml/5 tbsp lukewarm milk
450g/1lb/4 cups unbleached white bread flour
10ml/2 tsp salt
75g/3oz/6 tbsp butter
15 cardamom pods
2.5ml/½ tsp vanilla essence
50g/2oz/⅓ cup light brown soft sugar
grated rind of ½ lemon
2 eggs, lightly beaten
50g/2oz/¼ cup ready-to-eat dried apricots, chopped
50g/2oz/¼ cup glacé pineapple pieces, chopped
50g/2oz/¼ cup red and green glacé cherries, chopped
25g/1oz/3 tbsp dried dates, chopped
25g/1oz/2 tbsp crystallized stem ginger, chopped

For the Glaze
1 egg white
10ml/2 tsp water

For the Decoration
15ml/1 tbsp caster sugar
2.5ml/½ tsp ground cinnamon
8 pecan nuts or whole blanched almonds

MAKES 1 LOAF

1 Lightly grease a 23 × 13cm/9 × 5in loaf tin. In a measuring jug, cream the yeast with the milk.

2 Sift the flour and salt together into a large bowl. Add the butter and rub in. Make a well in the centre. Add the yeast mixture to the centre of the flour and butter mixture and stir in sufficient flour to form a thick batter. Sprinkle over a little of the remaining flour and set aside in a warm place for 15 minutes.

3 Remove the seeds from the cardamom pods. Put them in a mortar or strong bowl and crush with a pestle or the end of a rolling pin. Add the crushed seeds to the flour with the vanilla essence, sugar, lemon rind and eggs, then mix to a soft dough.

4 Turn out on to a lightly floured surface and knead for 8–10 minutes until smooth and elastic. Place in a lightly oiled bowl, cover with lightly oiled clear film and leave to rise, in a warm place, for 1–1½ hours, or until doubled in bulk.

5 Knock back the dough and turn it out on to a lightly floured surface. Flatten into a rectangle and sprinkle over half of the apricots, pineapple, cherries, dates and ginger. Fold the sides into the centre and then fold in half to contain the fruit. Flatten into a rectangle again and sprinkle over the remaining fruit. Fold and knead gently to distribute the fruit. Cover the fruited dough with lightly oiled clear film and leave to rest for 10 minutes.

6 Roll the fruited dough into a rectangle 38 × 25cm/15 × 10in. With a short side facing you, fold the bottom third up lengthways and the top third down, tucking in the sides, to form a 23 × 13cm/9 × 5in loaf. Place in the prepared tin, seam side down. Cover with lightly oiled clear film and leave to rise, in a warm place, for 1 hour, or until the dough has reached the top of the tin.

7 Meanwhile, preheat the oven to 180°C/350°F/Gas 4. Using a sharp knife, slash the top of the loaf lengthways and then make diagonal slits on either side.

8 Mix together the egg white and water for the glaze, and brush over the top. Mix the sugar and cinnamon in a bowl, then sprinkle over the top. Decorate with pecan nuts or almonds. Bake for 45–50 minutes, or until risen and browned. Transfer to a wire rack to cool.

VARIATIONS
• You can vary the fruits for this loaf. Try glacé peaches, yellow glacé cherries, sultanas, raisins, candied angelica, dried mango or dried pears and use in place of some or all of the fruits in the recipe. Use a mixture of colours and make sure that the total weight is the same as above.
• Use walnuts in place of the pecan nuts or almonds.

COOK'S TIP
Keep a close watch on the bread, especially during the final 15 minutes of cooking. If the top of the loaf starts to brown too quickly, cover loosely with foil or greaseproof paper.

450g/1lb/4 cups rye flour
5ml/1 tsp salt
50g/2oz/¼ cup butter
20g/¾ oz fresh yeast
275ml/9fl oz/generous 1 cup
lukewarm water
75g/3oz/2 cups wheat bran

MAKES 8 CRISPBREADS

COOK'S TIP
The hole in the centre of these crispbreads is a reminder of the days when breads were strung on a pole, which was hung across the rafters to dry. Make smaller crispbreads, if you like, and tie them together with bright red ribbon for an unusual Christmas gift.

KNACKERBRÖD

A very traditional Swedish crispbread with a lovely rye flavour.

1 Lightly grease 2 baking sheets. Preheat the oven to 230°C/450°F/Gas 8. Mix the rye flour and salt in a large bowl. Rub in the butter, then make a well in the centre.

2 Cream the yeast with a little water, then stir in the remainder. Pour into the centre of the flour, mix to a dough, then mix in the bran. Knead on a lightly floured surface for 5 minutes until smooth and elastic.

3 Divide the dough into 8 equal pieces and roll each one out on a lightly floured surface, to a 20cm/8in round.

4 Place 2 rounds on the prepared baking sheets and prick all over with a fork. Cut a hole in the centre of each round, using a 4cm/1½ in cutter.

5 Bake for 15–20 minutes, or until the crispbreads are golden and crisp. Transfer to a wire rack to cool. Repeat with the remaining crispbreads.

FINNISH BARLEY BREAD

In Northern Europe breads are often made using cereals such as barley and rye, which produce very satisfying, tasty breads. This quick-to-prepare flat bread is best served warm with lashings of butter.

225g/8oz/2 cups barley flour
5ml/1 tsp salt
10ml/2 tsp baking powder
25g/1oz/2 tbsp butter, melted
120ml/4fl oz/½ cup single cream
60ml/4 tbsp milk

MAKES 1 SMALL LOAF

COOK'S TIPS
• This flat bread tastes very good with cottage cheese, especially cottage cheese with chives.
• For a citrusy tang, add 10–15ml/ 2–3 tsp finely grated lemon, lime or orange rind to the flour mixture in step 1.

1 Lightly grease a baking sheet. Preheat the oven to 200°C/400°F/Gas 6. Sift the dry ingredients into a bowl. Add the butter, cream and milk. Mix to a dough.

2 Turn out the dough on to a lightly floured surface and shape into a flat round about 1cm/½ in thick.

3 Transfer to the prepared baking sheet and using a sharp knife, lightly mark the top into 6 sections.

4 Prick the surface of the round evenly with a fork. Bake for 15–18 minutes, or until pale golden. Cut into wedges and serve warm.

LUSSE BRÖD

120ml/4fl oz/½ cup milk
pinch of saffron threads
*400g/14oz/3½ cups unbleached white
bread flour*
50g/2oz/½ cup ground almonds
2.5ml/½ tsp salt
75g/3oz/6 tbsp caster sugar
25g/1oz fresh yeast
120ml/4fl oz/½ cup lukewarm water
few drops of almond essence
50g/2oz/¼ cup butter, softened

FOR THE GLAZE
1 egg
15ml/1 tbsp water

MAKES 12 BUNS

VARIATION
Gently knead in 40g/1½ oz/3 tbsp
currants after knocking back the
dough in step 4.

*Saint Lucia Day, the 12th of December, marks the beginning of Christmas in
Sweden. As part of the celebrations, young girls dressed in white robes wear
headbands topped with lighted candles and walk through the village
streets offering saffron buns to the townspeople.*

1 Lightly grease 2 baking sheets. Place
the milk in a small saucepan and bring
to the boil. Add the saffron, remove
from the heat and leave to infuse for
about 15 minutes. Meanwhile mix the
flour, ground almonds, salt and sugar
together in a large bowl.

2 Cream the yeast with the water. Add
the saffron liquid, yeast mixture and
almond essence to the flour mixture and
mix to a dough. Gradually beat in the
softened butter.

3 Turn out on to a lightly floured surface
and knead for 5 minutes until smooth
and elastic. Place in a lightly oiled bowl,
cover with lightly oiled clear film and
leave to rise, in a warm place, for about
1 hour, or until doubled in bulk.

4 Turn out on to a lightly floured surface
and knock back. Divide into 12 equal
pieces and make into different shapes:
roll into a long rope and shape into an
"S" shape; to make a star, cut a dough
piece in half and roll into two ropes,
cross one over the other and coil the
ends; make an upturned "U" shape and
coil the ends to represent curled hair;
divide a dough piece in half, roll into two
thin ropes and twist together.

5 Place on the prepared baking sheets,
spaced well apart, cover with lightly
oiled clear film and leave to rise, in a
warm place, for about 30 minutes.

6 Meanwhile, preheat the oven to 200°C/
400°F/Gas 6. Beat the egg with the
water for the glaze, and brush over the
rolls. Bake for 15 minutes, or until
golden. Transfer to a wire rack to cool
slightly to serve warm, or cool
completely to serve cold.

VÖRT LIMPA

*This festive Swedish bread is flavoured with warm spices and fresh orange.
The beer and port work nicely to soften the rye taste. The added sugars also
give the yeast a little extra to feed on and so help aerate and lighten the
bread. It is traditionally served with cheese.*

350g/12oz/3 cups rye flour
*350g/12oz/3 cups unbleached white
bread flour*
2.5ml/½ tsp salt
25g/1oz/2 tbsp caster sugar
5ml/1 tsp grated nutmeg
5ml/1 tsp ground cloves
5ml/1 tsp ground ginger
40g/1½ oz fresh yeast
300ml/½ pint/1¼ cups light ale
120ml/4fl oz/½ cup port
15ml/1 tbsp molasses
25g/1oz/2 tbsp butter, melted
15ml/1 tbsp grated orange rind
75g/3oz/½ cup raisins
15ml/1 tbsp malt extract, for glazing

MAKES 1 LARGE LOAF

VARIATION
This bread can be shaped into a
round or oval and baked on a baking
sheet if preferred.

5 Turn out the dough on to a lightly
floured surface and knock back. Gently
knead in the orange rind and raisins.
Roll into a 30cm/12in square.

6 Fold the bottom third of the dough
up and the top third down, sealing the
edges. Place in the prepared tin, cover
with lightly oiled clear film and leave to
rise, in a warm place, for 1 hour, or until
the dough reaches the top of the tin.

7 Meanwhile, preheat the oven to 190°C/
375°F/Gas 5. Bake for 35–40 minutes, or
until browned. Turn out on to a wire
rack, brush with malt extract and leave
to cool.

1 Lightly grease a 30 × 10cm/12 × 4in
loaf tin. Mix together the rye and white
flours, salt, sugar, nutmeg, cloves and
ginger in a large bowl.

2 In another large bowl, using a wooden
spoon, blend the yeast into the ale until
dissolved, then stir in the port, molasses
and melted butter.

3 Gradually add the flour mixture to the
yeast liquid, beating to make a smooth
batter. Continue adding the flour a little
at a time and mixing until the mixture
forms a soft dough.

4 Turn out on to a lightly floured surface
and knead for 8–10 minutes until
smooth and elastic. Place in a lightly
oiled bowl, cover with lightly oiled clear
film and leave to rise, in a warm place,
for 1 hour, or until doubled in size.

BREADS OF THE AMERICAS

Yeast breads, quick breads based on baking powder, Mexican flat breads and sweet breads are all part of the diverse range found in the Americas. Traditional American ingredients such as cornmeal, molasses, sweetcorn and pumpkin provide the distinctive flavours associated with Boston brown bread, Anadama bread, corn bread, Virginia spoon bread and pumpkin and walnut bread. There's a strong Jewish influence in specialities like challah, which is traditionally baked to celebrate religious holidays, and the ubiquitous bagel.

SAN FRANCISCO SOURDOUGH BREAD

In San Francisco this bread is leavened using a flour and water paste, which is left to ferment with the aid of airborne yeast. The finished loaves have a moist crumb and crispy crust, and will keep for several days.

FOR THE STARTER
50g/2oz/¹/2 cup wholemeal flour
pinch of ground cumin
15ml/1 tbsp milk
15–30ml/1–2 tbsp water
1ST REFRESHMENT
30ml/2 tbsp water
115g/4oz/1 cup wholemeal flour
2ND REFRESHMENT
60ml/4 tbsp water
115g/4oz/1 cup white bread flour

FOR THE BREAD
1ST REFRESHMENT
75ml/5 tbsp very warm water
75g/3oz/³/4 cup unbleached
plain flour
2ND REFRESHMENT
175ml/6fl oz/³/4 cup lukewarm water
200–225g/7–8oz/1³/4–2 cups
unbleached plain flour

FOR THE SOURDOUGH
280ml/9fl oz/1¹/4 cups warm water
500g/1¹/4lb/5 cups unbleached white
bread flour
15ml/1 tbsp salt
flour, for dusting
ice cubes, for baking

MAKES 2 ROUND LOAVES

1 Sift the flour and cumin for the starter into a bowl. Add the milk and sufficient water to make a firm but moist dough. Knead for 6–8 minutes to form a firm dough. Return the dough to the bowl, cover with a damp dish towel and leave in a warm place, 24–26°C/75–80°F, for about 2 days. When it is ready the starter will appear moist and wrinkled and will have developed a crust.

2 Pull off the hardened crust and discard. Scoop out the moist centre (about the size of a hazelnut), which will be aerated and sweet smelling, and place in a clean bowl. Mix in the water for the 1st refreshment. Gradually add the wholemeal flour and mix to a dough.

3 Cover with clear film and return to a warm place for 1–2 days. Discard the crust and gradually mix in the water for the 2nd refreshment to the starter, which by now will have a slightly sharper smell. Gradually mix in the white flour, cover and leave in a warm place for 8–10 hours.

4 For the bread, mix the sourdough starter with the water for the 1st refreshment. Gradually mix in the flour to form a firm dough. Knead for 6–8 minutes until firm. Cover with a damp dish towel and leave in a warm place for 8–12 hours, or until doubled in bulk.

5 Gradually mix in the water for the 2nd refreshment, then gradually mix in enough flour to form a soft, smooth elastic dough. Re-cover and leave in a warm place for 8–12 hours. Gradually stir in the water for the sourdough, then gradually work in the flour and salt. This will take 10–15 minutes. Turn out on to a lightly floured surface and knead until smooth and very elastic. Place in a large lightly oiled bowl, cover with lightly oiled clear film and leave to rise, in a warm place, for 8–12 hours.

6 Divide the dough in half and shape into 2 round loaves by folding the sides over to the centre and sealing.

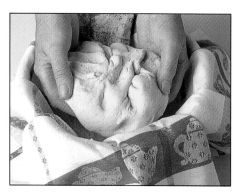

7 Place seam side up in flour-dusted *couronnes*, bowls or baskets lined with flour-dusted dish towels. Re-cover and leave to rise in a warm place for 4 hours.

8 Preheat the oven to 220°C/425°F/ Gas 7. Place an empty roasting tin in the bottom of the oven. Dust 2 baking sheets with flour. Turn out the loaves seam side down on the prepared baking sheets. Using a sharp knife, cut a criss-cross pattern by slashing the top of the loaves 4–5 times in each direction.

9 Place the baking sheets in the oven and immediately drop the ice cubes into the hot roasting tin to create steam. Bake the bread for 25 minutes, then reduce the oven temperature to 200°C/ 400°F/Gas 6 and bake for a further 15–20 minutes, or until sounding hollow when tapped on the base. Transfer to wire racks to cool.

COOK'S TIP
If you'd like to make sourdough bread regularly, keep a small amount of the starter covered in the fridge. It will keep for several days. Use the starter for the 2nd refreshment, then continue as directed.

7g/¹/₄ oz sachet easy-blend dried yeast
450g/1lb/4 cups unbleached white
bread flour
2.5ml/¹/₂ tsp salt
15ml/1 tbsp caster sugar
120ml/4fl oz/¹/₂ cup lukewarm milk
120ml/4fl oz/¹/₂ cup lukewarm water
1 egg, lightly beaten

FOR THE COATING
75g/3oz/¹/₂ cup sultanas
45ml/3 tbsp rum or brandy
115g/4oz/1 cup walnuts,
finely chopped
10ml/2 tsp ground cinnamon
115g/4oz/²/₃ cup soft light
brown sugar
50g/2oz/¹/₄ cup butter, melted

MAKES 1 LOAF

1 Lightly grease a 23cm/9in spring-form ring cake tin. Mix the dried yeast, flour, salt and caster sugar together in a large bowl and make a well in the centre.

2 Add the milk, water and egg to the centre of the flour and mix together to a soft dough. Turn out on to a lightly floured surface and knead for about 10 minutes until smooth and elastic. Place in a lightly oiled bowl, cover with lightly oiled clear film and leave to rise, in a warm place, for 45–60 minutes, or until doubled in bulk.

3 Place the sultanas in a small saucepan, pour over the rum or brandy and heat for 1–2 minutes, or until warm. Take care not to overheat. Remove from the heat and set aside. Mix the walnuts, cinnamon and sugar in a small bowl.

MONKEY BREAD

This American favourite is also called bubble bread – because of the "bubbles" of dough. The pieces of dough are tossed in a heavenly coating of butter, nuts, cinnamon and rum-soaked fruit.

4 Turn out the dough on to a lightly floured surface and knead gently. Divide into 30 equal pieces and shape into small balls. Dip the balls, one at a time into the melted butter, then roll them in the walnut mixture. Place half in the prepared tin, spaced slightly apart. Sprinkle over all the soaked sultanas.

VARIATION
Replace the easy-blend dried yeast with 20g/³/₄ oz fresh yeast. Mix with the liquid until creamy before adding to the flour.

5 Top with the remaining dough balls, dipping and coating as before. Sprinkle over any remaining walnut mixture and melted butter. Cover with lightly oiled clear film or slide the tin into a lightly oiled large polythene bag and leave to rise, in a warm place, for about 45 minutes, or until the dough reaches the top of the tin.

6 Meanwhile, preheat the oven to 190°C/ 375°F/Gas 5. Bake for 35–40 minutes, or until well risen and golden. Turn out on to a wire rack to cool.

PUMPKIN AND WALNUT BREAD

Pumpkin, nutmeg and walnuts combine to yield a moist, tangy and slightly sweet bread with an indescribably good flavour. Serve partnered with meats or cheese, or simply lightly buttered.

500g/1¼ lb pumpkin, peeled, seeded
and cut into chunks
75g/3oz/6 tbsp caster sugar
5ml/1 tsp grated nutmeg
50g/2oz/¼ cup butter, melted
3 eggs, lightly beaten
350g/12oz/3 cups unbleached white
bread flour
10ml/2 tsp baking powder
2.5ml/½ tsp salt
75g/3oz/¾ cup walnuts, chopped

MAKES 1 LOAF

1 Grease and neatly base line a loaf tin measuring 21.5 × 11cm/8½ × 4½ in. Preheat the oven to 180°C/350°F/Gas 4.

2 Place the pumpkin in a saucepan, add water to cover by about 5cm/2in, then bring to the boil. Cover, lower the heat and simmer for 20 minutes, or until the pumpkin is very tender. Drain well, then purée in a food processor or blender. Leave to cool.

3 Place 275g/10oz/1¼ cups of the purée in a large bowl. Add the sugar, nutmeg, melted butter and eggs to the purée and mix together. Sift the flour, baking powder and salt together into a large bowl and make a well in the centre.

4 Add the pumpkin mixture to the centre of the flour and stir until smooth. Mix in the walnuts.

COOK'S TIP
You may have slightly more pumpkin purée than you actually need – use the remainder in soup.

5 Transfer to the prepared tin and bake for 1 hour, or until golden and starting to shrink from the sides of the tin. Turn out on to a wire rack to cool.

90g/3¹/₂ oz/scant 1 cup cornmeal
90g/3¹/₂ oz/scant 1 cup unbleached
plain white flour or wholemeal flour
90g/3¹/₂ oz/scant 1 cup rye flour
2.5ml/¹/₂ tsp salt
5ml/1 tsp bicarbonate of soda
90g/3¹/₂ oz/generous ¹/₂ cup seedless
raisins
120ml/4fl oz/¹/₂ cup milk
120ml/4fl oz/¹/₂ cup water
120ml/4fl oz/¹/₂ cup molasses or
black treacle

MAKES 1 OR 2 LOAVES

COOK'S TIP
If you do not have empty coffee jugs,
tins or similar moulds, cook the bread
in one or two heatproof bowls of
equivalent capacity.

1 Line the base of one 1.2 litre/2 pint/
5 cup cylindrical metal or glass
container, such as a heatproof glass
coffee jug, with greased greaseproof
paper. Alternatively, remove the lids
from two 450g/1lb coffee tins, wash and
dry the tins thoroughly, then line with
greased greaseproof paper.

2 Mix together the cornmeal, plain
or wholemeal flour, rye flour, salt,
bicarbonate of soda and raisins in a large
bowl. Warm the milk and water in a
small saucepan and stir in the molasses
or black treacle.

3 Add the molasses mixture to the dry
ingredients and mix together using a
spoon until it just forms a moist dough.
Do not overmix.

BOSTON BROWN BREAD

*Rich, moist and dark, this bread is flavoured with molasses and can include
raisins. In Boston it is often served with savoury baked beans.*

4 Fill the jug or tins with the dough;
they should be about two-thirds full.
Cover neatly with foil or greased
greaseproof paper and tie securely.

5 Bring water to a depth of 5cm/2in
to the boil in a deep, heavy-based
saucepan large enough to accommodate
the jug or tins. Place a trivet in the pan,
stand the jug or tins on top, cover the
pan and steam for 1¹/₂ hours, adding
more boiling water to maintain the
required level as necessary.

6 Cool the loaves for a few minutes in
the jugs or tins, then turn them on their
sides and the loaves should slip out.
Serve warm, as a teabread or with
savoury dishes.

ANADAMA BREAD

*A traditional bread from Massachusetts, made with molasses, cornmeal,
wholemeal and unbleached white flour. According to legend, it was created by
the husband of a woman called Anna, who had left a cornmeal mush and
some molasses in the kitchen. On finding only these ingredients for supper
her husband mixed them with some flour, water and yeast to make this bread,
while muttering "Anna, damn her"!*

40g/1½ oz/3 tbsp butter
120ml/4fl oz/½ cup molasses
*560ml/scant 1 pint/scant 2½ cups
water*
50g/2oz/½ cup cornmeal
10ml/2 tsp salt
25g/1oz fresh yeast
30ml/2 tbsp lukewarm water
275g/10oz/2½ cups wholemeal flour
*450g/1lb/4 cups unbleached white
bread flour*

MAKES 2 LOAVES

1 Grease two 1.5 litre/2½ pint/6 cup
loaf tins. Heat the butter, molasses and
measured water in a pan until the butter
has melted. Stir in the cornmeal and salt
and stir over a low heat until boiling.
Cool until lukewarm.

2 In a small bowl, cream the yeast with
the lukewarm water, then set aside for
5 minutes.

3 Mix the cornmeal mixture and yeast
mixture together in a large bowl. Fold in
the wholemeal flour and then the
unbleached white bread flour to form a
sticky dough. Turn out on to a lightly
floured surface and knead for 10–15
minutes until the dough is smooth and
elastic. Add a little more flour if needed.

4 Place in a lightly oiled bowl, cover
with lightly oiled clear film and leave to
rise, in a warm place, for about 1 hour,
or until doubled in bulk.

VARIATION
Use a 7g/¼ oz sachet easy-blend
dried yeast instead of fresh. Mix it
with the wholemeal flour. Add to the
cornmeal mixture, then add the
lukewarm water, which would
conventionally be blended with the
fresh yeast.

5 Knead the dough lightly on a well
floured surface, shape into 2 loaves and
place in the prepared tins. Cover with
lightly oiled clear film and leave to rise,
in a warm place, for about 35–45
minutes, or until doubled in size and the
dough reaches the top of the tins.

6 Meanwhile, preheat the oven to 200°C/
400°F/Gas 6. Using a sharp knife, slash
the tops of the loaves 3–4 times. Bake
for 15 minutes, then reduce the oven
temperature to 180°C/350°F/Gas 4 and
bake for a further 35–40 minutes, or
until sounding hollow when tapped on
the base. Turn out on to a wire rack to
cool slightly. Serve warm.

500g/1¼ lb/5 cups unbleached white
bread flour
10ml/2 tsp salt
20g/¾ oz fresh yeast
200ml/7fl oz/scant 1 cup lukewarm
water
30ml/2 tbsp caster sugar
2 eggs
75g/3oz/6 tbsp butter or
margarine, melted

FOR THE GLAZE
1 egg yolk
15ml/1 tbsp water
10ml/2 tsp poppy seeds, for sprinkling

MAKES 1 LARGE LOAF

COOK'S TIP
If wished, divide the dough in half
and make two small challah, keeping
the plaits quite simple. Decorate with
the poppy seeds or leave plain.
Reduce the baking time by about
10 minutes.

1 Lightly grease a baking sheet. Sift the
flour and salt together into a large bowl
and make a well in the centre. Mix the
yeast with the water and sugar, add to
the centre of the flour with the eggs
and melted butter or margarine and
gradually mix in the surrounding flour
to form a soft dough.

2 Turn out on to a lightly floured surface
and knead for 10 minutes until smooth
and elastic. Place in a lightly oiled bowl,
cover with lightly oiled clear film and
leave to rise, in a warm place, for 1 hour,
or until doubled in bulk.

CHALLAH
—

*Challah is an egg-rich, light-textured bread baked for the Jewish Sabbath and
to celebrate religious holidays. It is usually plaited with 3 or 4 strands of
dough, but 8 strands or more may be used to create especially festive loaves.*

3 Knock back, re-cover and leave to rise
again in a warm place for about 1 hour.
Knock back, turn out on to a lightly
floured surface and knead gently. Divide
into 4 equal pieces. Roll each piece into
a rope about 45cm/18in long. Line up
next to each other. Pinch the ends
together at one end.

4 Starting from the right, lift the first
rope over the second and the third rope
over the fourth. Take the fourth rope
and place it between the first and
second ropes. Repeat, starting from the
right, and continue until plaited.

5 Tuck the ends under and place the
loaf on the prepared baking sheet. Cover
with lightly oiled clear film and leave to
rise in a warm place, for about 30–45
minutes, or until doubled in size.
Meanwhile, preheat the oven to 200°C/
400°F/Gas 6. Beat the egg yolk and
water for the glaze together.

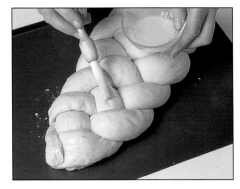

6 Brush the egg glaze gently over the
loaf. Sprinkle evenly with the poppy
seeds and bake for 35–40 minutes, or
until the challah is a deep golden brown.
Transfer to a wire rack and leave to cool
before slicing.

BAGELS

Bagels are eaten in many countries, especially where there is a Jewish community, and are very popular in the USA. They can be made from white, wholemeal or rye flour and finished with a variety of toppings, including caraway, poppy seeds, sesame seeds and onion.

350g/12oz/3 cups unbleached white bread flour
10ml/2 tsp salt
6g/1/4 oz sachet easy blend dried yeast
5ml/1 tsp malt extract
210ml/71/2 fl oz/scant 1 cup lukewarm water

FOR POACHING
2.5 litres/4 pints/21/2 quarts water
15ml/1 tbsp malt extract

FOR THE TOPPING
1 egg white
10ml/2 tsp cold water
30ml/2 tbsp poppy, sesame or caraway seeds

MAKES 10 BAGELS

5 Meanwhile, preheat the oven to 220°C/ 425°F/Gas 7. Place the water and malt extract for poaching in a large saucepan, bring to the boil, then reduce to a simmer. Place the bagels in the water 2 or 3 at a time and poach for about 1 minute. They will sink and then rise again when first added to the pan. Using a fish slice or large draining spoon, turn over and cook for 30 seconds. Remove and drain on a dish towel. Repeat with the remaining bagels.

1 Grease 2 baking sheets. Sift the flour and salt together into a large bowl. Stir in the dried yeast. Make a well in the centre. Mix the malt extract and water, add to the centre of the flour and mix to a dough. Knead on a floured surface until elastic.

2 Place in a lightly oiled bowl, cover with lightly oiled clear film and leave to rise, in a warm place, for about 1 hour, or until doubled in bulk.

3 Turn out on to a lightly floured surface and knock back. Knead for 1 minute, then divide into 10 equal pieces. Shape into balls, cover with clear film and leave to rest for 5 minutes.

4 Gently flatten each ball and make a hole through the centre with your thumb. Enlarge the hole slightly by turning your thumb around. Place on a floured tray; re-cover and leave in a warm place, for 10–20 minutes, or until they begin to rise.

6 Place five bagels on each prepared baking sheet, spacing them well apart. Beat the egg white with the water for the topping, brush the mixture over the top of each bagel and sprinkle with poppy, sesame or caraway seeds. Bake for 20–25 minutes, or until golden brown. Transfer to a wire rack to cool.

225g/8oz/2 cups unbleached
plain flour
5ml/1 tsp salt
4ml/³/4 tsp baking powder
40g/1¹/2 oz/3 tbsp lard or
vegetable fat
150ml/¹/4 pint/²/3 cup warm water

MAKES 12 TORTILLAS

WHEAT TORTILLAS

Tortillas are the staple flat bread in Mexico, where they are often made from
masa harina, a flour milled from corn. These soft wheat tortillas are also
popular in the South-western states of the USA.

1 Mix the flour, salt and baking powder
in a bowl. Rub in the fat, stir in the
water and knead lightly to a soft dough.
Cover with clear film and leave to rest
for 15 minutes. Divide into 12 equal
pieces and shape into balls. Roll out on a
lightly floured surface into 15–18cm/
6–7in rounds. Re-cover to keep moist.

2 Heat a heavy-based frying pan or
griddle, add one tortilla and cook for
1¹/2–2 minutes, turning over as soon as
the surface starts to bubble. It should
stay flexible. Remove from the pan and
wrap in a dish towel to keep warm while
cooking the remaining tortillas in the
same way.

DOUBLE CORN BREAD

In the American South, corn bread is made with white cornmeal and is fairly
flat, while in the North it is thicker and made with yellow cornmeal. Whatever
the version it's delicious – this recipe combines yellow cornmeal with
sweetcorn. It is marvellous served warm, cut into wedges and buttered.

75g/3oz/³/4 cup unbleached white
bread flour
150g/6oz/1¹/2 cups yellow cornmeal
5ml/1 tsp salt
25ml/1¹/2 tbsp baking powder
15ml/1 tbsp caster sugar
50g/2oz/4 tbsp butter, melted
250ml/8fl oz/1 cup milk
3 eggs
200g/7oz/scant 1¹/4 cups canned
sweetcorn, drained

MAKES 1 LARGE LOAF

1 Preheat the oven to 200°C/400°F/
Gas 6. Grease and base line a 22cm/
8¹/2 in round cake tin. Sift the flour,
cornmeal, salt and baking powder
together into a large bowl. Stir in the
sugar and make a well in the centre.

3 Using a wooden spoon, stir the
sweetcorn quickly into the mixture.
Pour into the prepared tin and bake for
20–25 minutes, or until a metal skewer
inserted into the centre comes out clean.

2 Mix the melted butter, milk and eggs
together. Add to the centre of the flour
mixture and beat until just combined.

4 Invert the bread on to a wire rack and
lift off the lining paper. Cool slightly.
Serve warm, cut into wedges.

VIRGINIA SPOON BREAD

450ml/³/4 pint/1³/4 cups milk
75g/3oz/²/3 cup cornmeal
15g/¹/2 oz/1 tbsp butter
75g/3oz/³/4 cup grated mature
Cheddar cheese
1 garlic clove
3 eggs, separated
75g/3oz/¹/2 cup sweetcorn
kernels (optional)
salt and freshly ground black pepper

MAKES 1 LARGE LOAF

VARIATIONS
Add 115g/4oz fried chopped bacon
or 5–10ml/1–2 tsp finely chopped
green chilli for different flavoured
spoon breads.

*Spoon bread is a traditional dish from the southern states of America, which,
according to legend, originated when too much water was added to a corn
bread batter and the baked bread had to be spooned out of the tin. Served hot
from the oven, this ethereally light offering – enhanced with Cheddar cheese
and a hint of garlic – is delicious.*

1 Preheat the oven to 180°C/350°F/
Gas 4. Grease a 1.5 litre/2¹/2 pint/6 cup
soufflé dish.

2 Place the milk in a large heavy-based
saucepan. Heat gently, then gradually
add the cornmeal, stirring. Add salt and
slowly bring to the boil, stirring all the
time. Cook for 5–10 minutes, stirring
frequently, until thick and smooth.

3 Remove from the heat and stir in the
butter, Cheddar cheese, garlic and egg
yolks. Season to taste.

4 In a bowl, whisk the egg whites until
they form soft peaks. Stir one-quarter
into the cornmeal mixture and then
gently fold in the remainder. Fold in the
well-drained corn, if using.

5 Spoon the mixture into the prepared
soufflé dish and bake for 45–50
minutes, or until puffed and beginning
to brown. Serve at once.

COOK'S TIPS
• Use a perfectly clean bowl and
whisk for whisking the egg whites and
make sure it is free of grease by
washing and drying thoroughly, then
wiping out with a little lemon juice.
• If any shell drops in with the egg,
scoop it out with another, larger
piece of shell.

NEW ENGLAND FANTANS

*These fantail rolls look stylish and are so versatile that they are equally
suitable for a simple snack, or a gourmet dinner party!*

1 Grease a muffin sheet with 9 × 7.5cm/
3in cups or foil cases. Mix the yeast
with the buttermilk and sugar and then
leave to stand for 15 minutes.

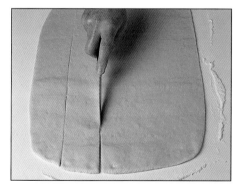

2 In a saucepan, heat the milk with
40g/1½ oz/3 tbsp of the butter until the
butter has melted. Cool until lukewarm.

3 Sift the flour and salt together into a
large bowl. Add the yeast mixture, milk
mixture and egg and mix to a soft
dough. Turn out on to a lightly floured
surface and knead for 5–8 minutes until
smooth and elastic. Place in a lightly
oiled bowl, cover with lightly oiled clear
film and leave to rise, in a warm place,
for about 1 hour, until doubled in size.

4 Turn out on to a lightly floured
surface, knock back and knead until
smooth and elastic. Roll into an oblong
measuring 45 × 30cm/18 × 12in and
about 5mm/¼ in thick. Melt the
remaining butter, brush over the dough
and cut it lengthways into 5 equal strips.
Stack on top of each other and cut
across into 9 equal 5cm/2in strips.

5 Pinch one side of each layered strip
together, then place pinched side down
into a prepared muffin cup or foil case.
Cover with lightly oiled clear film and
leave to rise, in a warm place, for
30–40 minutes, or until the fantans have
almost doubled in size. Meanwhile,
preheat the oven to 200°C/400°F/Gas 6.
Bake for 20 minutes, or until golden.
Turn out on to a wire rack to cool.

15g/½ oz fresh yeast
75ml/5 tbsp buttermilk, at room
temperature
10ml/2 tsp caster sugar
75ml/5 tbsp milk
65g/2½ oz/5 tbsp butter
375g/13oz/3¼ cups unbleached white
bread flour
5ml/1 tsp salt
1 egg, lightly beaten

MAKES 9 ROLLS

VARIATION
To make Cinnamon-spiced Fantans,
add 5ml/1 tsp ground cinnamon to the
remaining butter in step 4 before
brushing over the dough strips.
Sprinkle the rolls with a little icing
sugar as soon as they come out of
the oven, then leave to cool
before serving.

MEXICAN "BREAD OF THE DEAD"

3 star anise
90ml/6 tbsp cold water
675g/1½ lb/6 cups unbleached white bread flour
5ml/1 tsp salt
115g/4oz/½ cup caster sugar
25g/1oz fresh yeast
175ml/6fl oz/¾ cup lukewarm water
3 eggs
60ml/4 tbsp orange liqueur
115g/4oz/½ cup butter, melted
grated rind of 1 orange
icing sugar, for dusting

MAKES 1 LARGE LOAF

VARIATION
Top the baked bread with orange icing. Blend 60g/2oz/½ cup icing sugar and 15–30ml/1–2 tbsp orange liqueur. Pour the icing over the bread and let it dribble down the sides.

A celebratory loaf made for All Souls' Day. Even though the name of this bread suggests otherwise, it is actually a very happy day when both Mexicans and Spanish people pay their respects to the souls of their dead. Traditionally the bread is decorated with a dough skull, bones and tears.

1 Grease a 26cm/10½ in fluted round cake tin. Place the star anise in a small saucepan and add the cold water. Bring to the boil and boil for 3–4 minutes, or until the liquid has reduced to 45ml/3 tbsp. Discard the star anise and leave the liquid to cool.

2 Sift the flour and salt together into a large bowl. Stir in the sugar and make a well in the centre.

3 In a jug, dissolve the yeast in the lukewarm water. Pour into the centre of the flour and mix in a little flour, using your fingers, until a smooth, thick batter forms. Sprinkle over a little of the remaining flour, cover with clear film and leave the batter in a warm place for 30 minutes, or until the mixture starts to bubble.

4 Beat the eggs, the reserved liquid flavoured with star anise, orange liqueur and melted butter together. Gradually incorporate into the flour mixture to form a smooth dough.

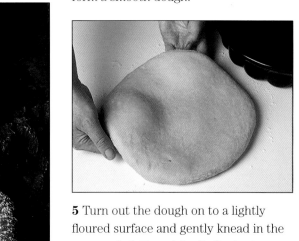

5 Turn out the dough on to a lightly floured surface and gently knead in the orange rind. Knead for 5–6 minutes until smooth and elastic. Shape into a 26cm/10½ in round and place in the prepared tin. Cover with lightly oiled clear film and leave to rise, in a warm place, for 2–3 hours, or until almost at the top of the tin and doubled in bulk.

6 Meanwhile, preheat the oven to 190°C/375°F/Gas 5. Bake the loaf for 45–50 minutes, or until golden. Turn out on to a wire rack to cool. Dust with icing sugar to serve.

WEST INDIAN ROTIS

Caribbean food is based on cuisines from many areas of the world, influenced by a wide range of cultures. It is the Anglo-Indian connection that brought the Indian flat bread called roti to Trinidad in the West Indies.

1 Mix the flour, baking powder and salt together in a large bowl, and make a well in the centre. Gradually mix in the water to make a firm dough.

2 Knead on a lightly floured surface until smooth. Place in a lightly oiled bowl, cover with lightly oiled clear film. Leave to stand for 20 minutes.

3 Divide the dough into 8 equal pieces and roll each one on a lightly floured surface into an 18cm/7in round. Brush the surface of each round with a little of the clarified butter or ghee, fold in half and half again. Cover the folded rounds with lightly oiled clear film and leave for 10 minutes.

450g/1lb/4 cups atta or fine wholemeal flour
5ml/1 tsp baking powder
5ml/1 tsp salt
300ml/¹/₂ pint/1¹/₄ cups water
115–150g/4–5oz/8–10 tbsp clarified butter or ghee

MAKES 8 ROTIS

4 Take one roti and roll out on a lightly floured surface into a round about 20–23cm/8–9in in diameter. Brush both sides with some clarified butter or ghee.

5 Heat a griddle or heavy-based frying pan, add the roti and cook for about 1 minute. Turn over and cook for 2 minutes, then turn over again and cook for 1 minute. Wrap in a dish towel to keep warm while cooking the remaining rotis. Serve warm.

BREADS OF INDIA
AND THE MIDDLE EAST

Chapatis, rotis and pooris are typical unleavened Indian flat breads. Chillies, herbs and spices are popular additions. The tradition of baking flat breads continues into the Middle East, although their specialities – crisp lavash, onion breads and barbari – include yeast. All these breads are perfect for serving with soups or dips. In southern India flour is replaced with rice and lentils or beans, which are fermented to make a pancake-style flat bread.

BHATURAS

*These light, fluffy leavened breads, made with semolina and flour and
flavoured with butter and yogurt, taste delicious served warm.*

15g/¹/₂ oz fresh yeast
5ml/1 tsp sugar
120ml/4fl oz/¹/₂ cup lukewarm water
200g/7oz/1³/₄ cups plain flour
50g/2oz/¹/₂ cup semolina
2.5ml/¹/₂ tsp salt
15g/¹/₂ oz/1 tbsp butter or ghee
30ml/2 tbsp natural yogurt
oil, for frying

MAKES 10 BHATURAS

COOK'S TIP

Ghee can be found in Asian and
Indian supermarkets, however, it is
easy to make at home. Melt unsalted
butter in a heavy-based pan over a
low heat. Simmer very gently until the
residue changes to a light golden
colour, then leave to cool. Strain
through muslin before using.

1 Mix the yeast with the sugar and
water in a jug. Sift the flour into a large
bowl and stir in the semolina and salt.
Rub in the butter or ghee.

2 Add the yeast mixture and yogurt and
mix to a dough. Turn out on to a lightly
floured surface and knead for
10 minutes until smooth and elastic.

3 Place in a lightly oiled bowl, cover
with lightly oiled clear film and leave to
rise, in a warm place, for about 1 hour,
or until doubled in bulk.

4 Turn out on to a lightly floured surface
and knock back. Divide into 10 equal
pieces and shape each one into a ball.
Flatten into discs with the palm of your
hand. Roll out on a lightly floured
surface into 13cm/5in rounds.

5 Heat oil to a depth of 1cm/¹/₂ in in a
deep frying pan and slide one bhatura
into the oil. Fry for about 1 minute,
turning over after 30 seconds, then
drain on kitchen paper. Keep warm in a
low oven while frying the remaining
bhaturas. Serve warm.

TANDOORI ROTIS

There are numerous varieties of breads in India, most of them unleavened. This one, as its name suggests, would normally be baked in a tandoor – a clay oven which is heated with charcoal or wood. The oven becomes extremely hot, cooking the bread in minutes.

350g/12oz/3 cups atta or fine
wholemeal flour
5ml/1 tsp salt
250ml/8fl oz/1 cup water
30–45ml/2–3 tbsp melted ghee or
butter, for brushing

MAKES 6 ROTIS

COOK'S TIP
The rotis are ready when light brown bubbles appear on the surface.

1 Sift the flour and salt into a large bowl. Add the water and mix to a soft dough. Knead on a lightly floured surface for 3–4 minutes until smooth. Place in a lightly oiled bowl, cover with lightly oiled clear film; leave to rest for 1 hour.

2 Turn out on to a lightly floured surface. Divide the dough into 6 pieces and shape each piece into a ball. Press out into a larger round with the palm of your hand, cover with lightly oiled clear film and leave to rest for 10 minutes.

3 Meanwhile, preheat the oven to 230°C/450°F/Gas 8. Place 3 baking sheets in the oven to heat. Roll the rotis into 15cm/6in rounds, place 2 on each baking sheet and bake for 8–10 minutes. Brush with ghee or butter and serve warm.

NAAN

225g/8oz/2 cups unbleached white
bread flour
2.5ml/1/2 tsp salt
15g/1/2 oz fresh yeast
60ml/4 tbsp lukewarm milk
15ml/1 tbsp vegetable oil
30ml/2 tbsp natural yogurt
1 egg
30–45ml/2–3 tbsp melted ghee or
butter, for brushing

MAKES 3 NAAN

From the Caucasus through the Punjab region of northwest India and beyond, all serve these leavened breads. Traditionally cooked in a very hot clay oven known as a tandoor, naan are usually eaten with dry meat or vegetable dishes, such as tandoori.

1 Sift the flour and salt together into a large bowl. In a smaller bowl, cream the yeast with the milk. Set aside for 15 minutes.

2 Add the yeast mixture, oil, yogurt and egg to the flour and mix to a soft dough.

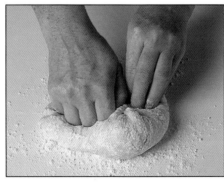

3 Turn out the dough on to a lightly floured surface and knead for about 10 minutes until smooth and elastic. Place in a lightly oiled bowl, cover with lightly oiled clear film and leave to rise, in a warm place, for 45 minutes, or until doubled in bulk.

4 Preheat the oven to its highest setting, at least 230°C/450°F/Gas 8. Place 3 heavy baking sheets in the oven to heat.

5 Turn the dough out on to a lightly floured surface and knock back. Divide into 3 equal pieces and shape into balls.

6 Cover two of the balls of dough with oiled clear film and roll out the third into a teardrop shape about 25cm/10in long, 13cm/5in wide and with a thickness of about 5mm–8mm/1/4–1/3 in.

7 Preheat the grill to its highest setting. Meanwhile, place the naan on the hot baking sheets and bake for 3–4 minutes, or until puffed up.

8 Remove the naan from the oven and place under the hot grill for a few seconds, or until the top of the naan browns slightly. Wrap the cooked naan in a dish towel to keep warm while rolling out and cooking the remaining naan. Brush with melted ghee or butter and serve warm.

VARIATIONS
You can flavour naan in numerous different ways:
• To make spicy naan, add 5ml/1 tsp each ground coriander and ground cumin to the flour in step 1. If you would like the naan to be extra fiery, add 2.5–5ml/1/2–1 tsp hot chilli powder.
• To make cardamom-flavoured naan, lightly crush the seeds from 4–5 green cardamom pods and add to the flour in step 1.
• To make poppy seed naan, brush the rolled-out naan with a little ghee and sprinkle with poppy seeds. Press lightly to make sure that they stick.
• To make peppered naan, brush the rolled-out naan with a little ghee and dust generously with coarsely ground black pepper.
• To make onion-flavoured naan, add 114g/4oz/1/2 cup finely chopped or coarsely grated onion to the dough in step 2. You may need to reduce the amount of egg if the onion is very moist to prevent making the dough too soft.
• To make wholemeal naan, substitute wholemeal bread flour for some or all of the white flour.

COOK'S TIP
To help the naan dough to puff up and brown, place the baking sheets in an oven preheated to the maximum temperature for at least 10 minutes before baking to ensure that they are hot. Preheat the grill while the naan are baking.

RED LENTIL DOSAS

Dosas and idlis are the breads of southern India. They are very different from traditional north Indian breads as they are made from lentils or beans and rice rather than flour. Dosas are more like pancakes; they are eaten freshly cooked, often at breakfast time, with chutney.

150g/5oz/³/4 cup long grain rice
50g/2oz/¹/4 cup red lentils
250ml/8fl oz/1 cup warm water
5ml/1 tsp salt
2.5ml/¹/2 tsp ground turmeric
2.5ml/¹/2 tsp freshly ground
black pepper
30ml/2 tbsp chopped
fresh coriander
oil, for frying and drizzling

MAKES 6 DOSAS

VARIATION
Add 60ml/4 tbsp grated coconut, 15ml/1 tbsp grated fresh root ginger and 1 finely chopped chilli to the batter just before cooking.

1 Place the rice and lentils in a bowl, cover with the water and leave to soak for 8 hours.

2 Drain off the water and reserve. Place the rice and lentils in a food processor and blend until smooth. Blend in the reserved water.

3 Scrape into a bowl, cover with clear film and leave in a warm place to ferment for about 24 hours.

4 Stir in the salt, turmeric, pepper and coriander. Heat a heavy-based frying pan over a medium heat for a few minutes until hot. Smear with oil and add about 30–45ml/2–3 tbsp batter.

5 Using the rounded bottom of a soup spoon, gently spread the batter out, using a circular motion, to make a 15cm/6in diameter dosa.

6 Cook for 1¹/2–2 minutes, or until set. Drizzle a little oil over the dosa and around the edges. Turn over and cook for about 1 minute, or until golden. Keep warm in a low oven over simmering water while cooking the remaining dosas. Serve warm.

PARATHAS

These triangular-shaped breads, made from a similar dough to that used for chapatis, are enriched with layers of ghee or butter to create a wonderfully rich, flaky bread.

1 Sift the flours and salt together into a large bowl. Add the oil with sufficient water to mix to a soft dough. Turn out the dough on to a lightly floured surface and knead vigorously for 8–10 minutes until smooth.

2 Place in a lightly oiled bowl and cover with a damp dish towel. Leave to rest for 30 minutes.

3 Turn out on to a lightly floured surface. Divide the dough into 9 equal pieces. Cover 8 pieces of dough with oiled clear film. Shape the remaining piece into a ball and then flatten it. Roll into a 15cm/6in round.

4 Brush with a little of the melted ghee or clarified butter and fold in half. Brush and fold again to form a triangular shape. Repeat with the remaining dough. Stack, layered between clear film, to keep moist. Heat a griddle or heavy-based frying pan.

*115g/4oz/1¼ cups unbleached
plain flour
115g/4oz/1 cup wholemeal flour
2.5ml/½ tsp salt
15ml/1 tbsp vegetable oil
120–150ml/4–5fl oz/½–⅔ cup water
90–120ml/3–4fl oz/scant ½ cup
melted ghee or clarified butter*

MAKES 9 PARATHAS

5 Keeping the shape, roll each piece of dough to a larger triangle, with each side measuring 15–18cm/6–7in. Brush with ghee or butter and place on the griddle or in the pan, brushed side down. Cook for about 1 minute, brush with ghee or butter and turn over. Cook for about 1 minute, or until crisp and dotted with brown speckles. Keep warm in a low oven while cooking the remaining parathas. Serve the parathas warm.

*115g/4oz/1 cup unbleached
plain flour
115g/4oz/1 cup wholemeal flour
2.5ml/1/2 tsp salt
2.5ml/1/2 tsp chilli powder (optional)
30ml/2 tbsp vegetable oil
100–120ml/31/2–4fl oz/scant
1/2 cup water
oil, for frying*

MAKES 12 POORIS

VARIATION
To make spinach-flavoured pooris,
thaw 50g/2oz frozen chopped spinach,
drain it well and add it to the dough
with a little grated fresh ginger root
and 2.5ml/1/2 tsp ground cumin.

*175g/6oz/11/2 cups atta or
wholemeal flour
2.5ml/1/2 tsp salt
100–120ml/scant 4fl oz/scant
1/2 cup water
5ml/1 tsp vegetable oil
melted ghee or butter, for brushing
(optional)*

MAKES 6 CHAPATIS

COOK'S TIP
Atta or *ata* is a very fine wholemeal
flour, which is only found in Indian
stores and supermarkets. It is
sometimes simply labelled chapati
flour. *Atta* can also be used for making
rotis and other Indian flat breads.

1 Sift the flour and salt into a bowl. Add
the water and mix to a soft dough.
Knead in the oil, then turn out on to a
lightly floured surface.

POORIS

*Pooris are small discs of dough that when fried, puff up into light airy breads.
They will melt in your mouth!*

1 Sift the flours, salt and chilli powder,
if using, into a large bowl. Add the
vegetable oil then add sufficient water
to mix to a dough. Turn out on to a
lightly floured surface and knead for
8–10 minutes until smooth.

2 Place in a lightly oiled bowl and cover
with lightly oiled clear film. Leave to rest
for 30 minutes.

3 Turn out on to a lightly floured
surface. Divide the dough into 12 equal
pieces. Keeping the rest of the dough
covered, roll one piece into a 13cm/5in
round. Repeat with the remaining
dough. Stack the pooris, layered
between clear film, to keep moist.

4 Heat oil to a depth of 2.5cm/1in in a
deep frying pan to 180°C/350°F. Using
a fish slice, lift one poori and gently slide
it into the oil; it will sink but return to
the surface and begin to sizzle. Gently
press the poori into the oil. It will puff
up. Turn over after a few seconds and
cook for 20–30 seconds.

5 Remove the poori from the pan and
drain on kitchen paper. Keep warm in a
low oven while cooking the remaining
pooris. Serve warm.

CHAPATIS

*These chewy, unleavened breads are eaten throughout Northern India. They
are usually served as an accompaniment to spicy dishes.*

2 Knead for 5–6 minutes until smooth.
Place in a lightly oiled bowl, cover with a
damp dish towel and leave to rest for
30 minutes. Turn out on to a floured
surface. Divide the dough into 6 equal
pieces. Shape each piece into a ball.

3 Press the dough into a larger round
with the palm of your hand, then roll
into a 13cm/5in round. Stack, layered
between clear film, to keep moist.

4 Heat a griddle or heavy-based frying
pan over a medium heat for a few
minutes until hot. Take one chapati,
brush off any excess flour, and place on
the griddle. Cook for 30–60 seconds, or
until the top begins to bubble and white
specks appear on the underside.

5 Turn the chapati over using a palette
knife and cook for a further 30 seconds.
Remove from the pan and keep warm,
layered between a folded dish towel,
while cooking the remaining chapatis.
If you like, the chapatis can be brushed
lightly with melted ghee or butter
immediately after cooking. Serve warm.

MISSI ROTIS

*These flavour-packed unleavened breads are eaten in northern India. They
are made with gram flour – grams or chana dhal are a variety of chick-pea,
which are milled to make this gluten-free flour.*

*115g/4oz/1 cup gram flour
115g/4oz/1 cup wholemeal flour
1 green chilli, seeded and chopped
1/2 onion, finely chopped
15ml/1 tbsp chopped fresh coriander
2.5ml/1/2 tsp ground turmeric
2.5ml/1/2 tsp salt
15ml/1 tbsp oil or melted butter
120–150ml/4–5fl oz/1/2–2/3 cup
lukewarm water
30–45ml/2–3 tbsp melted butter
or ghee*

MAKES 4 ROTIS

VARIATION
Use 1.25–2.5ml/1/4–1/2 tsp chilli
powder in place of the fresh chilli.

1 Mix the flours, chilli, onion, coriander, turmeric and salt together in a large bowl. Stir in the 15ml/1 tbsp oil or melted butter.

2 Mix in sufficient water to make a pliable soft dough. Turn out the dough on to a lightly floured surface and knead until smooth.

3 Place in a lightly oiled bowl, cover with lightly oiled clear film and leave to rest for 1 hour.

4 Turn the dough out on to a lightly floured surface. Divide into 4 equal pieces and shape into balls. Roll out each ball into a thick round 15–18cm/ 6–7in in diameter.

5 Heat a griddle or heavy-based frying pan over a medium heat for a few minutes until hot.

6 Brush both sides of one roti with the melted butter or ghee. Add it to the griddle or frying pan and cook for about 2 minutes, turning after 1 minute. Brush the cooked roti lightly with melted butter or ghee again, slide it on to a plate and keep warm in a low oven while cooking the remaining rotis in the same way. Serve the rotis warm.

LAVASH

Thin and crispy, this flat bread is universally eaten throughout the Middle East. It's ideal for serving with soups and starters, and can be made in any size and broken into pieces as desired.

275g/10oz/2½ cups unbleached white
bread flour
175g/6oz/1½ cups wholemeal
flour
5ml/1 tsp salt
15g/½ oz fresh yeast
250ml/8fl oz/1 cup lukewarm water
60ml/4 tbsp natural yogurt or milk

MAKES 10 LAVASH

1 Sift the white and wholemeal flours and salt together into a large bowl and make a well in the centre. Mix the yeast with half the lukewarm water until creamy, then stir in the remaining water.

2 Add the yeast mixture and yogurt or milk to the centre of the flour and mix to a soft dough. Turn out on to a lightly floured surface and knead for 8–10 minutes until smooth and elastic. Place in a lightly oiled bowl, cover with lightly oiled clear film and leave to rise, in a warm place, for about 1 hour, or until doubled in bulk. Knock back the dough, re-cover with lightly oiled cling film and leave to rise for 30 minutes.

3 Turn the dough back out on to a lightly floured surface. Knock back gently and divide into 10 equal pieces. Shape into balls, then flatten into discs with the palm of your hand. Cover and leave to rest for 5 minutes. Meanwhile, preheat the oven to the maximum temperature – at least 230°C/450°F/Gas 8. Place 3 or 4 baking sheets in the oven to heat.

4 Roll the dough as thinly as possible, then lift it over the backs of your hands and gently stretch and turn the dough. Let rest in between rolling for a few minutes if necessary to avoid tearing.

5 As soon as they are ready, place 4 lavash on the baking sheets and bake for 6–8 minutes, or until starting to brown. Stack the remaining uncooked lavash, layered between clear film or greaseproof paper, and cover, to keep moist. Transfer to a wire rack to cool and cook the remaining lavash.

*450g/1lb/4 cups unbleached white
bread flour
5ml/1 tsp salt
20g/3/4 oz fresh yeast
280ml/9fl oz/scant 1¼ cups
lukewarm water*

*FOR THE TOPPING
60ml/4 tbsp finely chopped onion
5ml/1 tsp ground cumin
10ml/2 tsp ground coriander
10ml/2 tsp chopped fresh mint
30ml/2 tbsp olive oil*

MAKES 8 BREADS

COOK'S TIP
If you haven't any fresh mint to hand,
then add 15ml/1 tbsp dried mint. Use
the freeze-dried variety if you can as
it has much more flavour.

SYRIAN ONION BREAD

*The basic Arab breads of the Levant and Gulf have traditionally been made
with a finely ground wholemeal flour similar to chapati flour, but now are
being made with white flour as well. This Syrian version has a tasty,
aromatic topping.*

1 Lightly flour 2 baking sheets. Sift the
flour and salt together into a large bowl
and make a well in the centre. Cream
the yeast with a little of the water, then
mix in the remainder.

2 Add the yeast mixture to the centre of
the flour and mix to a firm dough. Turn
out on to a lightly floured surface and
knead for 8–10 minutes until smooth
and elastic.

3 Place in a lightly oiled bowl, cover
with lightly oiled clear film and leave to
rise, in a warm place, for about 1 hour,
or until doubled in size.

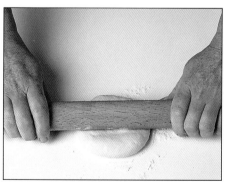

4 Knock back the dough and turn out on
to a lightly floured surface. Divide into
8 equal pieces and roll into 13–15cm/
5–6in rounds. Make them slightly
concave. Prick all over and space well
apart on the baking sheets. Cover with
lightly oiled clear film and leave to rise
for 15–20 minutes.

5 Meanwhile, preheat the oven to 200°C/
400°F/Gas 6. Mix the chopped onion,
ground cumin, ground coriander and
chopped mint in a bowl. Brush the
breads with the olive oil for the topping,
sprinkle them evenly with the spicy
onion mixture and bake for 15–20
minutes. Serve the onion breads warm.

BARBARI

*These small Iranian flat breads can be made in a variety of sizes. For a
change, make two large breads and break off pieces to scoop up dips.*

1 Lightly dust 2 baking sheets with flour.
Sift the flour and salt together into a
bowl and make a well in the centre.

2 Mix the yeast with the water. Pour
into the centre of the flour, sprinkle a
little flour over and leave in a warm
place for 15 minutes. Mix to a dough,
then turn out on to a lightly floured
surface and knead for 8–10 minutes
until smooth and elastic.

3 Place in a lightly oiled bowl, cover
with lightly oiled clear film and leave to
rise for 45–60 minutes, or until doubled.

4 Knock back the dough and turn out on
to a lightly floured surface. Divide into
6 equal pieces and shape into rectangles.
Roll each one out to about 10 × 5cm/
4 × 2in and about 1cm/½ in thick. Space
well apart on the baking sheets, and
make four slashes in the tops.

225g/8oz/2 cups unbleached white
bread flour
5ml/1 tsp salt
15g/½ oz fresh yeast
140ml/scant ¼ pint/scant ⅔ cup
lukewarm water
oil, for brushing

MAKES 6 BARBARI

VARIATION
Sprinkle with sesame or caraway
seeds before baking.

5 Cover the breads with lightly oiled
clear film and leave to rise, in a warm
place, for 20 minutes. Meanwhile,
preheat the oven to 200°C/400°F/Gas 6.
Brush the breads with oil and bake for
12–15 minutes, or until pale golden.
Serve warm.

SHOPPING FOR BREAD AND FLOUR

The following flour mills, bakeries and foodhalls are worth visiting. Most mills sell flour direct, but it is best to telephone before visiting.

AUSTRALIA

Bowan Island Bakery
202 Lyons Road
Drummoyne
NSW 2047
Tel: (02) 9181 3524

Brown's Bakeries
PO Box 1298
Windsor
VIC 3181
Tel: (03) 9510 9520

Dallas Bread
28 Cross Street
Brookvale
NSW 2100
Tel: (02) 9905 6021

David Jones Food Hall
Cnr. Market and
    Castlereagh Streets
Sydney
NSW 2000
Tel: (02) 9266 6065

Haberfield Bakery
153 Ramsay Road
Haberfield, Sydney
NSW
Tel: (02) 9797 7715

Il Gianfornaio
414 Victoria Avenue
Chatswood, Sydney
NSW
Tel: (02) 413 4833

Infinity Sourdough Bakery
225 Victoria Street
Darlinghurst
NSW 2031
Tel: (02) 9380 4320

La Gerbe d'Or
257 Glenmore Road
Paddington, Sydney
NSW Tel: (02) 9331 10710

New Norcia Bakeries
163A Scarborough
    Beach Road
Mt Hawthorn
WA 6016
Tel: (08) 9443 9437

Quinton's Sourdough and
    Danish Shop
179 The Mall
Leura
NSW 2780
Tel: (02) 9266 6065

Victoire
285 Darling Street
Balmain
Sydney
NSW
(02) 9818 5529

Simon Johnson Purveyor of
    Quality Foods
181 Harris Street
Pyrmont
Sydney NSW 2009
NSW 2009
Tel: (02) 9552 2522

and
12–14 Saint David Street
Fitzroy
VIC 3065
Tel: (03) 9486 9456

ENGLAND

& Clarke's
122 Kensington Church
    Street
Nottinghill Gate
London W8 4BII
Tel: 0171 229 2190

Baker & Spice
46 Walton Street
London SW3 1RB
Tel: 0171 589 4734

Country Market
139–146 Golder's Green Road
London NW11 8HB
Tel: 0181 455 3289

Crowdy Mill
Bow Road
Habertonford
Totnes
Devon TQ9 7HU
Tel: 01803 732 340

Euphorium Bakery
203 Upper Street
London N1 1RQ
Tel: 0171 359 7146

Funchal Patisserie
141 Stockwell Road
London SW9 9TN
Tel: 0171 733 3134

Harrods
Food Hall
Knightsbridge
London
SW1X 7XL
Tel: 0171 730 1234

Harvey Nichols
Food Hall
109–125 Knightsbridge
London SW1X 7RJ
Tel: 0171 235 5000

Hobb's House Bakery
39 High Street
Chipping Sodbury
Bristol
BS37 6BA
Tel: 01454 321 629

and
2 North Parade
Yate
South Gloucestershire
BS37 4AN
Tel: 01454 320 890

Konditor & Cook
22 Cornwall Street
London SE1 8TW
Tel: 0171 261 0456

and
10 Stoney Street
London SE1 9AD
Tel: 0171 407 5100

Letheringsett Watermill
Riverside Road
Letheringsett
Norfolk NR25 7YD
Tel: 01263 713 153

Maison Blanc
102 Holland Park Avenue
London W11 4UA
Tel: 0171 221 2494

Mortimer & Bennett
33 Turnham Green Terrace
London W4 1RG
Tel: 0181 995 4145

Neal's Yard Bakery
6 Neal's Yard
London WC2H 9DP
Tel: 0171 836 5199

Panadam Delicatessen
2 Marius Road
London SW17 7QQ
Tel: 0181 673 4062

Pimhill Organic Centre and
    Farm Shop
Lea Hall, Harmer Hill
Nr Shrewsbury
SY4 3DY
Tel: 01939 290 075

Rushall Mill
Rushall, Pewsey
Wiltshire SN9 6EB
Tel: 01980 630 335

Sally Lunn's
4 North Parade Passage
Bath BA1 1NX
Tel: 01225 461 634

Selfridges
Food Hall
400 Oxford Street
London W1A 1AB
Tel: 0171 620 1234

Shipton Mill Limited
Long Newton
nr Tetbury
Gloucestershire GL8 8RP
Tel: 01666 505 050

The Flour Bag
Burford Street
Lechlade
Gloucestershire GL7 3AP
Tel: 01367 252 322

The Old Farmhouse
    Bakery
Steventon
nr Abingdon
Oxon OX13 6RP
Tel: 01235 831 230

Villandry Foodstore
    Restaurant
170 Great Portland Street
London W1N 5TB
Tel: 0171 631 3131

SCOTLAND

Aberfeldy Water Mill
Mill Street
Aberfeldy
Tayside PH15 2BG
Tel: 01887 820 803

Fisher and Donaldson
21 Crossgate
Cupar
Fife KY15 5HA
Tel: 01334 652 551

and

3 Church Street
St Andrews
Fife KY16 9NW
Tel: 01334 472 201

Ian Mellis
30A Victoria Street
Edinburgh EH1 2JW
Tel: 0131 226 6215

and

205 Bruntsfield Place
Edinburgh EH10 4DH
Tel: 0131 447 8889

and

492 Great Western Road
Glasgow G12 8EW
Tel: 0141 339 8998

Star Continental Bakery
158 Fore Street
Scottoun
Glasgow G14 0AE
Tel: 0141 959 7307

Taylor's of Waterside Bakery
Waterside Street
Strathaven
ML10 6AW
Tel: 01357 521 260

Valvona & Crolla
19 Elm Row
Edinburgh EH7 4AA
Tel: 0131 556 6066

Victor Hugo
26-7 Melville Terrace
Edinburgh EH9 2PR
Tel: 0131 667 1827

WALES

The Village Bakery
Melmerby Road
Melberby
Penrith
Cumbria
CA10 1HE
Tel: 01768 881 515

Derwen Bakehouse
Museum of Welsh Life
St Fagans
Cardiff
Glamorgan
CF5 6XB
Tel: 01222 573 500

ACKNOWLEDGEMENTS

PUBLISHER'S ACKNOWLEDGEMENTS

The Publishers would like to thank Jo Lethaby and Jenni Fleetwood for their skilful editing; Jill Jones, who tracked down almost all the breads for the Breads of the World section; Jenny Blair for sourcing the Scottish breads; Amy Willenski, who tracked down or specially baked all the US breads; Angus Henderson and Jacky Lannel at Villandry Foodstore Restaurant, who specially baked the fougasse, épi and pane au cioccolato loaves; Christine Gough, the baker at the Welsh Museum of Life, for baking and supplying traditional Welsh breads; and Giacomo and Nuala Farruggia at Il Forno for baking and supplying many of the Italian breads, as well as the harvest loaf and hot cross buns.

PHOTOGRAPHY ACKNOWLEDGEMENTS

All recipe pictures and chapter openers are by Nicki Dowey. The pictures on pages 6–125 are by Amanda Heywood, except for the following that have been reproduced with the kind permission of those listed: p. 6t, p. 7t, p. 14b and p. 250 Maison Blanc Limited; p. 7b Jan Suttle/Life File; p. 9t and 13b Emma Lee/Life File; p. 12 t Lionel Moss/ Life File; p.12b Jeff Griffin/Life File; p. 8t and b e.t. archive; p. 9b English Heritage Photographic Library; p. 10t e.t. archive; p. 10b Biblioteca Estense, Modena/e.t. archive; p. 11t Andreas von Einsiedel/National Trust Photographic Library; p. 11b Eric Crichton/National Trust Photographic Library; p. 13 Food Features.

INDEX